DATE DUE

The Framing of Mumia Abu-Jamal

The Framing
of Mumia
Abu-Jamal

J. Patrick O'Connor

Lawrence Hill Books

Library of Congress Cataloging-in-Publication Data
O'Connor, J. Patrick.
  The framing of Mumia Abu-Jamal / J. Patrick O'Connor. — 1st ed.
    p. cm.
  Includes index.
  ISBN 978-1-55652-744-9
  1. Abu-Jamal, Mumia—Trials, litigation, etc. 2. Trials (Murder)—Pennsylva-
nia—Philadelphia. 3. Police murders—Pennsylvania—Philadelphia. I. Title.
  KF224.A354O256 2008
  345.748'1102523—dc22

                                                              2007048384

Cover and interior design: Scott Rattray
Front cover photo: © Reuters/CORBIS
Back cover and spine image: iStockPhoto.com, © Marie-france Bélanger

To my friend Herb Zucker and my son, Joe,
for their encouragement to write this book.

CONTENTS

ACKNOWLEDGMENTS

James Terry was of major assistance to me in the writing of this book. My editor, Yuval Taylor, helped me enormously with his deep sense of the issues involved. I owe them both a tremendous debt of gratitude.

I thank my sister, Paula O'Connor, and my friend Wendy Tell for proofreading the manuscript, Devon Freeny for guiding the book through the production process, and Janine Stanley-Dunham for her excellent copyediting.

Linn Washington was most gracious in providing me with background information on this case, and I am grateful to Michael Schiffmann for sharing resources he acquired in writing his book *Race Against Death: Mumia Abu-Jamal; A Black Revolutionary in White America* (Vienna, Austria: Promedia, 2006).

My research was greatly assisted by the Justice for Daniel Faulkner Web site. My sincerest hope is that this book may aid Officer Daniel Faulkner's family in finally achieving the justice it has been denied all these years.

David Lindorff's book *Killing Time: An Investigation into the Death Row Case of Mumia Abu-Jamal* (Monroe, ME: Common Courage Press, 2003) provides a seminal exploration of the case, particularly in the areas of corruption within the Philadelphia Police Department, prosecutorial abuse in the Philadelphia District Attorney's Office, and Federal District Judge William Yohn's flawed decision in upholding Abu-Jamal's conviction in 2003.

Other books that enlightened me in my research were Terry Bisson's biography *On a Move: The Story of Mumia Abu-Jamal* (Farmington, PA: Litmus Books, 2000) and Daniel Williams's *Executing*

Justice: An Inside Account of the Case of Mumia Abu-Jamal (New York: St. Martin's Press, 2001).

Along with former police commissioner and mayor Frank Rizzo, the radical back-to-nature group MOVE was and is at the center of the Abu-Jamal story in every respect. The group's International Concerned Family & Friends of Mumia Abu-Jamal kept Abu-Jamal's story alive against great odds. I wish to thank Kevin Price of that organization for his cooperation. MOVE's 1996 pamphlet "25 Years on the MOVE" tells its version of itself. *Burning Down the House: MOVE and the Tragedy of Philadelphia* (New York: Norton, 1987), by John Anderson and Hilary Hevenor, and *Discourse and Destruction: The City of Philadelphia Versus MOVE* (Chicago: University of Chicago Press, 1994), by Robin Wagner-Pacifici, are definitive accounts of the police/MOVE war.

Finally, I'd like to thank my steadfast agent, Barbara Casey.

PREFACE

When Mumia Abu-Jamal was sentenced to death on July 2, 1982, for the murder of Philadelphia police officer Daniel Faulkner, I was an associate editor for *TV Guide* at its headquarters in nearby Radnor, Pennsylvania. I had often listened to Abu-Jamal giving reports—in as distinctive a voice as I've ever heard—on the local public radio station during the twenty months he was employed there. I was impressed with his ability to make listeners feel what he was describing—they knew he cared.

I was surprised to hear that Abu-Jamal had been arrested for Officer Faulkner's killing. It did not seem to fit my image of him as a compassionate reporter. The major Philadelphia newspapers, the *Philadelphia Inquirer*, the *Philadelphia Bulletin*, and the *Philadelphia Daily News*, made the case seem an open-and-shut one, the verdict of death justified.

Sometime in the mid-1990s I began hearing and seeing the "Free Mumia" slogan. In 1996, when HBO premiered the one-hour documentary *Mumia Abu-Jamal: A Case for Reasonable Doubt?*, I developed some questions about the verdict. As the years passed and the Free Mumia movement intensified, those questions persisted. Shortly after Amnesty International published a report in 2000 stating it had "determined that numerous aspects of Mumia Abu-Jamal's case clearly failed to meet minimum international standards safeguarding the fairness of legal proceedings," I began to research the case. By this time I was editor of the Internet site Crime Magazine (www.crimemagazine.com), and I thought I should write an article about the case for it.

Running throughout much of Abu-Jamal's support is a subtext that his trial was unfair but that he probably killed Officer Faulkner in self-defense. As I read and reread the available material on the case—transcripts from both his trial and his Post-Conviction Relief Act hearings, newspaper accounts, and several books written about the case—I could see that Abu-Jamal's trial was a monumental miscarriage of justice, representing an extreme case of prosecutorial abuse and judicial bias. What I could not tell was whether Abu-Jamal had actually killed Officer Faulkner. The officer had been in the process of violently arresting Abu-Jamal's younger brother shortly before 4 A.M. in a sleazy section of Philadelphia when Abu-Jamal— moonlighting as a taxi driver—happened to be nearby and ran from a parking lot to assist his brother.

What makes getting to the truth of this case so difficult is that the prosecution built its case on perjured testimony with a calculated disregard for what the actual evidence established. When Abu-Jamal's insistence that MOVE founder—and nonlawyer—John Africa assist him in his defense caused the trial judge to strip Abu-Jamal of his right to self-representation during the opening of the trial, the search for the truth was abandoned and the verdict became a foregone conclusion. In a very real sense, Abu-Jamal sabotaged his own trial and was his own worst enemy. He was innocent but terribly misguided in courtroom tactics. He ruptured his own defense by emasculating his court-appointed defense attorney—calling him a "worthless sellout and shyster" during the sentencing phase of the trial—and doomed himself to the death verdict with his sneering contempt for the judicial process. His petulant, disrespectful courtroom protests resulted in his being banned for more than half of his trial.

This book shows how the Philadelphia Police Department and the Philadelphia District Attorney's Office framed Abu-Jamal for Faulkner's killing. It uses the preponderance of evidence to establish that Faulkner shot Abu-Jamal as the latter approached him and that a passenger in Abu-Jamal's brother's car, Kenneth Freeman, then killed Faulkner. In addition, unlike any other book or article on this subject, it describes the overarching roles of then-mayor Frank Rizzo and a small, radical back-to-nature cult called MOVE in the case.

MOVE was news, the biggest ongoing local news story in Philadelphia in the late 1970s and through the 1980s. On August 8, 1978, following a ten-month-long police blockade of the MOVE compound in the Powelton Village section of Philadelphia, hundreds of police fired an estimated ten thousand rounds of bullets into the MOVE house and ordered firefighters to flush the twelve adult MOVE members and eleven MOVE children out of the basement with water canons. In the mayhem of the police assault, a police officer was shot to death. Nine MOVE members would be convicted, and each would be sentenced to up to one hundred years in prison for the death of Officer James Ramp.

With his hair braided in the dreadlock style of MOVE members, a style he had adopted while attending rustic Goddard College in Vermont, Abu-Jamal covered the longest, most rancorous trial in Philadelphia history for a local public-radio station, his reports overtly sympathetic to the MOVE defendants.

The more the news media tried to paint MOVE as urban savages, the more Abu-Jamal felt compelled to portray the group as principled revolutionaries willing to stand up to police brutality, a stance that would cost him his full-time public-radio job and by 1981 force him to moonlight as a cabdriver. His coverage of MOVE also made him a marked man to Mayor Rizzo, who angrily threatened him publicly at a news conference in 1978. With that enmity came the full power of the Philadelphia Police Department and District Attorney's Office to railroad him for murder. And railroad him they did by knowingly using perjured, coerced, and bribed testimony at his trial.

Throughout Abu-Jamal's long incarceration on death row, the Pennsylvania Supreme Court has gone through contortions to prevent him from getting a new trial. Three years before it turned down Abu-Jamal's first appeal in 1989, it ruled in *Commonwealth v. Baker* to overturn Lawrence Baker's death sentence for first-degree murder on the grounds that the prosecutor improperly referenced the lengthy appeal process afforded those sentenced to death. That prosecutor, Assistant District Attorney Joseph McGill, was the same prosecutor who used similar improper language in his summation during both the guilt and sentencing phases of Abu-Jamal's trial. The judge who failed to strike the language in the *Baker* case was the same judge who presided at Abu-Jamal's trial, Common Pleas Court Judge Albert F. Sabo. The Pennsylvania Supreme Court ruled in *Baker* that the use of such language "minimize[ed] the jury's sense of responsibility for a verdict of death." When Abu-Jamal's appeal included the very same issue, the court reversed its own precedent in the matter, denying the claim in a unanimous decision. A year later, in *Commonwealth v. Beasley*, the Pennsylvania Supreme Court reinstated the death sentence of Leslie Beasley, convicted of murdering a police officer, but exerted its supervisory powers to adopt "a *per se* rule precluding all remarks about the appellate process in all future trials. We do so in the interest of justice, judicial economy and integrity of the system, and to provide clear-cut guidance to trial judges and members of the bar." Unlike in Abu-Jamal's case, Beasley's case presented no mitigating circumstances for the jury to weigh when considering whether his sentence should be life or death (this was his third conviction for homicide), but the *Baker* precedent was nonetheless reestablished.

In its review of Abu-Jamal's case, the Nobel Prize–winning Amnesty International concluded that such judicial machinations leave "the disturbing impression that the court invented a new standard of procedure to apply it to one case only: that of Mumia Abu-Jamal."

Robert R. Bryan, Abu-Jamal's lead attorney, said that in over three decades of litigating death penalty cases, he has not seen "one in which the government wants so badly to kill a client."

If ever there was a story of one man taking on a corrupt justice system without bridling, the case of Mumia Abu-Jamal is that story.

INTRODUCTION

A Cause Celebre

Mumia Abu-Jamal has been on death row since 1982. Over the years, as a result of his prison writings, the former radio reporter who prided himself on being "the voice of the voiceless" has attracted an astonishing level of national and international support that has turned the Free Mumia movement into the cause celebre of all thirty-six hundred death row cases in the United States. The Philadelphia Fraternal Order of Police (FOP) and the slain officer's widow, Maureen Faulkner, doggedly lead the "Fry Mumia" side of the controversy.

After years of denied appeals before the Pennsylvania Supreme Court, and a Post-Conviction Relief Act (PCRA) hearing conducted in the mid-1990s by the original trial judge in the case, Abu-Jamal's appeal finally made it to federal district court in December 2001 in the form of a habeas corpus petition. For the first time, Abu-Jamal's claim of constitutional violations at his trial was affirmed when U.S. District Court Judge William H. Yohn Jr. overturned Abu-Jamal's death sentence. However, in a ruling that evoked images of Solomon's decision to cut the baby in half, Yohn also upheld Abu-Jamal's conviction for murdering Officer Faulkner on December 9, 1981.

Yohn's 272-page ruling denied the twenty other defense claims of constitutional violations, but it did leave the door open a crack by "certifying" one of those claims—that is, declaring that the claim was eligible for appeal to a higher court. If Yohn had not certified that one claim, Abu-Jamal's appeals, for all practical purposes, would have been over. Barring an unlikely intervention by the U.S. Supreme Court or an even more unlikely offer of clemency by a future governor of Pennsylvania, Abu-Jamal would have been assured of spending the rest of his life in prison.

Overturning a death sentence normally means that the prisoner is taken off death row and placed among the regular prison population for the duration of the appeal process. But in a particularly spiteful maneuver, Philadelphia D.A. Lynne Abraham requested that Judge Yohn stay the order lifting Abu-Jamal's death sentence. The judge, incredibly, agreed. As a result, Abu-Jamal—who turned fifty-four on April 24, 2008—remains on death row twenty-two to twenty-three hours a day on weekdays and twenty-four hours a day on weekends in a cell at the super-max State Correctional Institution Greene in Waynesburg, Pennsylvania, fifty miles south of Pittsburgh on the border with West Virginia. He is allowed approved visitors for one two-hour period per week but must speak with them, in handcuffs, from behind one-inch-thick Plexiglas.

Four years after Abu-Jamal's sentence was overturned, his case took its next sharp turn. On December 6, 2005, a three-judge panel of the U.S. Court of Appeals for the Third Circuit issued an order to hear arguments on the claim certified by Judge Yohn—as well as two other claims raised by the defense and one raised by the state.

Abu-Jamal's new attorneys—led by Robert R. Bryan of San Francisco—had appealed, as they were entitled to, the one claim Yohn certified, but they added several other claims of constitutional violations arising from Abu-Jamal's trial and his PCRA hearing that they hoped the appeals court would consider. In a stunning victory for the defense, the Third Circuit agreed to hear arguments on two of those additional claims. One concerns the prosecutor's summation to the jury during the guilt phase of the trial, and the other the alleged bias of the judge who presided at Abu-Jamal's postconviction proceedings, Common Pleas Court Judge Albert Sabo, who was also Abu-Jamal's original trial judge.

The claim that Judge Yohn had certified for appeal in 2001, known as a *Batson* claim, pertained to the prosecutor's use of peremptory challenges to exclude qualified blacks from the jury.

The Third Circuit also agreed to hear the prosecution claim challenging Yohn's overturning Abu-Jamal's death sentence.

Robert Bryan called the Third Circuit's order "the most important decision affecting my client, Mumia Abu-Jamal, since the lower federal court ruling in December 2001," revoking Abu-Jamal's death sentence. Bryan, with over thirty-five years of experience in litigating death penalty cases, said all three defense claims "are of enormous constitutional significance and go to the very essence of Mumia's right to a fair trial, due process of law, and equal protection under the Fifth, Sixth, and Fourteenth Amendments to the U.S. Constitution." Hugh Burns, the Philadelphia D.A.'s Office appellate chief, called the order a "major blow."

The blow was so major that after over twenty-five years on death row, the probability of Abu-Jamal being granted a new trial is now high. Two of the claims the appellate court agreed to hear regard prima facie violations of his constitutional rights. At Abu-Jamal's trial prosecutor Joseph McGill told the jury in his summation that if they found Abu-Jamal guilty of first-degree murder, "there would be appeal after appeal and perhaps there could be a reversal of the case, or whatever, so that may not be final." This type of language undermines the jury's need to find the defendant guilty beyond a reasonable doubt. He brazenly said this despite the fact that in an earlier capital case when he had used similar language to coax a jury to a death-sentence verdict with Judge Sabo presiding, the Pennsylvania Supreme Court had overturned the verdict. (McGill used nearly the same language during the sentencing phase of Abu-Jamal's trial when he successfully argued for the imposition of the death penalty.)

On the *Batson* claim, McGill did use at least ten and most likely eleven peremptory challenges to exclude blacks from serving on Abu-Jamal's jury. In a city with a black population of 44 percent at the time of Abu-Jamal's trial, only three blacks were impaneled. One of those was dismissed—for violating jury sequestration—by Judge Sabo after the first day of testimony and replaced by a white male.

The other claim, that Sabo was biased against Abu-Jamal during his PCRA hearings, is a judgment call the appellate court judges will make based on the transcripts from those proceedings and the briefs filed by opposing counsel on the issue. If the judges were to find such bias, amply demonstrated by Judge Sabo throughout the hearings, they could order the hearings reopened. Those hearings could well lead to a new trial for Abu-Jamal on numerous other grounds that his new defense team could introduce there. And there will be no Judge Sabo presiding at these hearings; he died in 2002.

*   *   *

That Abu-Jamal's trial was, in so many different ways, a travesty of justice is irrefutable to his legions of supporters. And they are right: his trial was riddled with so many types of judicial and prosecutorial abuses that it was a sham from beginning to end. Judge Yohn's failure to overturn Abu-Jamal's conviction on legal and constitutional grounds in 2001 merely extended the sham.

But what really happened the night Officer Faulkner was killed? And how and why was an innocent man forced to pay for that tragic event?

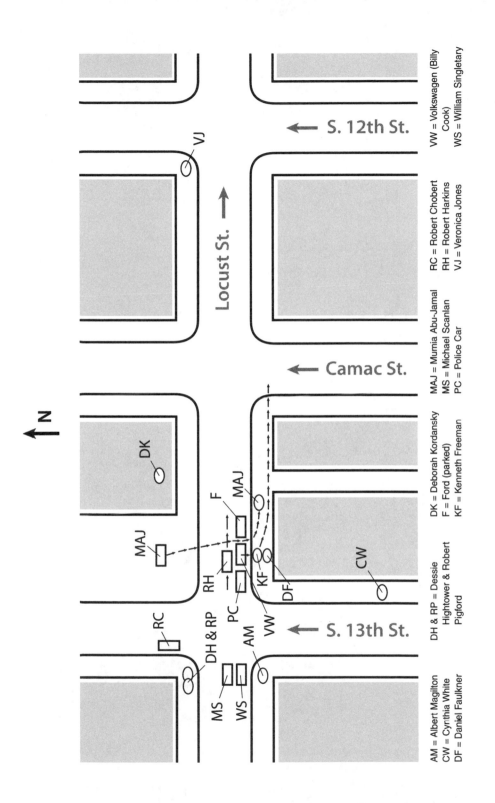

N

← S. 12th St.

Locust St. →

← Camac St.

← S. 13th St.

VJ

DK

MAJ

F

MAJ

RH

PC

VW

KF

DF

CW

RC

DH & RP

MS

WS

AM

AM = Albert Magilton
CW = Cynthia White
DF = Daniel Faulkner

DH & RP = Dessie Hightower & Robert Pigford

DK = Deborah Kordansky
F = Ford (parked)
KF = Kenneth Freeman

MAJ = Mumia Abu-Jamal
MS = Michael Scanlan
PC = Police Car

RC = Robert Chobert
RH = Robert Harkins
VJ = Veronica Jones

VW = Volkswagen (Billy Cook)
WS = William Singletary

1

DECEMBER 9, 1981

The early morning hours of December 9, 1981, were bitter cold, the temperature dropping to nine degrees Fahrenheit. It had been a busy evening for Abu-Jamal. He had had dinner with radio reporter E. Steven Collins, a friend since childhood, and then–state representative Milton Street, at Collins's house. From there, he told Terry Bisson, author of the biography *On a Move: The Story of Mumia Abu-Jamal*, he drove to his wife Wadiya's house in southwest Philadelphia and helped her put her children to bed before leaving in the United taxi he moonlighted in at about midnight. Because he had been robbed at gunpoint twice while driving the cab, Abu-Jamal now carried a short-barreled Charter Arms .38 for protection.

Officer Daniel Faulkner was only twenty-five but had already spent five years on the Philadelphia police force. The youngest of seven siblings, he was born in southwest Philadelphia. His father, a railroad worker, died of a heart attack five years later. A biographical sketch on the Web site www.danielfaulkner.com states that Faulkner dropped out of high school to join the army and while serving obtained his GED as well as an associate's degree in criminal justice. He began his law enforcement career as a corrections officer and then joined the Philadelphia Police Department in late 1975. He married for a second time in fall 1979.

By all accounts, Faulkner was a conscientious, dedicated police officer with a bright future ahead of him. His long-term ambition, according to the Web site, was to become a prosecutor in the Philadelphia

D.A.'s Office. At the time of his death, he was enrolled in a bachelor's program in criminal justice, in preparation for attending law school.

Faulkner usually worked with a partner, his best friend on the police force, Garry Bell. But owing to understaffing, he would work this night alone. He normally wore a bulletproof vest, but this night, a little pressed for time, he dressed in his uniform at home while his vest hung in his locker at the precinct. His wife, Maureen, told him to make sure to go get his vest. But Faulkner was busy and never got around to it. Sometime around 1:30 A.M. he was assigned a rape case, arresting the suspect and then driving the seven-year-old black victim to Jefferson University Hospital for treatment.

Around 3:55 A.M. Faulkner spotted Billy Cook, Abu-Jamal's twenty-five-year-old younger brother, in a battered blue Volkswagen with a wooden bumper, its license tag dangling in the rear. Faulkner turned on his red bubble light and pulled the VW over at the corner of 13th and Locust just behind a Ford parked there. Faulkner positioned his marked police car right behind the VW on the south side of Locust Street, a car-length east of the intersection with 13th Street. The intersection was the hub of a seedy nightspot section of downtown Philadelphia notorious for its prostitutes and drug users. The bars were in the process of closing, so a number of people were in the immediate area. Some taxis, including Abu-Jamal's, were waiting for fares.

That Faulkner knew Billy Cook and recognized him is a probability supported by Faulkner's own radio message to the police dispatcher before he got out of his patrol car to approach the VW. At first, Faulkner radioed for backup, but then he changed his mind and said, "On second thought, send me a wagon," meaning, according to police testimony at trial, that he had a prisoner and was planning to bring him in. Faulkner's request for a wagon could have also meant that there was more than one person in Cook's car. Although the prosecution estimated that Billy Cook, a down-on-his-luck street vendor with a drug problem, had up to $1,000 in outstanding parking tickets, Faulkner did not run a check of the VW's license plate.

Abu-Jamal's court-appointed defense counsel, Anthony E. Jackson, told a *Philadelphia Inquirer* reporter three days after Abu-Jamal was sentenced, "I'm reasonably convinced that they [Faulkner and Billy Cook] had some prior contact—once or twice before." Jackson said at one point during his investigation of Faulkner's slaying that he was shown a statement by a police officer who stated that Faulkner had spotted Billy Cook selling drugs in Center City some weeks before the incident but had lost him during a chase. Jackson said that Faulkner had told the officer that if he saw Cook again, he would arrest him. Thus, no license-plate check, thus the call for the wagon. (Cook would later deny ever previously meeting Faulkner.)

It is not clear what happened after Faulkner reached the VW, but it appears the officer first approached the passenger side—in a 2001 affidavit, Billy Cook would identify his street-vendor partner, Kenneth Freeman, as the passenger in the VW—and asked to see the passenger's identification. It would not become known until Abu-Jamal's postconviction hearing in 1995 that a duplicate license application bearing the name Arnold Howard was found in Faulkner's shirt pocket. Although the prosecution had included the license application in the evidence list it provided to Abu-Jamal's trial attorney, it did not inform the defense that it was found in Faulkner's pocket. Had it done so, the possibility of a shooter other than Abu-Jamal would have been material, particularly coupled with all the eyewitness testimony that one or more black men were seen fleeing the scene immediately after Faulkner was shot.

Homicide detectives thought enough of the license application's significance at the time to immediately send two detectives and several police to Howard's house before daybreak to bring him in for questioning. At Abu-Jamal's postconviction hearing, Howard testified that he was handcuffed and "still in his drawers" when hustled off to the Police Administration Building for questioning about Faulkner's murder. He testified that the homicide detectives held him without charges for the maximum seventy-two hours allowed, grilling him relentlessly, subjecting him to a trace metal test to determine if he had recently fired a gun. Either because Howard told investigators that he had given the duplicate license application to Freeman or because the police knew that Freeman was a passenger in the VW who had fled the scene, they also brought Freeman in for questioning hours after the shooting and put both him and Howard in several lineups.

Howard, a friend since childhood of both Abu-Jamal and Billy Cook, also testified at the PCRA hearing that Freeman kept getting singled out at the lineups. Howard informed the court that Freeman told him that the prosecution's star witness, prostitute Cynthia White, had picked him out twice. Howard said that he himself was finally released because he was able to produce a receipt from a convenience store in another part of the city where he had made a purchase at about the time Faulkner was killed.

Abu-Jamal happened to be directly across the street from where Faulkner had pulled Billy Cook over, sitting in his cab in a parking lot while making entries in his logbook and awaiting his next fare. The only credible eyewitness the prosecution chose to produce at trial, Michael Mark Scanlan, said he saw a man run across the street from the parking lot but saw no gun in his hand as he ran and the first shot rang out. Scanlan told police that the man he saw running toward Faulkner from the parking lot had an Afro and was wearing a black knit hat. Abu-Jamal wore his hair in dreadlocks and had on a green beret. When the police brought Scanlan to the paddy wagon to identify Abu-Jamal as the man he saw running toward Faulkner from parking lot—that is, as the shooter—Scanlan indicated he believed Abu-Jamal was the driver of the VW. At trial, he reiterated that he could not identify Abu-Jamal as the shooter but could identify him as the man running from the parking lot because of the clothing he wore.

The truth of the Faulkner shooting is buried in what happened during the one or two minutes after Faulkner pulled Cook over and got out of his patrol car to approach the VW. Scanlan, who was stopped at a traffic light at the intersection of 13th and Locust, was about forty feet away from where Faulkner pulled over the VW. Scanlan testified that he saw the police officer and the black driver of the VW in conversation as the latter was spread-eagled over the front of the police car. Scanlan said he saw the black man swing around and strike the police officer in the face with his fist. He then saw the officer react by hitting the black man two or three times in succession on the shoulders with a blackjack or a flashlight, the blows causing the black man's knees to buckle and the black man to duck down.

Cook's account of the scene adds some detail that Scanlan failed to observe. After being pulled over, Cook said, he got out of the VW and a heated verbal exchange ensued. He said Faulkner hit him three times in the back of his head with a flashlight, pushing him into the side of the police car and frisking him. Cook denies hitting Faulkner, saying he raised his hand only to ward off Faulkner's volley of blows. Cook said he was bleeding profusely as he got back into the driver's seat to look for his car's registration papers in the back seat. He said Kenneth Freeman was still in the car when he got in. Faulkner was now standing in front of the VW. When Cook first saw his brother, Abu-Jamal was just feet away from him, running toward him. Cook said Abu-Jamal had nothing in his hands. He heard a shot and saw his brother stumbling forward. Cook said he next noticed that the passenger door to his car was open and Kenneth Freeman had exited the car. Cook then heard more shots and saw sparks but did not see who shot Faulkner, because his back was to him. Cook said Freeman then fled the scene.

Abu-Jamal's account, as rendered in his own 2001 affidavit, picks up right after Faulkner had pummeled Cook with the flashlight. While parked across the street from where his brother had been pulled over, Abu-Jamal heard what sounded to him like gunshots. He said he looked into the rearview mirror and saw people running up and down Locust.

> As I scanned I recognized my brother standing in the street staggering and dizzy. . . . I immediately exited the cab and ran to his scream. . . . As I came across the street I saw a uniformed cop turn toward me gun in hand, saw a flash and went down to my knees. . . . I closed my eyes and sat still trying to breathe. . . . The next thing that I remember I felt myself being kicked, hit and being brought out of a stupor.

Kenneth Freeman is the wild card in this speculation, but he and an eyewitness the prosecution did not call to testify are the keys to everything about this case. Freeman was still sitting in the passenger seat of the VW when Cook, blood trickling down his neck, got back into the VW to look for his car's registration papers. Freeman, a hardscrabble U.S. Army veteran, saw Abu-Jamal running toward the VW, being shot point-blank range in the chest by Faulkner, and collapsing to the ground. Freeman got out of the VW.

At this point, Robert Harkins, a forty-two-year-old cabdriver, was driving east on Locust Street and approaching 13th Street. He saw Faulkner grab a man and watched as they scuffled. The man spun Faulkner around and threw him to the ground on his hands and knees, Faulkner's back now facing the man. As Faulkner tried to regain his balance, the assailant, from a foot or less away, shot him in the back, the bullet exiting his neck and knocking off his clip-on tie. Faulkner then rolled over onto his back. The assailant, again from a foot or less away, then fired two more shots directly at Faulkner's face, one apparently going through the collar of Faulkner's jacket, the other—fired execution style—hitting him in the right-hand corner of his left eye, killing him instantly.

Harkins's account of the shooting is supported by two important bits of physical evidence. Faulkner's pants were ripped at the knee, and his left knee bore a two-inch-wide, three-quarter-inch-high superficial skin denudation, indicating he had fallen down face first onto his hands and knees just as Harkins described. In the prosecution scenario, Faulkner fell down backward and while falling somehow managed to get off the shot that wounded Abu-Jamal in the chest.

Harkins said that as soon as he saw the officer shot in the face, he began fearing for his own life and immediately drove away to look for police to tell about the shooting. Within a block, Harkins came upon a police van and informed the two officers in it that a cop had been shot. Harkins did not return to the scene.

With Faulkner dead, a blacked-out Abu-Jamal was left to answer for his murder. Cook, to his credit, stayed behind.

Various witnesses said they saw a black man running from the scene right after the shooting, just as Cook said Freeman had done after Faulkner was shot. Some of the eyewitnesses said this man had an Afro and wore a green army jacket. Freeman did have an Afro, and the green army jacket he perpetually wore was his badge of honor from his days in the military. Michael Scanlan told police he thought the shooter had an Afro, as did another prosecution witness, cabdriver Robert Chobert.

About two hours later police brought Harkins to the station to take his statement. The framing of Abu-Jamal for Faulkner's killing was in high gear by the time Harkins arrived. The statement he gave was not at all what they wanted to hear.

> On 12-9-81 between 3:30 A.M. and 4 A.M. while traveling east on Locust Street from Broad Street, I was approaching 13th Street when I observed a police car with its dome lights on. And then I looked over and observed a police officer grab a guy. The guy then spun around and the officer went to the ground. [The officer] had his hands on the ground and then rolled over. At this time the male who was standing over the officer pointed a gun at the officer and fired one shot and then he fired a second shot. At this time the officer moved a little and then flat to the ground. I heard a total of three shots and saw what appeared to me to be three flashes from the gun of the man standing over the officer. When I saw the officer go flat to the ground I drove down the street and at 12th and Locust Streets I saw a police wagon which was traveling south on 12th Street and I told them that a cop got shot back there, and one of the officers, the passenger, said, "A cop"? and I said, "Yes, a cop."

Eight days later, Harkins gave a subsequent interview to a homicide detective.

> I was coming across the intersection of 13th Street on Locust when I saw the lights on the police car and I noticed the officer on the sidewalk. A guy grabbed him [Faulkner] and spun him around. He grabbed him with this hand and spun him and he went down (indicating the male spun the officer around with his right hand. Then stood over the officer who was on his hands.) The man stood right over the officer and shot him three times. I could see the flashes and hear the pops. It was like hearing a cap pistol. The officer turned over on his back and his leg went out straight. I think his right leg.

Q. Can you tell me how this man was dressed, the man that shot the officer?

A. The clothing didn't appear too dark and it wasn't light.

Q. Can you tell me about how tall this male was?

A. He was a little taller than the officer, heavier than the officer and he may have had a beard.

Q. Did you see another man on the sidewalk besides the officer and the shooter?

A. There was nobody in front of me.

Q. How many shots did you hear?

A. Three rapid like.

Harkins's description of the shooter, as being a little taller and heavier than the six-feet-one, 200-pound Faulkner, points directly to the burly Freeman, who was slightly taller than Faulkner and weighed about 225 pounds, the approximate weight another prosecution witness, Chobert, attributed to the shooter. It also excludes both Abu-Jamal and his brother, Billy Cook, from being the shooter. Abu-Jamal was about as tall as Faulkner but weighed a lean 170 pounds, and Cook, at five feet six inches in height, weighed less than 150 pounds. Both Abu-Jamal and Cook wore their hair in dreadlocks, while the shooter, according to both Scanlan and Chobert, had an Afro hairstyle.

Until Faulkner began clubbing Cook with his flashlight, there was little reason for any of the bystanders to focus on what appeared to be a routine traffic stop. None, for example, had noticed that Faulkner had placed some driver identification papers in his pocket—papers that Freeman had borrowed recently from Arnold Howard—before the situation began to get out of hand. (Scanlan did observe Faulkner, during his interaction with Cook, looking at some type of document.) As Faulkner began hitting Cook, the scene developed some interest. For those who were watching, Abu-Jamal soon became the focal point as he rushed across the street toward Faulkner. Scanlan, for one, assumed that the man running across the street must have been the one who shot Faulkner, although he admitted that he saw no flash coming from the running man as the first shot rang out and that the shooter he did observe had an Afro.

2

THE ARREST

Within two or three minutes of the shooting, police began arriving en masse at 13th and Locust. Among the first there were Officers Robert Shoemaker and James Forbes, the two Harkins had informed of the shooting. When they arrived, Faulkner was lying on his back within a few feet of the passenger door of the VW, Abu-Jamal was sitting on a curb about ten feet away, and Billy Cook was standing off to the side in front of a nearby building. Forbes went to assist Faulkner, while Shoemaker approached Abu-Jamal. At trial Shoemaker testified that he ordered Abu-Jamal "to freeze" and then kicked him in the face when he said he saw him move his hand toward a gun.

Numerous other police arrived in squad cars and wagons. Faulkner was carried to a police wagon to be taken to nearby Jefferson University Hospital.

In dragging Abu-Jamal to another police wagon, Officer Daniel Soboloski testified at trial, he and two other officers "unintentionally" rammed Abu-Jamal's head into a no-parking pole and dropped him to the ground.

Although it was now past 4 A.M., Abu-Jamal's involvement in the Faulkner shooting reached Police Inspector Alfonzo Giordano so quickly that he was able to make it to the crime scene while Abu-Jamal was still in the back of the paddy wagon. Giordano worked directly for George Fencl, the chief inspector of the police department's Civil Defense Bureau, which had monitored Abu-Jamal after he joined the Black Panther Party at age fifteen and had retained an

15

interest in him ever since. In his biography of Abu-Jamal, Terry Bisson relates that every time Fencl came across the young Black Panther, Fencl "would aim a finger and cock a thumb" at him, "the same thing he would do years later when Mumia was a newsman reporting . . . stories the cops didn't want told."

Normal police protocol would have been to send a homicide detective to the crime scene to take over the investigation of Faulkner's death, but instead Giordano was the ranking officer at the scene after the shooting. As corrupt a police officer as it is possible to imagine, Giordano did not take more than a few minutes to set the framing of Mumia Abu-Jamal on its course. It was Giordano who went inside the police wagon to interview Abu-Jamal, and it was Giordano who arranged for prostitute Cynthia White to be taken to the police station to give a statement and for a cabdriver with a felony conviction, Robert Chobert, to come to the paddy wagon and identify Abu-Jamal as the shooter.

Giordano and White would become the prosecution's only witnesses against Abu-Jamal at a preliminary hearing on January 8, 1982, to hold him over for trial. White testified that she saw Abu-Jamal run across the street and shoot at Faulkner and then shoot him in the face as he lay helplessly on the ground. Giordano testified that he asked Abu-Jamal in the paddy wagon where he had put his gun and quoted Abu-Jamal as responding, "I dropped it beside the car after I shot him [Faulkner]." No other officer in or around the paddy wagon would claim to have heard this confession.

As damning as Giordano's testimony would have proven to be if heard by a jury—and Judge Sabo ruled at Abu-Jamal's trial that it was admissible—the prosecution elected not to call Giordano as a witness at Abu-Jamal's trial. In his affidavit, Abu-Jamal refers to a police officer in a "white shirt"—most certainly Giordano—who struck him in the forehead with a walkie-talkie as he lay inside the paddy wagon and who repeatedly called him "nigger" and "a black motherfucker." In one of the more shameless and sinister aspects of Abu-Jamal's case, the police department made it clear why Giordano had not been called as a prosecution witness. On the first business day after Abu-Jamal's trial concluded, the police department "relieved" Giordano of his duties on what would prove to be well-founded "suspicions of corruption."

Four years later, an extensive federal probe of the rank corruption within the Philadelphia Police Department would lead to Giordano's conviction. The FBI had begun an undercover investigation in May 1981, more than six months before Faulkner's shooting, focusing on police corruption within the Sixth Precinct. The federal investigation—the largest the U.S. Justice Department had ever conducted of a police force—uncovered that Giordano and numerous other high-ranking Philadelphia police officials and officers, many of them involved in Abu-Jamal's arrest and trial, had been engaged for years in extorting kickbacks from pimps, prostitutes, and bar owners. The government presented evidence showing that Giordano had been receiving more than $3,000 per month in illegal payoffs. He pled guilty to tax fraud in connection with those payoffs. Numerous other police officers also were convicted, including Deputy Police Commissioner James Martin, and John DeBenedetto, head of the Central Division, to which Faulkner was assigned. James Carlini, head of the homicide unit, was named in a federal indictment as an unindicted coconspirator. Martin, the acknowledged ringleader of the Philadelphia Police Department's widespread extortion apparatus, was in charge of all major investigations, including Faulkner's death.

Giordano's involvement in extorting payments from prostitutes, pimps, and bar owners would explain his quick arrival at the Faulkner shooting scene. Nailing Abu-Jamal with Faulkner's killing was a clever way to explain Faulkner's death and even an old score against the police-bashing Abu-Jamal in the process.

Although Abu-Jamal had been shot in the chest and was blacking out from the trauma and loss of blood, the police were in no hurry to get him to the hospital. In addition to kicking him in the face, ramming his head into a pole and dropping him to the ground, and allowing Giordano to confront him in the paddy wagon, the police brought various eyewitnesses to the paddy wagon to try to identify him as the shooter. Abu-Jamal was taken to Jefferson University Hospital, arriving twenty-five to thirty minutes after Faulkner had been rushed there.

At the hospital, pandemonium reigned. Abu-Jamal, his hands cuffed behind his back and too weak to stand on his own, was dragged from the paddy wagon and placed on his side on the rubber floor mats just outside the emergency room's automatic doors by Officers Gary Wakshul and Stephen Trombetta. Numerous other police officers were there when Abu-Jamal was brought in. According to an emergency room doctor's testimony at trial, one of those officers raised his leg over Abu-Jamal and then the doctor heard Abu-Jamal "groan." She said her view of the officer's foot was obstructed so that she could not actually see the kick land. She also said another police officer then told her that if she were not directly involved in Abu-Jamal's medical care, she should not remain in that part of the ER.

Instead of taking Abu-Jamal to an operating room, hospital security guard Priscilla Durham had the police drag him to the family room. At about 4:30 A.M. Abu-Jamal was brought handcuffed to the emergency room for surgery.

As Dr. Anthony Coletta began treating Abu-Jamal, he noted that he was coherent but weak and on the verge of passing out from blood loss. Coletta testified at trial that Abu-Jamal had lost about one-fifth of his blood volume and was in "critical condition," meaning that if he had not gotten treatment right away, he would have died.

After surgery, Abu-Jamal was shackled to his hospital bed. Three police guarded the doorway to his room, and two others were posted inside it. That morning Common Pleas Judge Lynne Abraham arraigned Abu-Jamal at his bedside, charging him with murder, possession of an instrument of crime, and possession of an offensive weapon. Abraham also ordered him to be held without bail pending a hearing.

Five days after Faulkner's death, the Center City newsstand, where Kenneth Freeman and Billy Cook operated a vending stand, burned to the ground at about 3 A.M. Freeman told an *Inquirer* reporter hours after the blaze that "there was no question in my mind that the police are behind this." The *Inquirer* also quoted a Center City police officer who was on patrol in the area that morning as saying, "It's entirely possible" that "certain sick members" of his department were responsible. "All I know is when I got to the station to start my shift at 7:30 this morning, the station house was filled with Cheshire grins," said the officer, who asked not to be identified. Later the next year, a spokesperson for the fire marshal said the blaze had been classified as "suspicious," but the investigation had uncovered no suspects and the inquiry had been closed.

On March 29, 1982, Cook was tried on charges of aggravated assault of a police officer and resisting arrest, misdemeanors that carry a sentence of up to seven years. McGill was the prosecutor, and Cynthia White was the primary witness for the prosecution. Cook put up no defense. He was sentenced to six months to a year—his first conviction. He appealed the sentence to the Philadelphia Court of Common Pleas and posted bond. His appeal was not heard until a month after Abu-Jamal's trial concluded—a trial at which Cook did not testify. At the appeal, Cook pled guilty to simple assault and was given probation, an unusually light sentence for one involved in an altercation at the murder scene of a police officer.

3

THE ORIGINAL POLICE VERSION OF THE SHOOTING

The Philadelphia Police Department did not apply the notion of a person being presumed innocent until proven guilty in this case. Within hours of Abu-Jamal's arrest, the police department offered its version of Faulkner's shooting, and the media showed no restraint in disseminating it.

The *Philadelphia Inquirer* quoted the police the next day as stating that radio reporter Wesley Cook, known professionally as Mumia Abu-Jamal, shot Faulkner. The police said Faulkner had stopped the reporter's brother, Billy Cook, for driving the wrong way on 13th Street and was in the process of searching him when Cook struck Faulkner in the face. Faulkner then struck Cook. Abu-Jamal then ran across the street and fired at Faulkner's back from about ten yards away, causing Faulkner to fall down. Abu-Jamal then stood over the prone officer and fired several more shots at point-blank range at his face.

The police said, "Abu-Jamal was wounded when the dying officer managed to get off one shot, which struck him in the chest."

The police said that a .38 caliber revolver registered to Abu-Jamal—which he was not licensed to carry—was recovered at the scene with five spent cartridges, and it was the gun used to shoot Faulkner.

If this had been a tennis match, the police version would have been point, set, and match.

When an *Inquirer* reporter asked the police spokesperson about allegations from Abu-Jamal's family that the police had beaten Abu-Jamal several times, the spokesperson said there was "no evidence" of a beating.

One by one, major details of the police version would fall apart. Within two days the police backtracked on the .38. "Initial tests by police ballistics experts, who compared four bullets recovered at the shooting scene to a test bullet fired from (Abu-Jamal's) gun proved inconclusive," Captain Jerrold Kane of the homicide unit told reporters. It would not come out until trial that the police had not bothered to run any tests of Abu-Jamal's hands or clothing to determine if he had fired a gun or even if the .38 had been fired. (Tests such as these are so routine at murder scenes that it is almost inconceivable the police did not run them. It is more likely that they did not like the results of the tests.) The police further stated that the fingerprints on the gun were too smudged to determine who had fired it.

That same day police also undermined their account of the shooting—of Abu-Jamal standing over the prone officer and shooting several bullets into his face at point-blank range—by revealing that Faulkner had been shot only twice, once in the back and once in the face. The police said a single bullet was removed from Faulkner's head; a second bullet passed through Faulkner's body and struck a nearby building, and two other bullets missed Faulkner and were found lodged in the same building. They could not account for the fifth bullet they had claimed Abu-Jamal had fired. The police did not reveal that a preliminary report of Faulkner's autopsy had noted that the two bullets that struck Faulkner bore the markings of a .44 caliber revolver, not a .38. At trial, this potentially crucial revelation never emerged, because the defense failed to raise the issue. (This apparent discrepancy—potentially a smoking gun in reverse—would later become a mistaken focal point for Abu-Jamal's supporters. At Abu-Jamal's postconviction relief hearing in 1995, George Fassnacht, a ballistics expert called by the defense, testified that the deformed slug removed from Faulkner's head was most likely a .38 after all.)

What the police, or the prosecution later, would never try to explain was how Abu-Jamal could have possibly missed hitting Faulkner with the other bullets he was alleged to have fired directly at Faulkner's face from a distance of no more than twelve inches away. At trial, it was revealed that the bullet that struck Faulkner in the back also had been fired from within twelve inches, not from ten yards away, as the police had initially advanced. This finding sharply contradicted the original police version of events, which was based heavily on the statement given to police within thirty minutes of the shooting by key prosecution witness Cynthia White, the prostitute Inspector Giordano had arranged for detectives to interview. In her initial statement to police she said that Abu-Jamal, while running toward Faulkner, had gotten off four or five shots from about ten yards away before one of them struck the officer in the back, causing him to fall to the ground. According to White and two other prosecution witnesses, the shooter then stood over Faulkner and fired several more shots directly at his face. By White's account, Abu-Jamal had discharged seven or eight rounds, but the .38 registered to him had only five chambers. To fix that discrepancy at trial, White testified that Abu-Jamal had fired only one or two shots as he approached Faulkner.

Similarly, the police and the prosecution were never able to explain how Faulkner could have gotten off the shot that struck Abu-Jamal in the chest. At trial, Charles Tumosa, a criminalistics supervisor for the police department, testified that the bullet that struck Abu-Jamal was also fired from a distance of one foot or less. At Abu-Jamal's postconviction relief hearing, Dr. John A. Hayes, an assistant medical examiner for New York City, testified that the downward path of the bullet recovered from Abu-Jamal during his surgery was inconsistent with the police and prosecution theory advanced at his trial as to how Faulkner had shot Abu-Jamal. Their theory was that a wounded Faulkner was able to get that shot off, after he was shot in the back, by spinning around and firing as he was falling to the ground. In that scenario, Hayes said, the bullet in Abu-Jamal would have taken an upward path. The evidence indicated that Faulkner, while standing on the curb, had shot Abu-Jamal in the chest as he got within one foot of him on the street. That same evidence would automatically rule out Abu-Jamal as Faulkner's assailant because Faulkner was first shot in the back at near point-blank range.

4

FRANK RIZZO

To step back and attempt to understand why prosecutors and police were so determined to railroad Mumia Abu-Jamal, it is necessary to consider Frank Rizzo's Philadelphia as well as the small, rag-tag back-to-nature group called MOVE, which Rizzo detested and wanted to destroy. Over time, Abu-Jamal's fate had become inextricably tied to MOVE's.

Rizzo was not just a lightning rod for racial strife; he built his career on it, ascending from beat cop to precinct captain, to commander, to police chief (1967–71), to mayor (1972–79), promising along the way to make "Attila the Hun look like a faggot." Despite his bravado, Rizzo was less than willing to enforce the law when it came to corralling the high-profile mobsters who acted with virtual impunity during his long career. "On Frank Rizzo's watch, the South Philadelphia mob grew unabated," wrote Sal Paolantonio in his mostly fawning biography of Rizzo entitled *Frank Rizzo: The Last Big Man in Big City America*, published in 1993.

For Rizzo's willingness to wield a nightstick early in his career, his fellow officers nicknamed him "the Cisco Kid."

Blacks called him Rizzio. To many of his fellow Italian Americans in South Philly he was "the Bambino." To Paolantonio and other admirers he was simply "the Big Man."

In *On a Move*, Bisson recounted a classic Rizzo display that occurred in 1967, during Rizzo's first year as police chief, when three thousand black high school students marched on the Board of Education Building to demand black studies be included in the curriculum. Rizzo, like George Wallace at the University of Alabama, stood in the doorway as the students approached. Then he shouted his order to the police: "Get their black asses!" Police waded in among the young demonstrators with nightsticks, injuring dozens of students and beating fifteen of them so severely that they had to be hospitalized. While no police officer would be charged or disciplined for the assault, citations for resisting arrest and disorderly conduct were handed out to many students. Rizzo denied he had given the order to assault the students, until reporter Larry Kane at television station WFIL played it for him on videotape the next day. "When he saw that he had said it, he just turned his head and left," Kane said in an *Inquirer* interview.

Under Rizzo, police lawlessness was so commonplace and pervasive that the U.S. Justice Department sued the city's entire police force for civil rights violations in 1979. A federal court dismissed the suit on jurisdictional grounds. Later, President Carter and the majority of Philadelphians would come to view Rizzo as a national embarrassment. By the late 1970s police graft was so intertwined with underworld activities that the Philly Police Department, particularly the Center City precinct to which Faulkner was assigned, was the target of at least three ongoing FBI probes that would result in the indictments and convictions of more than thirty Central Division Philadelphia police officers, including Police Inspector Alfonzo Giordano, the ranking officer at the scene when Abu-Jamal was arrested for Faulkner's murder.

There have always been a lot of skeletons in the closet of the City of Brotherly Love. As Frederick Douglass wrote in 1862:

> There is not perhaps anywhere to be found a city in which prejudice against color is more rampant than in Philadelphia. . . . It has its white schools and its colored schools, its white churches and its colored churches, its white Christianity and its colored Christianity . . . and the line is everywhere tightly drawn between them.

Philadelphia remains, essentially, a city of ghettos. Its enormous inner-city black slums are hemmed in by a series of ethnic neighborhoods that stretch out to the south and east in miles and miles of nearly identical row houses. Further removed are the neighborhoods to the west, and beyond them, just outside the city's limits, the pristine suburbs roll, one after the other, along the storied Main Line.

In Rizzo, the Italians and the various Slavs, the Irish, and the Germans had their man who was more than willing to stand up to the expanding black population as it encroached on the boundaries of the city's ethnic neighborhoods. MOVE's ramshackle house in previously all-white West Philly would be the spot where Rizzo would draw a line in the sand.

5

MOVE

"In a certain universal sense, the group calling itself MOVE, from the early 1970s up to the current day, has acted like a vortex into which have flowed all of modern civilization's troubles."

—Robin Wagner-Pacifici, *Discourse and Destruction: The City of Philadelphia Versus MOVE*

Rizzo didn't create MOVE, but he might as well have, in the sense that every despot needs, in fact demands, a foil. In MOVE, Rizzo had the perfect one. The more he oppressed the group, the stronger, more determined, and politically savvy it became; the more he tried to destroy MOVE, the more he exposed his own lawlessness, causing his political career to collapse. When term limits barred him from seeking the mayoralty a third consecutive time, he put his career to a vote by spearheading a special referendum in 1978—in the wake of the Powelton MOVE debacle—to alter the city charter. In a massive denunciation, Philadelphia voters told Rizzo eight years was enough, rejecting the referendum 66 percent to 34 percent. "Sixty-six percent of the city's voters said no to charter change, no to Frank Rizzo, mayor for life," wrote Paolantonio. "The winners rejoiced as if the walls of totalitarianism had been pulled down."

Vincent Lopez Leaphart founded MOVE in the early 1970s in Philadelphia and subsequently changed his name to John Africa.

Leaphart, in his early forties at the time, was, like Rizzo, a high school dropout. IQ tests at age seven and fifteen revealed scores of 84 and 79, respectively. At age fifteen he transferred to a school for students with learning disabilities, only to drop out the following year. At age seventeen he was arrested for armed robbery and auto theft. Drafted in 1952, he served two years in the army, one of them in Korea. Like his father, Leaphart made what living he did as a handyman. In 1966 his wife of five years, Dorothy, brought charges against him for striking her, but the case was dismissed. They divorced the next year.

How Leaphart, who could barely read and write, was able to take on the messianic role he would carve out for himself is a matter of great mystery. His hold over his followers was similar in many respects to the incredibly magnetic pull other cult leaders such as Jim Jones and David Koresh had on their disciples. To this day—more than two decades after his gruesome death in 1985 at a bombed-out MOVE row house, where his beheaded corpse was found with buckshot in both its chest and buttocks—past and present MOVE members venerate him. "Long Live John Africa!" is their mantra.

In 1971 Leaphart moved into the Powelton Community Housing Project—known simply as "the Co-Op"—in the Powelton Village section of West Philadelphia, adjacent to Drexel University. This integrated neighborhood was a haven for free thinkers and 1960s-style radicals, home to students and faculty from both Drexel and the University of Pennsylvania. There Leaphart befriended Donald Glassey, a recent master's graduate in his early twenties from the School of Social Work at Penn. Together, with Leaphart dictating and Glassey taking notes, the two authored in a year's time what would turn out to be Leaphart's "naturalistic" philosophy, *The Book of Guidelines*. Later, this typewritten three-hundred-page manifesto would be known as *The Teachings of John Africa* and become the framework of the MOVE movement.

Less than two years after Leaphart moved into the Co-Op, its board began eviction proceedings against him for his failure to fumigate his apartment, the source of a major roach infestation now plaguing many of his neighbors. To Leaphart's naturalistic view, roaches and all living things were God's children, no different than humans.

When Glassey purchased half of a cavernous three-story Victorian house in Powelton in spring 1973, he allowed Leaphart—who now referred to himself as John Africa—to move in, bringing with him his sisters Louise James and LaVerne Sims, and their children, as well as a pack of dogs who followed him around and earned him the nickname "Dog Man" in the neighborhood. At first the Leapharts referred to themselves as the American Christian Movement for Life, but soon dropped the references to American and Christian, settling on MOVE. By the mid-1970s there were as many as thirty or forty MOVE members. They made money by washing cars in the street in front of the house, doing home repairs in the neighborhood, cutting wood, and, in season, selling watermelons and fruits from the front yard.

Most MOVE members were in their twenties and black, but a few were young white women looking for a family to belong to, for something to believe in. *In Burning Down the House: MOVE and the Tragedy of Philadelphia*, a white teenaged member, Jeanne Africa, is quoted as saying she joined MOVE to acquire "a solid, secure family." She said John Africa "gave us a lot of solutions to problems we had in The Lifestyle. We had people who were on drugs, he got them off drugs. He was like a messiah." The teachings of John Africa forbade the use of drugs.

At any one time there could be up to thirty or more MOVE members living in the Powelton house, including small children and infants. MOVE members didn't marry, but monogamous relationships were the rule. Pregnancies were common. In *Burning Down the House*, authors Anderson and Hevenor describe MOVE's approach to childbearing.

Progeniture was the order of the day at Headquarters. Sexual potency on the part of MOVE's men and childbearing on the part of its women were encouraged as part of "the natural order of life." . . . MOVE women were expected not only to bear many children, but to give birth naturally, licking their babies clean, biting off the umbilical cord with their teeth, then eating it.

John Africa's grand experiment was to have MOVE children grow up free of the addictions of the "System lifestyle." No school, no television, no clothes in summer, and a diet solely of raw fruits and vegetables. There would be no "Distortion Days" for the children like there were occasionally for MOVE adults; these were days when the adults could gorge themselves on all the junk food and meat they wanted. "Children were considered central figures in the MOVE organization. Babies did not diaper, but defecated in the yard along with the animals MOVE kept," wrote Robin Wagner-Pacifici.

In a pamphlet MOVE published in 1996 to mark its twenty-fifth anniversary, MOVE stated its mission.

> MOVE's work is to stop industry from poisoning the air, the water, the soil, and to put an end to the enslavement of life—people, animals, any form of life. The purpose of John Africa's revolution is to show people how corrupt, rotten, criminally enslaving this system is, show people through John Africa's teaching, the truth, that this system is the cause of all their problems (alcoholism, drug addiction, unemployment, wife abuse, child pornography, every problem in the world) and to set the example of revolution for people to follow when they realize how they've been oppressed, repressed, duped, tricked by the system, this government and see the need to rid themselves of this cancerous system as MOVE does.

It is beyond ironic that the rebellious MOVE cult took hold in the city William Penn founded as a Quaker colony in 1681. Penn's bronze statute—a beacon to liberty and tolerance—sits atop Philadelphia's ornate City Hall. Penn, just as MOVE would do three centuries later, issued tracts, lectured in public, got arrested for unlawful assembly, and scorned courtroom decorum. In 1670, Penn was imprisoned for "declining to doff his hat in court, for further unauthorized preaching, for refusing to take an oath of allegiance to the Crown," according to *The First American: The Life and Times of*

Benjamin Franklin, written by H. W. Brands in 2000. To rid England of the young, highborn firebrand, King Charles II granted Penn a large tract of land west of New Jersey to settle a debt he owed Penn's recently deceased father.

Characterized by dreadlock hair and the adopted surname Africa (*Africa* for the original homeland of all humankind), MOVE's members were controversial, confrontational, belligerent, and profane, calling their detractors "motherfuckers." The term *motherfucker*—particularly when MOVE members ranted over loudspeakers or bullhorns—would often be used three or four times in one sentence, in sentence after numbing sentence. They justified this obscenity by arguing that the real obscenity is the system that allows racism, exploitation, and injustice to flourish. "If our profanity offends you, look around you and see how destructively society is profaning itself. It is the rape of the land, the pollution of the environment, the betrayal and suffering of the masses by corrupt government that is the real obscenity."

According to the MOVE pamphlet, members saw themselves as "pilgrims with bullhorns" and their Powelton Village house as their *Mayflower*. MOVE picketed pet stores, circuses, veterinary offices, and the zoo ("Let the animals go free!"); challenged visiting celebrities to noisy debates; called Jane Fonda a racist and Jesse Jackson a liar. They took in the stray cats and dogs in the neighborhood, accumulating a pack of more than thirty unvaccinated dogs that roamed the premises. Although MOVE members were vegetarians, they fed their dogs with chunks of raw meat thrown into the yard. They also let their garbage pile up, "composting" in the front yard, a magnet for rats, termites, cockroaches, and swarms of insects. All life-forms were welcome at the MOVE house. They were the neighbors from hell.

The Teachings of John Africa prohibited bathing with soap and prescribed that men and women alike grow their hair to the fullest in "natural"-length dreadlocks. The uniform was unisex as well: blue jeans, blue denim jackets, and heavy-soled men's boots. Members were encouraged to chew garlic for its natural medicinal value.

Anderson and Hevenor described MOVE's Powelton house this way:

> The ramshackle headquarters at 309 N. 33rd in Powelton was turned into a compound. The whole of the front lawn was made into a stage for MOVE's drama. A wooden platform extended from the front porch all the way to an eight-foot-high outer fence. Electric bullhorns were mounted in treetops, and the neighborhood was treated to frequent lectures via the powerful sound system. Extemporaneous reading from *The Teachings of John Africa* blared through the night and into the early morning hours. Neighbors who dared complain soon found themselves denounced openly, loudly, and obscenely. Under such circumstances, powerful drama unfolded almost daily on North 33rd Street.

MOVE became the butt of many cocktail-party and local news broadcast jokes. Most Philadelphians readily bought the news media's version of MOVE as urban savages. By 1975 enough neighbors had complained to the city government about the stench emanating from MOVE's property that the Department of Licenses and Inspections had to respond. Later that year, the city filed a civil suit against MOVE to evict the group from its property. MOVE appealed to the state supreme court. The case would drag on for three years until Rizzo came up with his ultimate solution.

By the mid-1970s, MOVE was appearing in public with increasing frequency, demonstrating with bullhorns at political rallies, public forums, and media offices. MOVE, inevitably, made police abuse a focal point. Rizzo, now mayor, responded predictably; the police began to break up MOVE demonstrations and arrest MOVE members on disorderly conduct charges or other misdemeanor violations such as obscenity and failure to disperse. MOVE cases jammed the Philadelphia courts. During a seven-month period in late 1973 and early 1974, the *Inquirer* reported, forty different MOVE members were arrested 150 times. Some were sentenced to several years in jail.

The boiling point in the MOVE/police relationship was reached on Sunday, March 28, 1976, when seven jailed MOVE members were released in the afternoon and arrived at the Powelton house at around 4 P.M. A noisy celebration carried on into the late evening until neighbors called the police to complain. Upon their arrival, Chuck Sims Africa cursed the police. "Officer Daniel Palermo told reporters that as he was walking back to his car, a brick sailed through the air and caught him in the back of his head. More bricks flew. . . . Bedlam followed," Anderson and Hevenor reported in their book. Janine Africa told the authors "how the police had drawn their guns and billyclubs and begun to beat everyone present. The police, she said, 'were going crazy,' swinging their nightsticks, pushing and shoving the MOVE women away in order to get at their men. When Janine, the baby Life in her arms, tried to shield Phil (Africa), she too was pushed, then fell heavily to the ground. After that, the 'cops stepped all over me and on me.' Life Africa lay crushed to the earth."

Six MOVE men—including three who had been freed from jail that day—were arrested and charged with aggravated assault, riot, resisting arrest, and reckless endangerment. Six wounded Philadelphia police officers were taken to the hospital.

The next morning, MOVE held a news conference at its compound. One member displayed a broken, bloodstained police nightstick and a police officer's blue hat. Janine Africa told reporters that her three-week-old son, Life Africa, had been stomped to death on the floor after police knocked her down while she was holding the baby. "Police Department officials denied the story and hinted strongly that no such child as Life Africa had ever existed," reported Anderson and Hevenor. Since all MOVE children were home birthed, "there were, after all, no hospital records of the child's having been born."

To prove the baby boy's death to the media, MOVE invited a *Philadelphia Inquirer* photographer and reporter and several local politicians to dinner at their headquarters a number of days later. After the meal, the guests were shown the baby's corpse in a shoebox. The guests reported that the stench from the box was overwhelming.

A few weeks later, according to Bisson's biography, Abu-Jamal interviewed an eyewitness, an old man who had watched it all from a window across the street. "I saw that baby fall," he said. "They were clubbing the mother; I knew the baby was going to get hurt. I even reached for the phone to call the police, before I realized that it *was* the police. You know what I mean?"

No charges were filed against the police officers involved in the baby's death. Instead the D.A.'s office pursued prosecution of the six MOVE members arrested that night. Federal authorities informed MOVE that they would investigate the baby's death but would require an autopsy to do so. "The MOVE people demurred," Anderson and Hevenor reported. "Their organization was opposed to the perverted work of scientists and doctors." Instead, MOVE filed a $26 million civil suit against the city.

By 1976 hundreds of MOVE cases were clogging Philadelphia's justice system, preventing hundreds of non-MOVE-related cases from coming to court on time. "Thanks to MOVE, an already overloaded court system had virtually stalled," the *Inquirer* reported. To deal with this backlog, court administrators began dismissing numerous MOVE cases.

But three MOVE members were put on trial on charges of assault and resisting arrest in 1976. Robert, Conrad, and Jerry Africa—following the dictates of John Africa—refused to participate in their own defense, ignored courtroom decorum, and were eventually barred from their own trial. Common Pleas Judge Paul Ribner, who would later handle the preliminary hearings in Abu-Jamal's murder trial, tried them in absentia, found them guilty, and sentenced them to long prison terms.

By 1977 most MOVE efforts were directed toward getting the three released. On May 20, 1977, MOVE member Chuck Sims Africa was arrested when police stopped his car and found a gun and ammunition in it. Later that day, MOVE orchestrated its first major confrontation with the police. From a platform recently erected outside the MOVE house, various speakers, wearing khaki army-style uniforms, demanded over the loudspeaker system the release of their "political prisoners" and an end to the violent harassment by the city. A crowd formed. When the police began arriving, MOVE members brandished firearms—sawed-off shotguns, pistols, rifles, and clubs. This display brought SWAT and stakeout units. For nine tense hours, some two hundred police surrounded the compound and trained an arsenal of weaponry on the front porch. An unidentified MOVE member took the microphone and warned the police, shouting out, "The only way they will come in our headquarters is over our dead bodies. If those motherfuckers come in here, they're going to have to kill everyone in here to do it."

At 10:30 P.M., MOVE members took their weapons back inside and Police Commissioner Joseph O'Neill ordered the police to disperse.

"The May 20, 1977 confrontation gave MOVE the kind of credence that it had never possessed. News out of Powelton now played on front pages of local newspapers, and Philadelphia television stations often began their broadcasts with MOVE coverage. In a single day's time, MOVE had become a Story. The possibility of violence commanded attention as no amount of bullhorns and pickets ever could," Anderson and Hevenor reported.

The confrontation also brought round-the-clock police surveillance to the compound, which would continue unabated for the next ten months.

Four days after the confrontation, Judge Lynne Abraham (currently the Philadelphia district attorney) issued eleven warrants for MOVE members on riot charges and "possession of an instrument of crime." Included in the warrants was one for Chuck Sims Africa. The gun taken from his car earlier on May 20 was traced to the gun shop where it was purchased. Records there showed that Leaphart's old friend, Donald Glassey, had purchased two shotguns and two hundred rounds of ammunition eight weeks earlier. Glassey was arrested on June 3 and charged by the U.S. Attorney's Office with falsifying information on the firearms forms. Unable to make the $25,000 bail and facing a possible five-year prison sentence, Glassey "turned." On July 21—in exchange for a reduced sentence, a recommendation of early parole, and a place in the Federal Witness Protection Program—he led federal agents to two cars he had stocked with most of the MOVE weapons—guns, bombs, and ammunition—that he had collected from various MOVE locations to set up the bust. As a result of the bust, federal arrest warrants were issued against Leaphart and Alfonso "Mo Africa" Robbins. Leaphart and Robbins went underground for the next four years until their arrest in Rochester, New York. Delbert Orr Africa became MOVE's interim leader.

One purpose of the twenty-four-hour watch the police set up around the MOVE house was to arrest members when they came off the property. Sue Africa left the premises and was apprehended a few blocks away and jailed. The other members remained at the house as months passed. (MOVE's $26 million civil suit against the city in connection with the March 28 death of Life Africa and other alleged police brutalities was dismissed during this period when the standoff prevented MOVE members from attending a hearing.)

Various community mediators tried to broker a deal between the city and MOVE in order to end the standoff, but MOVE's demand for the release of Sue Africa and the three MOVE members sentenced to prison by Judge Ribner always brought these discussions to an impasse.

The now nearly yearlong standoff was a major public relations debacle for the macho mayor. In March 1978, Rizzo decided to starve MOVE members out by ordering the water and electricity to the MOVE house cut off and the police to set up numerous sand-bagged sniper posts. "Police covered a truck with sandbags, armed it with machine guns, and pulled it up before MOVE headquarters. They stationed sharpshooters in the surrounding buildings. This development heightened the crisis and precipitated a new flurry of intermediary efforts," reported Hizkias Assefa and Paul Wahrhaftig in their 1990 book *The MOVE Crisis in Philadelphia: Extremist Groups and Conflict Resolution*. The police established checkpoints, sealing off a four-block area. Rizzo boasted that the perimeter was so tight "a fly couldn't get through."

With bullhorns and loudspeakers at the Poweltown house, MOVE members mocked the city government for spending thousands of dollars a day on police overtime just to stand around and listen to them decry the police and spew revolutionary rant. The media reveled in the street theater, making the Rizzo-versus-MOVE confrontation a staple of daily news coverage.

For the next two months, the city's quarantine of MOVE continued with great inconvenience to the neighbors who were now forced to drive around blockades and show identification going to and from their homes. The *Philadelphia Daily News* reported that city spending for police overtime had passed the $1 million mark. Area residents held a massive demonstration on Sunday, April 4, 1978, when several thousand ringed City Hall to protest the police blockade at the MOVE house. Rizzo had accomplished the near impossible in making MOVE the object of public sympathy.

With a nudge from the Carter administration to end the stalemate, the city's managing director, Hillel Levinson, announced a ten-point agreement in early May that had been brokered with MOVE counsel Oscar N. Gaskins. Judge Fred DiBona, City Solicitor Sheldon Albert, and Gaskins signed the agreement. "MOVE agreed to turn over its remaining weapons and allow police to search the Powelton compound," Anderson and Hevenor detailed. "In return, 18 MOVE members, charged with felonies and misdemeanors, would be freed from jail on their own recognizance. The MOVE organization would then have a 90-day grace period—or until midnight, Aug. 1, 1978—to vacate 307–309 N. 33rd Street entirely. At that point, all outstanding charges would be dropped against the [18 released] MOVE members." MOVE also agreed to dismantle the platform at the front of the house within two weeks, to remove its animals, and to cease dumping garbage in its backyard. The city agreed to assist MOVE in obtaining replacement housing.

No mention in the agreement was made of MOVE's three "political prisoners"—Jerry, Conrad, and Robert Africa. Their release "had been accomplished by an oral arrangement and had already been carried out as a precondition to MOVE's assent to the May 5 agreement," according to Assefa and Wahrhaftig.

Implementation of the agreement began that day with the police searching the MOVE compound with metal detectors. When only inoperable weapons were found, the barricades and roadblocks surrounding the area were pulled open. A May 24 news article in the *Inquirer* reported that health inspectors had found the MOVE house to be clean.

In gaining the release of its political prisoners, MOVE thought it had felled Goliath without hurling a stone. Its interpretation of the agreement, based on oral understandings shuttled back and forth between the city and MOVE during the negotiations of the settlement agreement, was that all charges against each of the twenty-one recently released MOVE members would be dropped pending the successful relocation of MOVE members. In fact, during the ninety-day grace period the office of District Attorney Edward Rendell (who became governor of Pennsylvania in 2003) began taking actions to bring some of those MOVE members to trial in connection with the May 20, 1977, standoff with police. MOVE saw this as a double cross.

When the city pressed MOVE to tear down its fence, get rid of all of its animals except for a few puppies, and turn over its loudspeakers to the police, MOVE did not comply. "As soon as the city knew MOVE had no guns or explosives, they began modifying and restating the terms of the agreement," the group's pamphlet states. "It soon became apparent that D.A. Rendell's promise to dispose of all pending MOVE cases within four-to-six weeks was a blatant lie. The ninety-day time period, which had been described to MOVE as a working timetable, was misrepresented to the media as an absolute deadline. The promise to assist MOVE in finding a new place to live was never completed, and the city began demanding that the house be razed."

The city did offer MOVE five dilapidated houses in an all-black North Philadelphia neighborhood. "At least one of the five North Philadelphia houses offered to MOVE for taking rental for $1 a year has been declared unfit for human habitation," the *Philadelphia Daily News* stated in an editorial dated April 4, 1978, noting that the other four were "run-down properties." The *Daily News* found this quite odd. "The ludicrous thing is that the city is trying to drive the MOVE people out of this property [the Powelton compound] on the claim that it is unfit for human habitation."

At a hearing on August 2, 1978—the day after the ninety-day deadline for MOVE to vacate its Powelton compound—that quickly turned intemperate and would lead to MOVE attorney Gaskins being jailed for contempt of court, Judge DiBona ruled that MOVE was in violation of the ninety-day deadline to vacate the Powelton house. He proceeded to sign bench warrants for twenty-one MOVE members, regardless of where they happened to live. This action would set in motion the horrific seizure of the Powelton compound within the week.

At dawn on August 8 hundreds of police in flak jackets and riot helmets surrounded the MOVE house. Inside were twelve MOVE adults and eleven children, some of them infants. Over MOVE's loudspeakers, Chuck Africa stated: "Testing, motherfuckers, testing. You're trying to kill breastfeeding mothers and breastfeeding children. We're not backing down. If you want us out, you'll have to bring us out dead." Other MOVE speakers asked if the police had their life insurance policies paid up, warning that there would be "lots of widows."

At 6:04 A.M. George Fencl, head of the Civil Affairs Bureau, announced over a bullhorn, "You have exactly two minutes in which to come out." A MOVE member responded, "The gate's open. Stop playin' games." Fencl then said, "Come out. No one will hurt you." He then handed the bullhorn to longtime community activist Monsignor Charles Devlin to make his plea: "Come on out. No one's going to get hurt. Let me come in, and I'll walk out with you."

"Fuck you, priest," was the reply, according to Anderson and Hevenor.

Police then rolled in specially modified construction vehicles and tore down the fence and smashed out the windows of the house. Just before 7 A.M. MOVE was notified by bullhorn: "Uniformed officers will enter your house for the purpose of taking each of you into custody. Any resistance or use of force will be met with force." In the next hour about thirty flak-jacketed police entered and searched the three-story house, determining that all twenty-three MOVE members were barricaded in the basement. As firefighters began prying off the boarded up basement windows, they saw a gun sticking out of a basement window. Deputy Police Commissioner Morton Solomon ordered the firefighters to blast water into the basement, flushing the basement with hundreds of gallons of water in minutes.

With the police still in the house and with firefighters just outside it, gunshots suddenly rang out at about 8:15 A.M., setting off a torrent of bullets into the house from the police sniper posts. During the ninety-second period of sustained gunfire, Officer James Ramp was fatally wounded. Four other police officers and four firefighters were also shot. For the next half hour, firefighters pumped more water into the basement, raising the standing water level in the basement to several feet. Finally, a MOVE woman and three naked small children climbed out of a front basement window and walked toward the police.

In the next few minutes, all of the remaining MOVE members, except Delbert Orr Africa, climbed out of the front of the house and surrendered. When Delbert, the nominal head of MOVE since John Africa went underground to avoid arrest, crawled out a side window and raised his arms up in a posture of surrender, he was about to become the only MOVE member seriously injured during the ordeal. With one police officer pointing a rifle at his chin, Officer Joseph Zagame smashed him in the face with his police helmet and Officer Lawrence D'Ulisse struck him in the chest with the butt of a rifle, knocking him to the ground. Police then dragged Delbert by his dreadlocks across the street where other officers kicked him in the head, kidneys, and groin.

Immediately following the arrests the police version of the events was that MOVE had fired the first shot and that no beatings had accompanied the arrests. The police were forced to abandon the second part of their claims when later that day local TV news broadcasts began airing videotaped footage of Delbert Africa's brutal arrest. Philadelphians were duly shocked. (The resulting public outcry forced the D.A.'s office to impanel a special grand jury, which eventually handed down indictments against three police officers, but no trial would be held for another two and a half years.)

The police claim that MOVE had fired the first shot also came into immediate dispute. Radio reporters Richard Maloney and Larry

Rosen both recalled hearing the first shot come from a house diagonally across the street where they said they saw an arm holding a pistol out of a second-story window. Most of the reporters at the scene, though, reported that the first shot came from a basement window of the MOVE compound. The next day, police interviewed three of the eleven MOVE children. An eight-year-old MOVE girl told them all MOVE adults had guns, and a five-year-old boy said he saw Phil, Eddie, Delbert, Janet, and Merle fire their guns—and that MOVE adults were the first to shoot.

Although the death of Officer Ramp had caused the MOVE house to become a murder scene, the compound would be bulldozed that day by noon. Crushed in the debris was a wooden sign that read "Long Live the House That John Africa Built."

Later that afternoon, Abu-Jamal attended Mayor Rizzo's news conference at City Hall. Rizzo blamed the "new breed of journalism" for the death of Officer Ramp and then, in response to a question from Abu-Jamal, said, "They believe what you write, what you say. And it's got to stop. And one day, and I hope it's in my career, that you're going to have to be held responsible and accountable for what you do."

All twelve MOVE adults arrested on August 8 were charged with the murder of Officer Ramp, as well as with attempted murder, conspiracy, and aggravated and simple assault.

At a preliminary hearing, MOVE's court-appointed lawyers entered a motion to dismiss the charges based on destruction of evidence, arguing that the demolition of the house prevented MOVE from proving that it was impossible for any of its members to have shot Ramp. Judge Merna Marshall denied that petition and held the defendants over for trial. Prior to trial, prosecutors dismissed charges against two of the defendants who agreed to disavow MOVE. Another defendant, Consuella Dotson Africa, refused to disavow the group but would be tried separately, because the prosecution could not establish that she was a MOVE member.

When the remaining nine MOVE defendants all elected self-representation, the court appointed separate backup counsel for each. The hearings for pretrial motions would last more than a year and frequently provide raucous and uproarious street theater. The media feasted on every twist and turn and played up every confrontation between the unruly MOVE defendants and the prosecution.

The nonjury trial—presided over by Common Pleas Judge Edwin Malmed—would not begin until December 10, 1979, and would go on for the next five months, becoming the longest trial in Philadelphia history. Nearly one hundred witnesses would testify, about two hundred exhibits would be introduced, and there would be three hundred defense motions for dismissal.

One of the first prosecution witnesses was Chief Inspector George Fencl, head of the Civil Affairs Bureau, a police official whom MOVE considered to be Rizzo's main architect in the plot to eliminate it. MOVE defendants cross-examined Fencl for four days until Judge Malmed ordered the witness excused. On Friday, January 18, Malmed removed all defendants from the courtroom for disorderly behavior, ordering their backup attorneys to take over the case. Each Monday after that, according to Anderson and Hevenor, "the MOVE defendants were taken into court and again asked to pledge to obey the judge's orders." They never did and were never again allowed to be present during the trial.

Eight defense witnesses, including several reporters, a number of neighbors, and one of the negotiators, testified that the first shot fired had been fired from outside the MOVE compound, contradicting earlier prosecution testimony from various police officers that the first shot was fired from the basement of the MOVE house.

In closing arguments held on May 5, the various court-appointed MOVE attorneys urged the judge to weigh just how circumstantial the evidence in this case was: no fingerprints on the weapons the police claimed to have recovered from the house, no ballistics to prove that Officer Ramp was killed by a bullet fired from the compound, and no eyewitness testimony of anyone claiming to have seen a MOVE member shoot Ramp. How could the judge even consider convicting nine people for the murder of one man who had been shot only once?

It took Judge Malmed just three days to reach his verdict. The sixty-eight-year-old jurist pronounced Chuck Sims Africa, Deborah Sims Africa, Delbert Orr Africa, Edward Goodman Africa, Janet Holloway Africa, Janine Phillips Africa, Merle Austin Africa, Michael Davis Africa, and William Phillips Africa guilty of third-degree murder, conspiracy, and multiple counts of attempted murder and aggravated assault. On August 4, Malmed sentenced each defendant to thirty to one hundred years in state prison. Consuella Dotson Africa was later sentenced to ten to twenty years by Common Pleas Judge Levy Anderson, who added on another three-and-a-half years for contempt. (Dotson was paroled in 1994. Merle Austin Africa died in prison in 2000. The other eight become eligible for parole in August 2008.)

After the trial, when Judge Malmed was asked on a radio call-in program who actually fired the fatal shot that killed Officer Ramp, the judge, according to Bisson, replied, "I haven't the faintest idea. They call themselves a family. I sentenced them as a family."

The trial of the three police officers indicted for brutalizing the now convicted Delbert Africa would not be held until 1981. D.A. Rendell's office brought to trial Officers Zagame, Charles Geist, and Terrence Mulvihill on assault charges. (No charges were brought against Officer D'Ulisse, who was photographed wielding the rifle butt.) Attorneys for the D.A.'s office presented photographic evidence of these police officers assaulting Delbert Africa. Just before the jury was to start its deliberations, Judge Stanley Kubacki ordered the jury dismissed and the officers acquitted. (Geist would be shot by his police officer wife during a "domestic dispute" three months after his acquittal, go into a coma, and die eight months later. Mulvihill would commit suicide in 1989.)

6

THE ARREST AND TRIAL OF JOHN AFRICA

On May 13, 1981, Bureau of Alcohol, Tobacco, and Firearms agents arrested Vincent Lopez "John Africa" Leaphart and Alfonso "Mo Africa" Robbins in Rochester, New York. The two had been fugitives since September 1977 when a federal grand jury indicted them on bomb-making and gunrunning charges. In July 1981 John and Alfonso went on trial at the federal courthouse in Philadelphia. The media dubbed the case "John Africa vs. the System." Abu-Jamal was among the reporters who covered the trial.

Unlike previous MOVE trials, in which the defendants had been banished from the courtroom for unruly behavior, John Africa insisted that his "advisors" (his court-appointed attorneys) neither raise objections nor cross-examine any witnesses. Throughout the trial, he sat impassively at the defense table, appearing to nod off to sleep through great stretches of it, according to Abu-Jamal biographer Bisson.

The government's star witness was Donald Glassey, the young, white master's graduate who had assisted Leaphart in writing *The Teachings of John Africa* and who had allowed Leaphart to take over the house in Powelton that became MOVE headquarters. Glassey testified that Leaphart had ordered him to purchase two shotguns in 1977 to add to the arsenal of weapons Leaphart was amassing at the MOVE house in preparation for the May 20 confrontation. That was the day when MOVE members brandished weapons from their front porch most of the day and warned the police that they intended to return violence with violence.

When it came time for the defense to present its closing statement to the jury, John Africa rose and delivered his only formal remarks to the court. He began by saying, "I'm not a guilty man. I am an innocent man. I didn't come here to bring trouble but to bring the truth. And goddamn it, that's what I'm going to do."

In an impassioned, hour-long harangue, he made no direct rebuttal to the government's evidence and testimony. In a resonant, deep voice, he told the jury, "I'm fighting for the air you breathe. I'm fighting for the water you drink, and if it gets any worse, you're not going to be drinking that water. I'm fighting for the food you eat, and if it gets any worse, you're not going to be eating that food. I've been a revolutionary all my life, and I remain a revolutionary, because don't you see, revolution simply means to turn, to generate, to activate. It simply means to be right."

Just before he sat down, he said, "I just want to say that I don't have anything against anyone in this courtroom. It isn't the people I'm against, but the idea that controls the people."

The jury deliberated the government's mostly circumstantial case for four days. When it returned, its verdict was jaw dropping. The jury found both defendants not guilty, acquitting them on all counts.

Abu-Jamal, who had attended the entire trial, was amazed, according to his biographer. So was everyone else. John Africa had pulled off a Houdini act. For the first time in a criminal court, a MOVE defendant had won an acquittal. "Calmly but completely, John Africa had turned the courtroom on its head. It was a lesson to be pondered," Bisson wrote. It was a lesson Abu-Jamal would badly misapply at his own murder trial just months away.

7

MUMIA

To those who knew Mumia Abu-Jamal, the news that he had been arrested and charged with the cold-blooded murder of a Philadelphia police officer was a shock. The day after the killing, the *Philadelphia Daily News* ran a story headlined "The Accused: Friends Can't Fathom 'Brilliant' Newsman as Murder Suspect."

Abu-Jamal, twenty-seven then, had never been known for violence. Quite the opposite. While he was willing to argue his point of view with conviction, those who knew him said he did so without raising his voice. With his deepening interest in the laid-back, Jamaican-based Rastafarian religious movement, which he had become interested in while attending ultraprogressive Goddard College, he was even less likely to be involved in a senseless murder. "I can't tell you how stunned I am about this," respected *Philadelphia Daily News* columnist Chuck Stone said the day after the killing. "Abu-Jamal has always been a peaceful person. You would never hear him raise his voice. When you would call his home, he'd say 'Peace,' before talking."

A couple months later Stone visited Abu-Jamal for two hours at the Detention Center in Philadelphia. "A white prison guard walked briskly past the visitors' stalls separated by wooden partitions that are raised about a foot off the floor," Stone wrote in his column:

Abu-Jamal nodded affably. "How you doing"?
"Hi, big fella," replied the guard.

49

"Abu-Jamal's basically a friendly person," observed prison superintendent David Owen.

Stone wrote that Abu-Jamal declined to discuss details "of that fateful Wednesday night in December," telling Stone, "I've talked with no one about it." "I know this. They tried to kill me that night," Stone quoted him as saying. "Their star witness said she saw me shoot a cop, but didn't see anything happen to me. What the D.A.'s office has yet to say is how I got shot."

Stone reported that Abu-Jamal "vigorously denied a reported confession," which Inspector Giordano had attributed to him, but avoided details of Officer Faulkner's slaying.

According to Stone, Abu-Jamal's "most vivid recollection of that tragic night are the beatings he said were administered by the police." Stone's column reported Abu-Jamal detailing being beaten before he was put in the police wagon, having his head rammed into a pole by two cops, and being beaten again inside the wagon by the inspector (Giordano). "When I finally got to Jefferson Hospital, two cops came in—I was handcuffed—pulled me out, dropped me to the street, kicked, punched and blackjacked me. Then I was beaten inside Jefferson again.

"I'm sure that they're surprised I'm not dead. The D.A. and the state are proceeding in a legal way to kill me when they failed illegally in the street," Abu-Jamal told Stone.

Tommie St. Hill, the City Hall reporter for the *Philadelphia Journal*, grew up five blocks from Abu-Jamal, attended high school with him, and considered him one of his closest friends. "Abu-Jamal was smart enough not to get into any dumb trouble. . . . He didn't have the warmest feelings toward police, but he wasn't going to assassinate any, either. I don't think he'd have invited any police to dinner, but he wouldn't kill any," St. Hill told a columnist for the *Inquirer*.

Abu-Jamal was well known throughout the black community and, thanks to his radio reporting, had begun to make a name for himself throughout the Philadelphia area. His voice, a rich, melodious baritone, was his gift. It was a voice unlike any other heard on radio in Philadelphia. When listeners heard it, if they had ever heard it before, they knew it instantly. Behind the voice was compassion. Abu-Jamal was a champion of the downtrodden, "the voice of the voiceless," to his admirers.

Abu-Jamal, a twin, was born Wesley Cook in Philadelphia on April 24, 1954. His mother, Edith, migrated after World War II from North Carolina to Philadelphia, where she married Bill Cook, also a transplanted Southerner, and had three boys with him. She also had two sons and a daughter from her first marriage. The Cooks raised their six children in the projects—known as the PJs—of North Philadelphia in a strict but nurturing household. Mrs. Cook worked as an inspector in the mail-order division of Sears, Mr. Cook at various odd jobs. At the time of Abu-Jamal's trial, his eldest half-brother, Keith, was a master sergeant in the army, stationed in West Germany. His twin brother, Wayne, was serving in the army in Germany. His half-sister, Lydia, was a nurse.

According to Bisson, young Wesley was a precocious child, learning to read before entering first grade in Philadelphia's racially segregated school system. At age fourteen, two years after his father died of a heart attack, Wesley Cook adopted Mumia as his first name. One of his high school teachers, Timone Ombima, was from Kenya; he taught the boys and girls some words in Swahili, and assigned Swahili names to the male students and had them use those names in class. (When Mumia became a father at age seventeen and named his son Jamal, he dropped his surname and became Mumia Abu-Jamal. In Arabic, *abu* means "father of.")

Abu-Jamal got his earliest dose of Philadelphia's law and order soon after changing his first name. With three friends, he attended a George Wallace for President rally at South Philly's Spectrum arena. To counter the rally's chants of "Segregation forever," they yelled, "Black power." In *On a Move*, Bisson recounts what happened next.

> The boys were pounced upon and beaten, [and] when they called out for
> help from the police the police beat the boys all over again, with nightsticks
> and sappers and kicks. Then they handcuffed and arrested them, for

assault. The police took them to the hospital on the way to the police station. When his mother came to the emergency room to see him she said "that's not my boy." He had been beaten so badly she couldn't recognize him. Two days later at the arraignment, the judge heard the cop's testimony and said "Assault? This kid's face assaulted your fist. Case dismissed."

The following year, Abu-Jamal joined the Philadelphia chapter of the Black Panther Party (BPP) and the next year—at age sixteen—he was named "lieutenant of information" for the chapter. The day after his appointment, a picture of him at Panther headquarters ran on the front page of the *Philadelphia Inquirer*. A prophetic poster over his left shoulder read "Free All Political Prisoners."

To the FBI's J. Edgar Hoover, the BPP was "the greatest threat to the internal security of the United States." Hoover countered the Panthers, and a number of other radical groups such as Students for a Democratic Society, the Weathermen, and the American Indian Movement, by creating COINTELPRO (for COunter INTELligence PROgram) in 1967 to monitor, harass, and disrupt U.S. dissidents. Before the decade was out, at least thirty-eight Panthers had died in clashes with local police and hundreds more were imprisoned.

Abu-Jamal's FBI file, released in 1991, contained approximately seven hundred pages. From age fifteen, when he was placed on the FBI's Security Index of subversives to be rounded up and jailed during times of national crisis, Abu-Jamal was one of the most surveilled citizens in the nation. An FBI field report dated October 24, 1969, stated, "In spite of the subject's age (15 years), in view of [Wesley] Cook's position of authority within the BPP, it is recommended that he be included in the Security Index. . . . Copies of this report are being designated to NISO [Naval Intelligence Services Office], OSI [Office of Special Investigation], SS [Secret Service] and MI [Military Intelligence]." (An FBI field report in 1974 revealed that Abu-Jamal had been deleted from the Security Index in March 1973, stating that "he has not displayed a propensity for violence" although "he has continued to associate with individuals and organizations engaged in extremist activities.")

In October 1970, Abu-Jamal resigned from the BPP when the Philly branch of the party decided to close rather than choose sides in an internal BPP power struggle between the East Coast and West Coast factions of the party's leadership.

At Ben Franklin High School, Abu-Jamal led a campaign to change the school's name to Malcolm X. The campaign got him elected president of the student body, but the school's name was not changed, and he was later expelled for being too confrontational.

After passing a GED exam, Abu-Jamal was accepted at freethinking, bucolic Goddard College in Vermont in fall 1971. Goddard had been founded in 1938 on the progressive ideas of John Dewey. Abu-Jamal studied anthropology, East Asian civilization, educational psychology, and black theater, and he worked at the college's small radio station. His FBI files showed that the FBI monitored him there. During his second semester, his girlfriend Fran Hart, the mother of his son Jamal, was admitted to Goddard. After she became pregnant again, they married. But Vermont was not for her. She moved back to Philly and had their daughter, Latifah. Abu-Jamal moved back home too, but his marriage fell apart.

At Temple University in Philadelphia, Abu-Jamal got his start in broadcasting, working as a non-enrolled volunteer at the university's student-run radio station, WRTI, where he did a commentary show on black issues through 1973. He got his first job in radio at WKDU in 1974, a station that featured itself as "the black experience in music." He hopped from station to station, learning engineering, photography, news writing, and how to edit his own tapes. To gather stories, he pedaled around the city on his bicycle with his radio equipment strapped to his back.

By 1975 he was still doing the show *The Black Experience* on WKDU and *Black Times Audio* for the Temple station, when he landed his first commercial job at WHAT, as a broadcaster on a popular morning radio show. The show's host, Mary Mason, told a *Daily News* reporter after Abu-Jamal had been charged with Faulkner's murder that she thought he "was the best in the business. He was an extraordinary newsperson. Abu-Jamal could have been

a network anchor. As a man, he was very aware of his 'blackness.'"
She described him as "a Malcolm X, Dr. Martin Luther King Jr. and
the Rev. Jesse Jackson all rolled into one." She said this despite Abu-
Jamal's having led a walkout of other station employees that resulted
in Mason's show being off the air for a time.

After the walkout at WHAT, Abu-Jamal landed a weekend job
at WPEN, a top-40 station. The station manager had him change his
on-air name to the more mainstream handle of William Wellington
Cole. While working at WPEN, Abu-Jamal married his second wife,
Marilyn, a schoolteacher. Their son Mazi was born in September
1977.

Based on his success at WPEN, Abu-Jamal got the job he most
wanted, and his adopted name back, at Philadelphia's highly
regarded public radio station WUHY (now WHYY). (The station is
home to Terry Gross's long-running National Public Radio program
Fresh Air.) His short tenure at WUHY—from July 1979 to March
6, 1981—was long enough for his talents as a journalist and a broadcaster to gain wider recognition. His "91 Report," which he worked
on with America Rodriguez, won several local broadcasting awards,
including one from the Society of Professional Journalists, Sigma
Delta Chi. Rodriguez, who would go on to be the Los Angeles cor-
respondent for NPR for ten years, said Abu-Jamal "had a dramatic
flair. It was a sincere flair. . . . He didn't make [his stories] dramatic.
He could draw out the drama of an event." *Philadelphia Magazine*
took note by naming him one of eighty-one "people to watch" in
1981, saying his advocacy-journalism approach to issues was bringing "a special dimension to radio reporting." Concomitantly, Abu-
Jamal was elected president of the city's Association of Black
Journalists.

That Abu-Jamal lasted as long as he did at the politically sensi-
tive public radio station was something of a miracle. He was never
so much a reporter as he was a crusader, a righter of wrongs. The
initial appeal of that approach can wear off rapidly with the wine-
and-brie set that sits on the boards of public radio stations, particularly when Abu-Jamal began championing the cause of local law

enforcement's most detested counterculture group, MOVE. Abu-Jamal, with that mahogany voice, was safe when he talked about racism, oppression, and police brutality in the abstract. WUHY's educated listeners were likewise against all that. When he began reporting about those issues in terms of the Philadelphia Police Department's brutalizing of MOVE members, the phone in the station's general manager's office started to ring. The station manager, Nick Peters, forced Abu-Jamal to resign over what he termed a "dispute over the objective reporting of the news." Peters said, "On some stories, he would not show any objectivity, and I would have to pound him over the head to get the other side." The day after Abu-Jamal's arrest for Faulkner's slaying, Peters told a *Daily News* reporter that his former reporter "had an incredible voice, he was a very good writer and an excellent producer. He could do wonders with sound."

By 1981, because of his coverage of MOVE, Abu-Jamal was unemployed, but still doing regular freelance stories on Mutual Black Network and NPR, landing high-profile interviews with Julius Erving, Bob Marley, and Alex Haley. He was now living alternately with Wadiya, his third wife, and at his mother's. Strapped for income, he also got a job two nights a week driving a cab. He joked to fellow reporter Linn Washington that he didn't want to become known as the "wheels of the wheel-less."

By 1982, he was on trial for his life.

8

PRETRIAL HEARINGS

Abu-Jamal's pretrial hearings were presided over by Common Pleas Judge Paul Ribner, who in 1977—with great antipathy—had tried three MOVE members in absentia on charges of assault and resisting arrest and had sentenced each to long prison terms. Abu-Jamal was represented by attorney Anthony Jackson—at first of the defendant's own accord; his family had retained Jackson to look into charges of police brutality during his arrest.

At a March 18 hearing, Jackson requested that a jury questionnaire be sent to anyone receiving a jury summons for this case. A jury questionnaire—a common practice in many states in capital cases—is a tool designed to test potential biases of prospective jurors. Jackson's concern in asking for a questionnaire was to make it more difficult for the prosecution to use peremptory challenges to exclude qualified blacks from the jury. "It has been the custom and the tradition of the district attorney's office to strike each and every black juror that comes up peremptorily. That has been my experience since I have been practicing law, as well as the experience of the defense bar; the majority of the defense bar knows that that occurs," Jackson told the judge. The judge ruled that the county would not pay for such a survey. (No survey was conducted.)

On April 1, Ribner denied Abu-Jamal's pretrial motion that the two prosecution witnesses who had identified him as the shooter—White and Chobert—be ordered to attempt to identify him in a police lineup.

On April 29, Jackson told Ribner at another hearing that he was having difficulty locating prosecution witnesses so that he could question them in preparation for trial. Back in January, Ribner had denied Abu-Jamal's request for the prosecution to provide the defense with the names, addresses, and phone numbers of its witnesses—a standard request that is normally granted except in organized-crime cases. Ribner likewise denied Jackson's request for the court to assign another attorney to assist him. Jackson did not even have a secretary at the time.

Judge Ribner's—and later Judge Sabo's—hold on the purse strings would further cripple the defense's ability to mount an adequate defense. In all, the total budget authorized for defense investigators and experts paid by the court was a meager $1,400. Pretrial, Judge Ribner approved just $150 for Jackson to hire an investigator to track down witnesses. Although the police had conducted more than 125 witness interviews, by the time the trial started, the investigator had located only two eyewitnesses.

About forty minutes into the hearing, Abu-Jamal rose and announced he was going back to his cell. "You try the case," he shouted at the judge. "You're going to decide what you want to hear. . . . What are you afraid of? What are you scared of?" He also told the judge to "go to hell" and accused him of orchestrating the case against him.

Abu-Jamal asked for permission to defend himself. At a pretrial hearing on May 13, 1982, Ribner granted his request but appointed Jackson as his backup counsel. Jackson told the judge he was not trained for such a role and requested that the judge appoint another attorney in his place. Ribner refused. Jackson, now believing that his role would be limited to supporting Abu-Jamal, essentially stepped away from preparing any sort of defense for his headstrong client. Ribner, at Jackson's request, then directed the lead prosecutor in the case, Assistant D.A. Joseph McGill, to proceed with the investigation of Abu-Jamal's complaint of police brutality after his arrest.

In late February, the D.A.'s office, along with the police's internal affairs unit, had already held hearings to investigate Abu-Jamal's claims. No charges against police officers resulted. Two of the great ironies of this case evolved from Abu-Jamal's attempts to disprove the police department's contention that the arresting officers and other officers at the hospital had not beaten him. One was that Jackson, whom he had hired to investigate the brutality charges, unwillingly became backup counsel for his murder trial. The other was that the D.A.'s investigation into Abu-Jamal's allegations led to the development of the strongest evidence of his guilt presented at trial: his alleged confession. Two of the witnesses the D.A.'s office interviewed, Officer Garry Bell and hospital security guard Priscilla Durham, would testify at trial that they heard Abu-Jamal boast loudly and defiantly at the hospital about shooting Faulkner, quoting him as saying, "I shot the motherfucker, and I hope the motherfucker dies."

9

THE WITNESSES

Eyewitness testimony, even in broad daylight under normal circumstances, is often unreliable. Not only do different people notice different things, but eyewitnesses can also view the same incident unfolding and see aspects of it differently or not even recall seeing crucial details that occurred. Eyewitnesses, like people in general, have varying levels of observation, memory, and comprehension. While Faulkner's attempted arrest of Cook covered just a minute or two, the shooting took a matter of seconds. Each of the eyewitnesses, at different vantage points, was viewing parts of a heart-stopping shooting or its immediate aftermath in the wee hours of a frigid night through the flashing red lights of a police car.

In addition to Faulkner, Cook, and Abu-Jamal, there were at least twelve people—not counting the one or two people who various witnesses alleged they saw flee—who claimed to see or hear parts of the activities leading up to or directly following Faulkner's slaying. The police reported interviewing seven people within an hour of the shooting who had witnessed parts of the incident. The prosecution would call on only four of them to testify at trial: Cynthia White, an African American prostitute with thirty-eight arrests in the last eighteen months; Robert Chobert, a twenty-three-year-old white cabdriver with a suspended driver's license who was on probation for felony arson; Michael Scanlan, a twenty-five-year-old white man from Haddonfield, New Jersey, who was returning from a date; and Albert Magilton, a pedestrian whom Faulkner had questioned just moments before he stopped Cook because the officer had spotted

61

Magilton looking into the back seat of a parked limousine. Only Scanlan, who acknowledged having had a few cocktails earlier that evening, had solid credibility, and he was unable to identify the person who shot Faulkner, only the clothes Abu-Jamal was wearing as he ran from the parking lot toward Faulkner. This left the prosecution needing the testimony of its other three witnesses, but only one of them, Cynthia White, claimed to have seen a gun in Abu-Jamal's hand.

The defense would call two eyewitnesses: Dessie Hightower, a young accounting student with no police record who only heard the gunshots from a nearby parking lot but who told arriving police that he saw someone run from the scene after the shooting; and Veronica Jones, a prostitute who told the police that she had left the scene right after the shooting. Police picked her up the first week of January and questioned her for five hours, promising her, according to her testimony at trial, that she could continue to work the area if she would corroborate prostitute Cynthia White's testimony. She declined the offer. In her first statement to police she was quoted as saying that she had heard three shots and had turned to see "a policeman fall down." She then observed "two black guys walk across Locust Street and then they started sort of jogging" away from the scene.

What became of the other six eyewitnesses? Each of the prostitutes reported being with a man. The man with key prosecution witness Cynthia White was interviewed by a Highway Patrol officer at the scene, but his statement was never produced nor was his name provided to the defense. Late at trial, the Highway Patrol officer was identified by the detective in charge of the case as Vernon Jones. Jones was not called to testify. The man with prostitute Veronica Jones was never identified. The man in the parking lot with Dessie Hightower, Robert Pigford, was not called as a witness. Deborah Kordansky, who lived in a shabby hotel that overlooked the crime scene, told police she saw a man running from the scene right after the shooting, but she refused defense counsel's requests for her to testify at trial. William Singletary, a tow-truck operator who told police within hours of the shooting that he saw someone other than Abu-Jamal shoot Faulkner, testified at Abu-Jamal's 1995 postconviction hearing that a detective tore up his two original statements and forced him to sign a false one. The other eyewitness, Robert Harkins, was the cabdriver who was the first to alert police that a police officer had been shot. He had observed, more clearly than all the other eyewitnesses, how Faulkner had come to die. The police took two statements from Harkins, but he would not be called as a witness by either side. The prosecution did not call him because his statements exculpated Abu-Jamal as Faulkner's killer. Abu-Jamal's defense did not call him because it was underfinanced, overwhelmed, and in total disarray.

10

THE PLAYERS

THE JUDGE

Albert F. Sabo, a short, wiry, mercurial man, was elected to the Philadelphia Court of Common Pleas in 1973. A proud member of the Fraternal Order of Police, he campaigned on a "law and order" platform and became the first person of Slovak decent to become a city judge. For sixteen years prior to his election, he held the post of undersheriff of Philadelphia—the legal adviser to the sheriff.

"He's somebody who is regarded as not simply a prosecutor's judge, but . . . somebody who gets actively involved in the trial and demonstrates a prosecutorial bent," said Temple University law professor Edward D. Ohlbaum.

Prominent defense lawyer Richard A. Sprague once referred to Judge Sabo as a "prosecutor in robes." The *Inquirer* termed him "a defendant's worst nightmare."

Sabo tried capital cases exclusively for fourteen years, and an *Inquirer* survey in the early 1990s found that no judge in the nation had been involved in more trials that resulted in the defendants receiving the death penalty. At the time, 20 percent of the state's 115 death row inmates were from trials Judge Sabo had conducted. Half of the state's death row inmates are from Philadelphia, and 90 percent of those are black. Of thirty-one death sentences in Sabo trials, five have been overturned on appeal, an indication of extreme judicial prejudice.

In an *Inquirer* article by Melissa Dribben, written in August of 1995 during Abu-Jamal's Post-Conviction Relief Act hearing conducted by Judge Sabo, she described him this way:

65

He yawns. A lot.

He pouts. He fumes. Strokes his eyebrows. Chews his tongue. Glares. Huffs. And loses his composure.

Mr. Magoo with an attitude.

This is the Judge Albert Sabo you see on the bench. . . . It's not the kind of behavior that inspires confidence in the court's impartiality. Which only helps to reinforce the Abu-Jamal camp's conviction that a radical black man can't get justice in America.

Especially not in Philadelphia. . . .

Abu-Jamal's attorneys protest his rulings. He snaps, "I don't care."

They make a point. He shrugs, "So what?" They complain. He tells them, "I know, I know, take it up with the Supreme Court." Or "don't give me that stuff."

On August 21, 2001, Terri Maurer-Carter, a former court stenographer for the Philadelphia Court of Common Pleas, signed an affidavit declaring that she overhead Judge Sabo tell someone at the courthouse during Abu-Jamal's trial, "Yeah, and I am going to help them fry the nigger."

Professor Cornel West, then of Harvard and now of Princeton, attended a hearing concerning Abu-Jamal's Post-Conviction Relief Act proceedings on July 2, 1995, and made this observation: "The atmosphere—including the judge's mockery and flippancy—was that of a Jim Crow court. For instance, at one point, the judge exclaimed roughly, 'What's the rush? He's not being executed tomorrow; he's got a few more weeks.' Abu-Jamal's family was in the front row."

Two years later, Judge Sabo's incivility would finally catch up with him. He was unceremoniously dumped when the Pennsylvania Supreme Court opted to reduce from fourteen to ten the number of senior judges employed at the Philadelphia Court of Common Pleas. Sabo told an *Inquirer* reporter that he was "angry about the procedure that was followed," claiming court officials were arbitrary in selecting him to get the ax. The same article reported that a Supreme Court official stated that the decision of whom to cut was based on "productivity and temperament."

THE PROSECUTOR

Assistant D.A. Joseph McGill, having already won death penalty verdicts in five previous capital cases, was selected by D.A. Ed Rendell to prosecute Abu-Jamal. A tall man with angular features, deep-set dark eyes, and a salt-and-pepper mustache, McGill viewed the staging of a trial as closely akin to the staging of a play. He was wily and combative, and there was something terribly dissembling about him. He played various roles depending on the courtroom audience he was appealing to. To crusty Judge Sabo, McGill was obsequious; to the jury he was the slightly rumpled big-brother crusader who would protect them by avenging cop killers; to his overmatched and underfinanced defense counsel opponent, he was tolerant. McGill saved the considerable venom he was able to muster at a moment's notice for the defendant. In this case, throughout the trial, McGill would put on display his palpable, sneering loathing of the former Black Panther.

The trial of Mumia Abu-Jamal for the murder of Officer Daniel Faulkner would be the highest profile case McGill would ever prosecute. He would prosecute it as though he had a slam dunk, and only a death penalty verdict would vindicate his effort.

McGill so much wanted to send Abu-Jamal to the electric chair that he would go over the top time and again to do so, from his pretrial dealings through his summation at the sentencing phase of the trial. During pretrial discovery, where the prosecution has been required since 1963 by the U.S. Supreme Court (*Brady v. Maryland*) to provide the defense with any information it has that is favorable to the defendant, McGill withheld or failed to fully explain numerous pieces of "*Brady* material" that would have undermined the state's case against Abu-Jamal.

- McGill knew that there was another person in Billy Cook's VW. He knew that another man—Arnold Howard—had loaned his driver's application to Cook's street-vendor partner, Kenneth Freeman, and that application was in Faulkner's shirt pocket when the officer was killed. (McGill turned over a copy of the driver's application but did not divulge it was in Faulkner's shirt pocket.) McGill knew but did not divulge that his star witness, prostitute Cynthia White, had several times during the hours after Faulkner died picked Freeman out of a police lineup.

- McGill knew that the police detectives had polygraphed defense witness Dessie Hightower, who reported to police soon after Faulkner's shooting that he had seen a black man flee the scene, but the prosecutor did not inform the defense of the forty-five-minute polygraph test or its results. The results of the exam were favorable to the defense in all respects, except when Hightower responded that he had not seen Abu-Jamal holding a gun.

- As would be revealed to the defense for the first time when prostitute Veronica Jones testified at Abu-Jamal's trial as a defense witness, uniformed Philadelphia police arrested her in early January and brought her to the police station. There, over a five-hour period, detectives reinterviewed her—and, as she would testify at trial, attempted to coerce her to corroborate Cynthia White's account of naming Abu-Jamal as the shooter.

In an *Inquirer* article written by reporters Marc Kaufman and Julia Cass during Abu-Jamal's postconviction relief hearing in July 1995, former prosecutor McGill, true to form, denied any *Brady* violations, saying, "This was a high-profile case, and we wanted to make sure everything was done just right. We gave them everything we had."

Brady violations were not McGill's only sleight-of-hand maneuvers.

- At an early pretrial hearing, after the defense requested that Cynthia White be required to pick Abu-Jamal out of a lineup, McGill stood silent when Judge Ribner, in ruling against the defense, characterized the prosecution's star witness as only "a link in the chain of evidence."

- During jury selection, McGill used ten and probably eleven peremptory challenges to exclude blacks.
- At trial he used perjured and most likely coerced testimony to have Cynthia White testify that she saw Abu-Jamal murder Faulkner in cold blood, and he used perjured and definitely coerced testimony to have Veronica Jones disavow testifying that she saw two black men flee the scene after Faulkner was shot.
- McGill blatantly violated Abu-Jamal's constitutional rights in both his summation to the jury during the guilt phase of the trial and during the sentencing by telling the jurors that the defendant would get appeal after appeal. He did this knowing that when he had used similar language in another trial, the Pennsylvania Supreme Court had overturned the verdict.

McGill went into private practice in 1986, following his prosecution of Ramona Africa, the lone adult MOVE member to survive when police firebombed MOVE headquarters on Osage Avenue the year before, destroying sixty-one row houses. A jury found her guilty of criminal conspiracy and riot in connection with her role in the police confrontation that day but acquitted her on ten counts of simple and aggravated assault. She was sentenced to a maximum of seven years. The *Philadelphia City Paper* reported that the Pennsylvania Parole Board "offered her freedom after 16 months, on the sole condition that she cut her ties to MOVE. She refused and wound up serving the full seven years." Before her trial, she was hospitalized for a month, receiving skin grafts for burns to her legs, arms, and back sustained during the firebombing of MOVE. (In the City of Philadelphia's settlement with MOVE over the Osage Avenue bombing, it paid Ramona Africa $1.3 million in damages.)

THE DEFENSE ATTORNEY

Unlike the veteran, battle-hardened McGill, Anthony E. Jackson had never acted as lead defense counsel on a capital case—much less a high-profile one—when Common Pleas Judge Paul Ribner appointed him Abu-Jamal's counsel. Jackson had been admitted to the bar in 1974 after attending law school at Temple University in Philadelphia. His first job, as a prosecutor in the Philadelphia District Attorney's Office, lasted only six months. For the next several years he was in private practice, working without distinction as a criminal defense lawyer. He readily gave up that practice in 1978 to go to work as a staff attorney for the Public Interest Law Center of Philadelphia, an organization federally funded by the Law Enforcement Assistance Administration to improve police-community relations. Promoted to director, Jackson assisted the U.S. Justice Department in filing the lawsuit against the City of Philadelphia referenced in chapter 4. The suit, unprecedented in U.S. annals, charged Mayor Rizzo and eighteen senior police officials with systematically condoning police brutality, particularly in its treatment of minority residents. (A federal court dismissed the suit on the grounds that the Justice Department did not have standing to file suit. Subsequently, the U.S. Supreme Court denied to take the case on appeal.)

By the end of 1981, Jackson practically stood alone in Philadelphia as the one black attorney with a record of combating police abuses. When Abu-Jamal was recuperating in the hospital, it would be to Jackson that Abu-Jamal's friends and family turned for help in exposing the beatings Abu-Jamal had sustained from various police officers following his arrest for Faulkner's murder.

As Jackson visited Abu-Jamal in his hospital room on December 11, he was at another crossroads in his life. He was in the process of returning to private practice but had yet to set up an office or hire any staff. For Abu-Jamal, the criminal justice system was churning rapidly. With Abu-Jamal's arraignment to be conducted at his hospital bedside within two days, Jackson, on December 12, accepted the offer from Judge Ribner to become Abu-Jamal's court-appointed attorney.

Jackson's first court appearance on behalf of Abu-Jamal occurred on January 5, 1982, before Judge Ribner, during which McGill nearly dumbfounded Jackson by informing the judge that the state was prepared to proceed with Abu-Jamal's preliminary hearing—a hearing where the prosecution presents evidence to establish that it has probable cause to hold the defendant over for trial. Jackson told the judge he had assumed that the preliminary hearing would not be held until January 8 and that he would not be available on that date because of a prior appointment in New York.

Ribner denied Jackson's request to postpone the hearing and issued an advisory to Jackson that would go unheeded throughout the course of his representation of Abu-Jamal: "Well, this is the kind of case you want to keep on top of."

11

JURY SELECTION

Jury selection began on June 7 with Abu-Jamal acting as his
own defense counsel and Jackson as his court-appointed
backup counsel. The day before, Judge Sabo had denied all of
Abu-Jamal's requests that John Africa replace Jackson as backup
counsel. The *Philadelphia Inquirer*'s news story of the first day of
jury selection reported that Abu-Jamal was "intent and business
like." One juror was selected. On the second day no jurors were
selected, although by this point fifty potential jurors had been questioned by both sides. On the third day, after McGill elicited from a
particularly nervous prospective juror that having the defendant in
a murder trial question her was unsettling, Sabo, wanting to speed
up the jury-selection process, used that comment as justification to
bar Abu-Jamal from questioning any more prospective jurors. Abu-
Jamal asked the judge, "Am I [still] going to be allowed to represent myself in this case?" Sabo said he would be, adding that the
issue of who questions jurors would not affect his status as his own
counsel. In protest from being excluded from the jury-selection
process, Abu-Jamal instructed Jackson not to participate in it either.
For the next two hours, Judge Sabo took over the questioning for
the defense. When the afternoon session began, Abu-Jamal, under
protest, allowed Jackson to conduct the questioning of the potential jurors for him, informing the court that he would refuse to
speak during the process. Again, no jurors were selected.

Because this was a capital case, where a death penalty could be
sought, the prosecution was allowed to remove for cause any poten-

tial juror who expressed an unwillingness to impose a sentence of death. McGill was thus able to remove more than half of the prospective black jurors interviewed for that reason. This process is called "death penalty qualifying." The impact of ridding the jury of all those opposed to the death sentence is a profound one on the accused. "People who advocate the death penalty tend to be conservative politically, tend to believe authorities, particularly prosecutors and police, and are conviction prone," David Lindorff, citing studies on the subject, reported in a *Salon* magazine feature entitled "The Death Penalty's Other Victims," published in 2001.

Prosecutor McGill used fifteen of his allotted twenty peremptory challenges. In ten or most probably eleven of them, he struck blacks. He used others to turn down younger people. He also nixed a Catholic priest.

The defense would run out of peremptory challenges before jury selection was complete. During that brief, two-hour period when Judge Sabo took over questioning prospective jurors, Abu-Jamal, in a state of miff, spent at least four of the defense's allotted twenty peremptory challenges. The *Inquirer* reported that Abu-Jamal and Jackson used most of the defense's peremptory challenges to reject ethnic whites from inner-city neighborhoods. One juror that Jackson failed to challenge for cause or to exclude peremptorily stated that a police officer friend of his had been wounded in the line of duty. The one time Jackson did use a peremptory challenge to strike a black potential juror, Sabo made a record of it, the only such record of a juror's race in the court transcript.

Jury selection was completed after seven days of questioning 157 potential jurors. Those selected were:

1. Jennie Dawley
2. James Mattiace
3. Richard Tomczak
4. Joseph Mangan
5. Maurice Simovetch
6. Miriam Adelman
7. Savanna Davis
8. Lois Pekala
9. George Ewalt
10. Basil Malone
11. Domenic Durso
12. Louis Godfrey

Despite the 44 percent black population in Philadelphia at the time, the jury selected was composed of nine whites, eight of whom were males, and only three blacks; one of the blacks, Jennie Dawley, was the sole juror selected while Abu-Jamal was handling the voir dire. The jury impaneled was composed of four retired persons, two unemployed persons, two mechanics, one letter carrier, one telephone lineman, one supervisor with the federal government, and one mail clerk. In addition, the four alternate jurors selected were all white, one the wife of a police officer. One of the alternate jurors selected was Edward Courchain, a middle-aged postal worker who during the jury questioning repeatedly stated that owing to all the negative pretrial publicity about Abu-Jamal he was not sure he could be unbiased toward the defendant. Jackson, by then out of peremptory challenges, attempted to have him removed from consideration for cause. Judge Sabo, inexplicably, rejected Jackson's request.

In contrast, the jury-selection process in the murder trial of former professional football player Rae Carruth lasted five weeks. It produced a jury of nine whites (seven male, two female) and three black women. The alternates were one black man and two white women. In a split decision, the jury on January 19, 2001, found Carruth not guilty of first-degree murder but convicted him of conspiring to murder, shooting into an occupied vehicle, and using a gun to try to kill a baby. Carruth thereby escaped the death penalty sought by the prosecution. Instead he received a sentence of up to twenty-five years.

At the O. J. Simpson murder case in 1995, it took nearly two months to pick the jury. Despite the fact that the racial composition of the initial jury pool was 40 percent white, 28 percent black, 17 percent Hispanic, and 15 percent Asian, Simpson's jury ended up with nine blacks, one Hispanic and just two whites. Although the murders Simpson was on trial for occurred in upscale, predominantly white Santa Monica, the prosecutors chose to file the case in downtown Los Angeles. Vincent Bugliosi, the prosecutor in the Charles Manson case, said that mistake "dwarfed anything the prosecution did" in losing the case.

Most prosecutors and defense attorneys believe jury selection is such a crucial factor in the outcome of a high-profile case that they routinely retain jury consultants to assist them during the process. Both Carruth and Simpson did, and so did their prosecutors. At Abu-Jamal's trial, not only was no such luxury even sought for the indigent defendant, but after two days of jury selection, the judge barred Abu-Jamal from exercising his right to participate in the process even though the court had previously granted him his right to self-representation.

12

THE TRIAL OPENS

The right to self-representation in a judicial proceeding is a fundamental right in U.S. judicial proceedings, but it is subject to the discretion of the court. The judge's assessment of the defendant's competency to conduct his or her own defense is the major criterion deployed in granting a defendant this right. In Abu-Jamal's case, his request to defend himself was granted during a mid-May pretrial hearing by Common Pleas Court Judge Ribner but then rescinded by Judge Sabo.

When Abu-Jamal's murder trial opened on the morning of June 17, 1982, Abu-Jamal was acting as his own counsel, with Jackson his court-appointed backup counsel. After the jury was impaneled and seated, Abu-Jamal launched his John Africa–inspired defense. When Judge Sabo asked him how he wanted to plead to the charge of murder of Faulkner, he gave no response. The second charge—possession of an instrument of crime—brought no response. The judge said he took both nonanswers as pleas of innocence, and entered the pleas. He then asked if Abu-Jamal wanted a jury trial or to be tried by a judge without a jury. Again no response.

Abu-Jamal then began his drive to have John Africa replace Jackson as his backup counsel. Sabo denied the request each time Abu-Jamal made it but displayed uncharacteristic restraint in permitting Abu-Jamal to keep on making it, right up until the trial was recessed that afternoon. As a way of getting past this impasse, the judge encouraged Jackson—right after Jackson informed the court that he wished to withdraw as backup counsel—to petition the Pennsylvania Supreme Court later that afternoon to determine if he must defend Abu-Jamal and to decide if John Africa could sit at the defense table and act as Abu-Jamal's counsel. At an open hearing the next morning, Justice James T. McDermott of the Pennsylvania Supreme Court ruled that Jackson must continue to serve as backup defense counsel and upheld Judge Sabo's decision to bar John Africa from sitting at the defense table.

That evening juror No. 1, Jennie Dawley, went home to take her sick cat to a veterinarian. One of only three blacks on the jury and the only juror selected while Abu-Jamal was allowed to handle the jury-selection process, Dawley had informed the court earlier that day of her need to take her cat to a vet that evening, but Judge Sabo had denied her that permission. The next day the judge removed her from the jury. Courchain, the alternate juror who said he was unsure he could not be biased against Abu-Jamal, replaced her. (Later during the trial, when a white juror requested permission to take a previously scheduled civil service exam, the trial was recessed in the afternoon so that a marshal could accompany that juror to the examination.)

The second day of the trial began as the first day had ended, with Abu-Jamal insisting for several hours that MOVE leader John Africa replace Jackson as his backup counsel—to the point that McGill was prevented from making his opening statement to the jury. Judge Sabo had to keep excusing the jury from the proceedings. Both the judge and the prosecutor attempted to reach a compromise with Abu-Jamal about John Africa's presence at the proceedings. Both agreed that John Africa could sit in the second row behind the defense table, confer with Abu-Jamal during recesses, meet with him before the trial opened each day, and visit him in his jail cell. He simply could not sit at the defense table, because he was not an attorney.

Having John Africa as his backup counsel was nonnegotiable for Abu-Jamal. He wanted him at the defense table and Jackson sitting in the audience.

Late in the afternoon, as Abu-Jamal was arguing with the judge and the jury was re-entering the courtroom, the following exchange took place in front of the jury.

McGILL: Your honor, may I proceed?

ABU-JAMAL: I'm not finished.

JUDGE SABO: We're finished.

ABU-JAMAL: I'm not finished. We are not finished.

McGILL: May I proceed with the opening [statement] before this jury that's
   been waiting two days?

JUDGE SABO: Yes.

ABU-JAMAL: I don't care.

McGILL: You don't care what?

ABU-JAMAL: I have a right to the defense of my choice.

JUDGE SABO: Let's move the jury out just for a minute.

ABU-JAMAL: This does not mean anything to me. They mean absolutely
   nothing to me.

The jury was excused, and Judge Sabo ordered Abu-Jamal removed from the courtroom.

As Abu-Jamal was being removed, two of his brothers, Billy and Wayne Cook, stood. One shouted, "This is a fucking railroad, I say. What are you trying to do here?"

The second shouted, "What is this?"

Judge Sabo had both men brought forward—"You both are in criminal contempt of this court. . . . I am summarily fining [*sic*] you to sixty days in the County Prison. That's it."

McGill told Sabo he believed that Abu-Jamal's disruptiveness was part of a carefully planned effort to sway the jurors, adding, "He is the most intelligent defendant I've ever had, and he's not just spouting off. He knows exactly what he's doing."

Judge Sabo, notorious for his short fuse, ignored McGill's strong endorsement of Abu-Jamal's intelligence—the main criterion in determining a defendant's fitness to self-representation—and stripped Abu-Jamal of his right to defend himself on the well-founded grounds that he was "too disruptive." Sabo then ordered Jackson to stand in as Abu-Jamal's counsel.

Abu-Jamal's misguided strategy of having John Africa act as his backup counsel—even after the state supreme court ruled that impermissible—would put to rout the possibility of a fair trial, coloring every aspect of the proceedings, tainting all that followed. Is this really what Abu-Jamal wanted? In his push for John Africa, Abu-Jamal humiliated Anthony Jackson, alienated the jury, and enabled Judge Sabo to strip him of his right to represent himself. Whatever he thought his strategy was, it was a disaster in all respects. As for John Africa, he never made a courtroom appearance.

McGill made his opening statement in the afternoon of the second day of the trial, telling the jurors he would prove that Abu-Jamal shot Faulkner right between the eyes at point-blank range—from only twelve inches away—and "literally blew away his brains."

McGill next introduced the alleged confession, saying that Abu-Jamal had boasted to Faulkner's partner at the hospital, "I shot the motherfucker and I hope he dies."

Jackson, who up until that day had been functioning in the role of backup counsel and was not prepared to make an opening statement on the spot, offered no opening remarks. When he told the court he would hold his opening remarks until the prosecution had presented its case, the rout was on.

McGill's first witness would send the primary message the prosecutor wanted the jury to lock into and never release: A young, valiant police officer had been gunned down in cold blood, and there was now hell to pay. He called the slain officer's widow, Maureen, to the stand to identify her husband's hat and bloodstained clothing. Choked with tears, she did, and then quickly left the stand, rushing out of the courtroom to collect herself. She, along with members of the Fraternal Order of Police, would attend the remainder of the trial and sentencing, her emotions on continuous display.

13

Testimony of Robert Chobert

On the third day of the trial, the prosecution called its first eyewitness, cabdriver Robert Chobert. He testified he had just let a fare out at the southeast corner of 13th and Locust. "I heard a shot. I looked up, I saw the cop fall to the ground, and then I saw Abu-Jamal standing over him and firing some more shots into him. . . . Then I saw him [Abu-Jamal] walking back about ten feet and he just fell to the curb."

Before Jackson could begin his cross-examination, McGill asked the judge for a sidebar conference. McGill told Judge Sabo and Jackson that Chobert was currently on five years of probation for arson. Jackson said that such a crime constitutes *crimen falsi* and as such entitled Jackson to let the jury know that about Chobert, thus undermining his credibility with the jury. Other charges related to the arson against Chobert were "causing a catastrophe" and "criminal mischief." Plus he had two recent arrests for driving while intoxicated and was driving his cab with a suspended driver's license—a violation for which he had not been charged.

Chobert was an extremely compromised witness. For driving a cab without a license, he was in continuous violation of his parole and was facing a possible thirty years in prison if his probation were revoked. He was one of two witnesses—Cynthia White was the other—whom Inspector Giordano lined up to identify Abu-Jamal as Faulkner's shooter.

At the sidebar, when McGill told Chobert to tell the judge what he was found guilty of, Chobert stated, "I threw a bomb into a school. A Molotov cocktail."

JUDGE SABO: You just threw it into a school building?

CHOBERT: Yes.

McGILL: He was eighteen when he did it. Threw it into John Bartram, a school he attended.

JUDGE SABO: And that's why you threw it in there?

CHOBERT: No, that ain't why. I got paid for doing it.

JACKSON: That's the reason, that's the *crimen falsi*.

JUDGE SABO: That's not *crimen falsi*.

McGILL: That's not *crimen falsi*. He got paid for doing it.

The judge decided that Chobert could continue his testimony, ruling that his being on probation for arson and other offenses related to that felony would be kept from the jury, as would his two arrests for driving while intoxicated and his driving a cab with a suspended license. As a point of law, Chobert being on probation and continuing to operate a taxi with a suspended license were grounds for allowing the jury to become aware of Chobert's current legal status and the potential bias such a witness represented. As Jackson would testify at Abu-Jamal's postconviction hearing in 1995, he was unaware of the law governing such a witness.

When cross-examination resumed, Chobert testified he was parked one car length behind Faulkner's police car when he heard a shot. He said he got out of his cab and walked toward the sound of the shot, a highly improbable course of action for a paroled felon who was operating a taxi without a driver's license, and a completely reckless course of action for anyone who has just heard gunfire within feet of a police car. He said he didn't see a gun in Abu-Jamal's hand or see the firing of the bullets but saw Abu-Jamal position his hand down at the fallen officer, saw his hand "jerk back" several times, and heard shots after each jerk. He said Abu-Jamal then ran about ten feet away from Faulkner and collapsed. Chobert also testified that he saw another man (Billy Cook) "walk away from the scene after the shooting. He moved down about ten feet." He described Cook accurately as having a full beard, being about five feet six, and wearing a red-and-green beanie-type hat and a dark coat.

Chobert had given two statements to the police, the first shortly after the shooting and the second six months later. Jackson had him reread both and got him to acknowledge that his memory of the incident would have been better at the time of the original statement.

In the December 9 statement, Chobert said the man who shot Faulkner was in his midthirties; was "heavy-set," weighing 200 to 225 pounds; was six feet tall; and wore a gray-colored dress shirt that had a green picture on the back. When Jackson asked him if that was the description he gave police, Chobert answered, "I guess so. That's what I said. Yes." (Abu-Jamal is just over six feet tall, but he weighed about 170 pounds in 1981. That night he wore a waist-length, red-quilted ski jacket with a vertical blue stripe crossing the front. There was no picture on it, front or back.)

In addition, Chobert had originally told police that Abu-Jamal had run about thirty feet before collapsing, not the ten feet he was testifying to now, and that the other man (Cook) "had started running as soon as the shots were fired and then he got about half a block away. Then the cops came and he just stopped."

Jackson asked Chobert why in court he was saying that the other man (Cook) walked, when he had earlier told police he had run. He said he had made a mistake. When Jackson asked him if his memory was better at trial than it had been before, Chobert answered, "No, not really. No."

Jackson then asked Chobert to explain why his recollection was that Faulkner was shot between the police car and the Volkswagen. "We've got several witnesses who indicate that the officer was shot between the Volkswagen and the Ford. Can you tell us why?" Chobert said he did not remember seeing the Ford that night and that he saw Abu-Jamal between the police car and the VW.

When Jackson asked Chobert if he saw the police strike Abu-Jamal, he said he did not. He said he saw the police drag Abu-Jamal to the police wagon but didn't see the police walk him into a pole or drop him to the ground.

Asked if there were any civilians at the scene, Chobert testified there were no civilians other than Abu-Jamal and Cook. This assertion would corroborate the subsequent testimony of all the other eyewitnesses except for that of Cynthia White, the prosecution's key eyewitness, who would soon testify that she was standing on the same corner that Chobert was, just feet away from Abu-Jamal as he shot Faulkner.

Jackson then asked Chobert if he saw an officer kick Abu-Jamal. He said he did. He told Jackson he did not see Abu-Jamal get shot, nor did he see Officer Faulkner shoot his gun.

In saying he saw Abu-Jamal stand over Faulkner and position his hand down at the fallen officer, saw his hand "jerk back" several times, and heard shots after each jerk, Chobert's testimony was damaging to Abu-Jamal. But, as Jackson's cross-examination brought out, his testimony was so riddled with inconsistencies from his original statement to police that it eroded his credibility. In addition Jackson showed that Chobert's observations were deficient in three important matters: Chobert had not even noticed the parked Ford; he had Faulkner standing between the VW and the patrol car rather than where he actually was, between the VW and the Ford; and he had not seen the police ram Abu-Jamal's head into a pole on his way to the paddy wagon. Chobert had the police dragging Abu-Jamal straight to the paddy wagon.

If Judge Sabo had allowed Chobert's probation—a probation he had violated at least twice by being arrested for driving while intoxicated and had violated further still by driving a cab with a suspended license—to be disclosed to the jury, Chobert's integrity as a witness would have been irreparably impugned and his motive for testifying as a prosecution witness put to challenge. As it was, his testimony was a near disaster for the prosecution: his description of the shooter was that of a man other than Abu-Jamal; and his saying he did not see any civilians at the scene would undermine the soon-to-be introduced testimony of the prosecution's only witness who claimed to have seen Abu-Jamal shoot Faulkner, Cynthia White.

Although to a lesser degree than White, Chobert was a corrupted witness, motivated by his own fear of having his probation revoked and his hope of having McGill assist him in getting his chauffeur's license reinstated. At Abu-Jamal's postconviction hearing in 1995, Chobert admitted on the stand that sometime before or during the trial he had asked McGill for such help and that McGill had told him he would look into it. Like White, he altered his testimony from his original statement to fit the prosecution's version of the case.

Just prior to Abu-Jamal's postconviction hearing, a private legal investigator interviewed Chobert at his residence at the behest of Abu-Jamal's defense attorney, Leonard Weinglass. The investigator, Michael Newman of San Diego, California, stated in an affidavit signed in 2001 that after he visited Chobert at his home, he called him on the phone to clarify some points. Newman said that Chobert admitted to him he had been parked in his taxi on 13th Street, north of Locust, and had not seen Faulkner shot. At trial Chobert had testified that he had been parked on Locust, east of 13th Street, and had watched the officer being shot.

"[Chobert] said what actually happened was that he was sitting in his taxi when he heard gunfire. He exited the taxi and saw a black man standing next to a police car that was parked on Locust, east of 13th Street. The black man slumped down. Chobert walked toward that area and when he got closer saw a police officer sprawled on his back on the sidewalk and a black man sitting nearby," Newman declared in the affidavit.

14

CYNTHIA WHITE'S FIRST DAY OF TESTIMONY

From the outset, the investigation into the shooting death of Daniel Faulkner was conducted with one goal in mind: to hang the crime on Mumia Abu-Jamal, no matter what it took. There was no search for truth, no attempt at providing the slain officer with the justice he deserved. Faulkner himself was just a pawn, his widow and the Fraternal Order of Police turned into unwitting dupes, and dupes they remain. Predicating the prosecution's case on the concocted testimony of prostitute Cynthia White and Abu-Jamal's fabricated "confession" at the hospital, the police and the prosecution proved only that they would stop at nothing to bring Abu-Jamal down.

Without White's testimony, there would have been no evidentiary case against Abu-Jamal, just a patchwork of inconsistent, contradictory eyewitness testimony that even Anthony Jackson could have turned into reasonable doubt. McGill was only too aware that both of the police officers who had accompanied Abu-Jamal from the time of his arrest until he went into surgery—Gary Wakshul and Stephen Trombetta—had signed statements reporting that Abu-Jamal had made no statements. McGill knew that testimony would destroy the confession.

McGill really had only White. With White saying she saw it all from beginning to end, and willing to testify that she saw Abu-Jamal blow the helpless Faulkner's brains out in ruthless cold blood, McGill had his case made, providing White's credibility could survive Jackson's cross-examination. McGill bet the entire case that it could, and he, despite the utter web of lies she told the jury, was right.

Before Cynthia White took the stand on day four of the trial, McGill asked the judge for a sidebar conference.

> McGILL: Your honor, this question that I wish to ask the court, really, rather than stopping in the middle of her testimony—Cynthia White is my next witness. I haven't been as generous as I should have been. Apparently, she has, well basically, three pages plus two, three-and-a-half I guess you'd call it, pages of prostitution arrests. I want to alert the court and Mr. Jackson that our knowledge is that she has three open prostitution charges.
>
> JUDGE SABO: Here in the City of Philadelphia?
>
> McGILL: Here in the City of Philadelphia—and they will be prosecuted. [They never were.] She is currently incarcerated in Massachusetts for a prostitution offense, which she was guilty of and then she appealed and she's awaiting a trial.
>
> We brought her down here on an Interstate Agreement Witness Act . . . under the law we are unable to prosecute her while she's here. . . . You cannot use [her] for any other purpose than a witness. That's specifically stated in the act, but we do intend to prosecute her when she returns, and if she finishes her other trial to bring her down for purposes of prosecution for those three offenses.
>
> There have been no dealings . . . and there has been no agreement in reference to her charges. As a matter of fact, she's already been tried on one of her charges that she had not been tried before the hearing. She has four open charges . . . and now she has three. She was tried before Judge Bednarek, before April, later part of April. She was due to be tried in the end of May for her second prostitution case, but at that time she was incarcerated in Massachusetts. I know of no deals related to her in connection with this case. [That was not true, as McGill would proceed to admit in his next statement.]
>
> There was one thing the court should be made aware of to the extent that this could be or will be a question, I think. A friend of hers by the name of Smith, who's not a relative but is a very close friend,

was or has been present with her at several hearings. He at one time was arrested last month, I believe. . . . [White] was in Massachusetts at the time. But he was arrested down here and there was some concern over his safety in the prison because of his connection with her . . . and for that reason we allowed him—this was a theft charge—to sign his own bail for that theft charge with the assurance that he would appear in court.

She was not made aware of this until a couple of days ago, actually when I told her about it. I'm trying to think if there was anything else. There was no other deal that I know of at this time for Miss White.

McGill has such a penchant for the bald-faced lie that at times such as these he does not seem able to harness himself. What McGill did not disclose, but would come out during White's trial testimony, was that the man McGill was telling Judge Sabo was her "very close friend" was actually her live-in pimp, and that for testifying against Abu-Jamal, the police had allowed White to continue to work as a prostitute with impunity during the six months leading up to Abu-Jamal's trial. Prior to her becoming a prosecution witness in Abu-Jamal's case, White had been arrested thirty-eight times for prostitution. None of the arrests were more than forty days apart. After she gave her third statement to police, on December 17, 1981, she would not be arrested for prostitution in Philadelphia ever again even though she admitted at Billy Cook's trial that she continued to be "actively working."

Early in his direct examination of White, McGill had some tidying up to do regarding White's previous testimony at Billy Cook's March 29 trial for assaulting Officer Faulkner. McGill handled that case as well. He assumed, correctly, that Jackson had seen the transcript from it. McGill's questioning of White at Cook's trial indicated that both he and his star witness knew there was a passenger in Cook's VW at the time Faulkner pulled the car over.

McGILL: When the officer [Faulkner] went up to the car, which side of the car did the officer go up to?
WHITE: The driver side.
McGILL: The driver's side?

WHITE: Yes.

McGILL: What did the passenger do?

WHITE: He had got out.

McGILL: What did the driver do?

WHITE: He got out of the car.

McGILL: He got out of the car?

WHITE: Yes.

Now, with White just settling in on the witness stand at Abu-Jamal's trial, McGill wanted to get on the record the exact opposite testimony from her.

McGill began by asking her if anyone else was there besides the defendant (Abu-Jamal); the police officer (Faulkner), who was on the ground; and Billy Cook. White said "No."

Getting White to limit the people at the crime scene to Abu-Jamal, Faulkner, and Cook was an essential deception McGill needed to establish before Jackson had his opportunity to cross-examine her. If Jackson were to read her the testimony she gave at Cook's trial and then ask her to describe the passenger, the genie would have been out of the bottle. Judge Sabo and the jury would know that someone did escape after Faulkner was shot and that someone other than Abu-Jamal may have killed Faulkner. As it turned out, Jackson did not question her about the passenger she claimed to have seen when testifying at Cook's trial, although Jackson did use her testimony from that trial to ask her about the man she said was with her.

It is suborning perjury—a felony offense—when an attorney leads a witness to testify under oath to something the attorney knows is not true and the attorney knows the witness knows is not true.

McGill asked White to tell the jury where she was when Faulkner stopped Cook's VW. She answered that she was on the southeast corner of 13th and Locust—that is, within fifteen feet of Faulkner's police car.

WHITE: The policeman got out of his car and walked over towards the Volkswagen. The driver of the Volkswagen got out of the car. A few words passed. They both walked between the police car and the Volkswagen up to the sidewalk. A few more words passed again between them. The driver of the Volkswagen then struck the police officer with a closed fist to his cheek, and the police officer turned the driver of the Volkswagen around in a position to handcuff him.

I looked across the street in the parking lot and I noticed [Abu-Jamal] was running out of the parking lot and he was practically on the curb when he shot two times at the police officer. It was the back. The police officer turned around and staggered and seemed like he was grabbing for something. Then he fell. Then [Abu-Jamal] came over and he came on top of the police officer and shot some more times. After that he went over and he slouched down and he sat on the curb.

White then stated that the shots fired at Faulkner's back were both "from two or three feet away." She said that Abu-Jamal had run up between the police car and the Volkswagen.

Jackson began his cross-examination by asking White if she had ever given any false statements to the police. She said she had not and reconfirmed that denial when Jackson asked her a second time.

Jackson then proceeded to demonstrate a long list of false names and false addresses White had given to the police during her thirty-eight arrests for prostitution over the past eighteen months. White said she could not remember where she lived as recently as the time of her arrest on December 17, 1981, and at many other periods of time relative to some of her other arrests.

Jackson asked White how many statements she had given to police in connection with Faulkner's slaying. She said she had given four, plus one statement that was not written up but taped.

When Jackson asked her how many times she had discussed this case with the D.A.'s office, she declined to say or estimate how often. She would not even estimate how many times she had seen McGill since arriving in Philadelphia from Massachusetts on May 28. Jackson did get her to admit that she had had two meetings with McGill—one two days before and one before the trial reconvened that day. She told Jackson she could not remember what they had discussed.

White gave her first statement to police within thirty minutes of the shooting. (Inspector Giordano, who knew White and many other prostitutes and their pimps from years of shaking them down for kickbacks, had arranged for her to be taken directly to the police station in a police car to give her statement.) She testified that she had been on the corner for thirty or thirty-five minutes, standing there with a man for the last five or ten minutes. She said that the man with her saw the incident as well and that she did not lose sight of this man until the police "put me in a car and took me to [the police station at] 8th and Race to take my statement down. That's when I didn't see him no more." She said she did see the man who had been with her talking to the "highway police."

After White testified that she had seen several police officers struggling with Abu-Jamal, using their blackjacks while trying to handcuff and subdue him, Jackson had her read her original statement to the police and asked her if she had told the truth in it. She answered, "Yes," and then "Yes" again when Jackson asked her if she were certain of that. He then had her read aloud from page 3 of her original statement, where she stated she had seen no struggle.

In White's original statement to police at the scene, she said she saw Abu-Jamal with a gun in his hand. "He fired the gun at the police officer four or five times. The police officer fell to the ground, starting screaming."

After further questioning, White said her first statement differed from what she subsequently told the police on December 17 in that "[Faulkner] was shot that many times but it wasn't all at once and he didn't fall to the ground." On December 12, White gave her second statement to homicide detectives after she was arrested and brought to the police station. Homicide had been unable to locate White because she had given the police a false address after providing her original statement, so her picture was posted on a police bulletin board, asking her to contact the homicide department. The only substantive change in her second statement was that she saw Billy Cook strike Faulkner in the face. When she was arrested again on

December 17, her statement was fine-tuned to comport with her eventual trial testimony.

Jackson's cross-examination showed how White's subsequent statements to the police had been "enhanced" after each of her arrests to fit the police and prosecution's version of Faulkner's slaying. Her original statement, that Abu-Jamal had begun firing his gun from as far as ten yards away and had gotten off four or five shots before Faulkner fell, had been transformed to Abu-Jamal's firing his gun at Faulkner's back once or twice at close range, from as near as two or so feet away.

It is axiomatic of manipulated witnesses such as White and Chobert, who have not seen what they claimed to have seen, to require multiple witness statements to get their stories straight. Unlike credible witnesses, their memory improves the farther away from the event time takes them.

15

WHITE'S TESTIMONY,
PART II

On day five of the trial, Abu-Jamal informed Judge Sabo's clerk that he wished to address the judge before the jury was called in, but Sabo had the jury brought in anyway. As Jackson informed the judge that Abu-Jamal wanted to address him about his right to self-representation, Abu-Jamal stood and asked to address the judge. At a sidebar conference, Sabo told Abu-Jamal he could not address the court. After a minute of bickering, he excused the jury.

After Sabo ruled that only Jackson could address the court on Abu-Jamal's behalf, McGill volunteered that with the jury out of the room perhaps the court should hear what Abu-Jamal had to say. The judge refused, ordering Jackson to make any statements or motions.

Jackson reiterated Abu-Jamal's claim to self-representation, asking that the trial be delayed until a federal district court could rule on his request. Sabo denied all parts of Jackson's motion. When Abu-Jamal restated that he did not want Jackson to represent him any longer, Sabo had Abu-Jamal removed from the courtroom.

With Cynthia White back on the witness stand, Jackson began by asking her if she had "participated in any agreement with the Commonwealth?" She said she had not. The truth, although Jackson did not know it, was that since White's December 17 statement to homicide detectives she had been allowed to work as a prostitute in Philadelphia without being arrested again. Jackson was aware that White had more than the three pending cases against her that she claimed in her testimony the day before, and he got her to admit to that on the stand.

Jackson asked White if one of the bench warrants was because she had failed to appear in court on December 10, the day after Faulkner's shooting. She said she could not remember.

Later, Jackson asked White how tall she was and she answered, "I don't know." When he asked her if she knew the difference between one and a half feet and six feet, she said, "No."

In her statement to police on December 9, White gave this description of Cook: "He was a black male, about 27 years, dark complexion, 5′8″, wearing his hair in dreadlocks with a tan cap on." Her description of Abu-Jamal: "He was a black male, short, in his 20s and he also wore his hair in dreadlocks." In her third statement to police, the one she gave at the police station on December 17, she described Abu-Jamal: "Black male, late 20s, just a little shorter than the police officer he shot, medium build, 160 pounds, dark complexion, dreadlock hair, wearing a tan hat, dark in color, mustache."

When McGill conducted his redirect examination of White, she did not ask him to repeat a single question or respond to any of his questions by saying she could not remember, a response she had used dozens of times during Jackson's cross-examination. To most of McGill's questions, she replied either "yes" or "no."

In Jackson's re-cross-examination, he read an answer that White had given in her second statement to police (December 12). She had been asked that when the shooter "began to shoot, did he fire all at once, or were the shots staggered." She had answered, "It sounded like all at once. It sounded like firecrackers."

JACKSON: Do you remember that statement, the question and answer?
WHITE: Yes.
JACKSON: It's incorrect, though, right?
WHITE: It did sound like all at once. That's the way it sounded.
JACKSON: I thought you told us earlier that it was . . . one or two and then three or four shots?

WHITE: I'm saying what it sounded like.

Jackson then asked White about her testimony on January 11 at Abu-Jamal's preliminary hearing before Judge Ribner, when she had said that when Abu-Jamal stood over Faulkner, she had not actually seen the shooting but was only able to hear the gunshots. "I couldn't see the shots but I could see the gun," she answered.

Jackson said, "Okay. Fine. I'm glad you said that. Page 96, same date, same hearing," as he read the next question and answer from her January 11 testimony: "Q. 'Did you see him fire the gun?' A. 'I knew he was firing. I didn't see the gun.'"

JACKSON: That's what you said on Jan. 11, 1982, before the Honorable Judge Ribner. Now is what you're saying today true, or what you were saying then true?

WHITE: I told you what I seen.

JACKSON: I know what you told us. I am asking what is true?

WHITE: Well, that's it.

JACKSON: What?

WHITE: I seen part of the gun.

Jackson concluded by asking White to look at the crime scene diagram she had given to police on the night of the shooting and compare it with the diagram she gave the police on December 17.

JACKSON: You have the officer between the patrol car and the Volkswagen; is that right? You just said yes.

WHITE: Yes.

JACKSON: And you've got the shooter now between the Ford and the Volkswagen?

WHITE: Yes.

JACKSON: Okay. Now is that the way you remember the events of December 9?

WHITE: No.

JACKSON: So that was wrong.

WHITE: Yes.

JACKSON: But you gave them that on December 9?
WHITE: Yes.

When White stepped down from the stand after two grueling days of cross-examination, her testimony was in shambles. Who would know what to believe from all the different versions of the shooting that she advanced? Jackson succeeded in displaying how each of her subsequent statements to police conflicted sharply with the statements she had given within thirty minutes of the shooting and how altering her testimony to fit the police and prosecution's version of the shooting had benefited her personally.

*   *   *

Twenty years after the death of Officer Faulkner, in an affidavit signed on January 28, 2002, and subsequently filed by Abu-Jamal's new defense attorneys with the U.S. Court of Appeals in Philadelphia a few days later, Yvette Williams, who was in police custody with key prosecution witness Cynthia White in December 1981 after Faulkner was killed, swore that White had told her that Philadelphia police detectives forced her to identify Abu-Jamal as Faulkner's killer even though White did not witness the shooting.

Williams stated in paragraph two of her affidavit: "Cynthia White told me the police were making her lie and say she saw Mr. Jamal shoot Officer Faulkner when she really did not see who did it. She said she knew Mumia from seeing him drive a cab."

Williams stated that White used a lot of different names, that she knew her as "Lucky," and that "the word on the street was that she was a snitch for the police."

Both Williams and White were locked up in protective custody, White for her involvement in the Faulkner case, Williams because the police thought she knew something about another homicide. "I didn't, but they wanted to get information out of me."

Williams noticed that when White would return to her cell after meeting with detectives, she would bring back contraband such as "cigarettes and candy and even hoagies, syringes and white powders."

According to Williams, White was "nervous and frightened and glad to have someone to talk to. She was always crying and sad. She told me she was scared for her life. I asked her, 'Scared of who'? She stated, 'The guards and Vice.'"

Williams's affidavit contained fourteen assertions. In the sixth she stated, "When Lucky [Cynthia White] told me she didn't even see who shot Officer Faulkner, I asked her why she was 'lying on that man' [Mumia Abu-Jamal]. She told me it was because the police and vice threatened her life. Additionally, the police were giving her money for tricks . . . the police told her they would consolidate all her cases and send her 'up' to Muncy, a women's prison, for a long time if she didn't testify to what they told her to say." Williams also said White told her that she "was scared her pimp 'would get pissed off' at all the money she was losing when she was locked up, and off the street. She was afraid that when she got out he would beat her up or kill her."

White, according to Williams, was also afraid "the police would kill her if she didn't say what they wanted."

Not only did White not see who killed Faulkner, but Williams also stated that White told her she "was high on drugs when it happened," and that she tried to run away after the shooting. Williams said that White told her the cops had grabbed her and wouldn't let go. "They took her in the car first and told her that she saw Mumia shoot Officer Faulkner."

Why was Williams coming forward now? "I feel like I've almost had a nervous breakdown over keeping quiet about this all these years," she stated in assertion number ten. "I didn't say anything because I was afraid. I was afraid of the police. They're dangerous. They can hurt you and get away with it. I know, I've been in trouble with the law and they know me." She stated she was still afraid of what the police might do to her, but when Abu-Jamal's case was back in the news in mid-December 2001 after Federal District Court Judge Yohn issued his ruling overturning Abu-Jamal's death sentence, "I couldn't get it out of my mind, I kept thinking that man could die because of all the lies that Lucky told on that witness stand and Mrs. Faulkner would never know the truth."

*   *   *

Police and prosecution favors continued to fall White's way long after Abu-Jamal was sentenced to death. In a review of Abu-Jamal's case by Amnesty International in 2000, the human rights organization reported that in June 1987 White was incarcerated on charges of armed robbery, aggravated assault, and possession of illegal weapons. At her bail hearing, Douglas Culbreth, the detective who took White's first statement within a half-hour of Faulkner's shooting and who served as White's police escort during Abu-Jamal's trial, appeared on her behalf to request that she be given bail. Culbreth informed the judge of White's cooperation in Abu-Jamal's trial. Even though the judge stated that he was reluctant to release her because of her record of "seventeen failures to appear" and "page after page" of arrests, the prosecution consented to the request that she be allowed to sign her own bail and the judge released her. According to information received by Amnesty International, White failed to appear in court on the charges and the authorities have since been unable to locate her.

16

THE ALLEGED CONFESSION

On day six of the trial, McGill called several expert witnesses. Joseph Grimes, the latent print examiner for the police department, testified both that there were no fingerprints taken at the crime scene and that there were no prints on either Faulkner's or Abu-Jamal's gun. Anthony Paul, a police ballistics expert, testified that the bullet removed from Faulkner was so mutilated, it could not be determined what type of gun had fired it. When McGill asked him if Faulkner's police revolver was in working condition when he tested it, Paul stated it was "operable," but he added that it had a cracked hammer spur, which prevented it from being fired in a single-action mode, because it would not cock on its own. For Faulkner to have fired this gun, he would have had to first cock the hammer with his thumb and then squeeze the trigger. During cross-examination, Jackson did not pursue this revelation to establish how even more unlikely it would have been for Faulkner to have gotten off the shot that hit Abu-Jamal in the chest as the officer was falling down backward. Jackson did elicit an estimate from Paul that there are millions of guns that could have fired the bullet that killed Faulkner.

As the afternoon session convened, Abu-Jamal stood and addressed Judge Sabo, whereupon the judge ordered the jury out. Abu-Jamal said he did not want Jackson to represent him; he wanted John Africa. After further exchange in this vein, Sabo had Abu-Jamal removed from the courtroom.

On day seven of the trial, June 23, 1982, after McGill had taken the testimony of Officer Roy Land and Jackson had completed his cross-examination, Abu-Jamal attempted to question Land. As he did, Judge Sabo sent the jury back out. Abu-Jamal then restated his request to have John Africa replace Jackson.

Later that day, McGill called two witnesses who claimed to have heard Abu-Jamal confess that he had shot Faulkner. Priscilla Durham, a security guard at Jefferson University Hospital, was the first. She said she had been employed at Jefferson for five years and had been a security guard for eight or nine years, including being a store detective two different times. Durham testified that as soon as Abu-Jamal was brought into the area just outside the ER, she heard him say, "I shot the motherfucker, and I hope the motherfucker dies." She said that Abu-Jamal was directly at her feet when she heard him confess.

Durham said she then heard a police officer say to Abu-Jamal, "If he dies, you die." She then identified that officer as Garry Bell. She testified that she again heard—some ten minutes later as Abu-Jamal was being brought into the operating room—Abu-Jamal shout out, "Yeah, I shot the motherfucker, and I hope the motherfucker dies."

Under further questioning from McGill, Durham testified that she did not know Faulkner but had seen him several times, including two hours earlier, when he had brought a seven-year-old black rape victim to the hospital. She said that Faulkner had apprehended the suspect.

Under cross-examination, Durham at first again denied knowing Faulkner, but she added that she had "seen him several times" and spoken with him a number of times when he had taken some time out for coffee. Jackson asked her how often she had had an occasion to see and speak to officers from the Sixth Precinct. She estimated six days a week, some days more than once. Did she ever give statements to those police in connection with her work as a security guard? Yes, she said she did.

Jackson then asked her when she first let the police or the district attorney know that she had heard Abu-Jamal's confession.

JACKSON: Isn't it a fact that you didn't tell them until sometime in March?

DURHAM: Okay. Yes, I did not talk to the D.A.'s office until—what was it—February or whenever.

JACKSON: Did you try to contact them before?

DURHAM: No.

JACKSON: This incident happened in December, right?

DURHAM: Yes.

JACKSON: You saw police after that, didn't you?

DURHAM: Yes.

JACKSON: And you saw police in February, didn't you?

DURHAM: Maybe not. I was out of work.

JACKSON: The entire month of February?

DURHAM: You said—I'm not sure of the dates but I was out of work for about six weeks, six-to-eight weeks from December up until the time that I was questioned [by the D.A. in connection with its investigation into the allegations that the arresting officers had beaten Abu-Jamal].

Jackson failed to pursue why Durham had been out of work from shortly after Abu-Jamal's arrest or how she had come to get her job back at the hospital soon after she informed the D.A.'s investigators about Abu-Jamal's alleged confession. Instead Jackson asked her why she had not initiated any efforts to let the authorities know that she had heard Abu-Jamal's confession. She said she had not because she had already given a statement to Jefferson Hospital investigators. Jackson asked her when she had done that, and she said, "The very next day."

Jackson asked the court if he could suspend his cross-examination of Durham until he could see a copy of that statement. Judge Sabo responded: "Cross-examine her about something else. You call her later on." McGill said he would attempt to have a police officer obtain a copy of it.

Jackson resumed his cross by asking Durham, "Whom did you give it to?" She said she gave it to "[James] Bartelli of the Jefferson [University Hospital] Investigator Department."

JACKSON: You never told the police that you gave that statement to anyone, did you?

DURHAM: I assume that's why I was contacted was because of that. I didn't, you know—

JACKSON: You assume that—the question is did you ever tell the police that you gave a statement to someone?

DURHAM: No. Nobody asked.

After an objection from McGill, Jackson honed in on why Durham had been contacted by the police.

JACKSON: Weren't you contacted by the police because . . . I on behalf of Mr. Jamal had accused the police department of beating him?

DURHAM: Internal Affairs, yes.

JACKSON: So that's the reason you were contacted. So why did you say you assumed it was because of your statement?

DURHAM: Well, I don't know.

JACKSON: So when you said that you assumed that they were calling you or contacting you about your statement to Bartelli you were incorrect, is that right?

DURHAM: Yes. I didn't know whether [Bartelli] had given them the statement or not. You know, I just gave it to him.

JACKSON: Now did you ever tell the police that you gave the statement to Bartelli?

DURHAM: No. . . .

JACKSON: Do you know at this point what, in fact, Bartelli did with the statement you gave him?

DURHAM: No. I do not.

JACKSON: Was it a written statement?

DURHAM: No. I believe I just dictated it to him.

JACKSON: You just dictated it to him?

DURHAM: Yes.

JACKSON: And he took it down?

DURHAM: Yes, and I think I signed it.

Jackson then returned to questioning Durham about the scene at the hospital when Abu-Jamal was brought in, asking her how many police officers were around. "That's all there was around was police officers. I could tell you fifty, a hundred, and still be wrong," Durham answered. Jackson asked her to estimate how many police were around Abu-Jamal. She answered, "Fifteen, twenty." He asked her what these police were doing. "Sir, I don't know. When the doors opened Mr. Abu-Jamal was hollering, the police were hollering. I immediately left the area." Pressed further about what the police were doing, Durham said, "One was holding his legs, somebody had his arms; they were trying to control their prisoner. I did not stand there and watch and see what they did."

Durham testified that Abu-Jamal was brought to the hospital thirty to forty-five minutes after Faulkner. The police had placed him on the floor just outside the ER. Abu-Jamal was handcuffed, his hands behind his back, lying on his back. She said she did not know that he had been shot and that was why she had the police drag him to the family room rather than to one of the ER treatment areas. She said at no time did she see any blood on Abu-Jamal or any injury to his head. When Jackson asked her if she had filed an "incident report" about that evening's activities, she answered that she did not view the activities as an "incident."

Jackson asked Durham how close she had gotten to Abu-Jamal. "I was on him. I was on top of him—his head was at my feet," she said.

After Jackson completed that section of his cross-examination, Abu-Jamal stood to address the court. Judge Sabo excused the jury. Abu-Jamal then again told the judge that Jackson did not represent him and that he wanted John Africa in his place. Sabo ordered Abu-Jamal removed from the courtroom.

The statement that Durham alleged she had given to Bartelli was then brought in and given to McGill, who provided it to Jackson. The statement was typed, undated, and unsigned. Jackson should have demanded that Bartelli be brought to the courtroom and put on the stand to verify the document before questioning Durham about it, but instead he just pressed on, recklessly adopting the document as a defense exhibit.

> JACKSON: Earlier when I questioned you with regard to the statement that you gave to your supervisor at Jefferson Hospital, you indicated that you dictated a statement orally. Is that correct?
>
> DURHAM: Yes.
>
> JACKSON: Is this the statement?
>
> DURHAM: Yes.
>
> JACKSON: As it was being dictated it was being typed immediately onto a typewriter?
>
> DURHAM: No.
>
> JACKSON: So again we still don't have the statement that you gave. Is that correct?
>
> DURHAM: Not the handwritten one.
>
> JACKSON: And you signed the handwritten statement?
>
> DURHAM: No. I said I believe I may have signed the statement. I didn't say whether I had or not. I didn't remember.
>
> JACKSON: Did you review the statement after you gave it to see if it was accurate?
>
> DURHAM: No.
>
> JACKSON: So in other words you don't know what was written?
>
> DURHAM: No.
>
> JACKSON: So anything that would be brought in here you'd have no idea at all when it was written. Is that correct?
>
> DURHAM: I'd know if I said it.

Jackson then brought out that the typed statement referenced Durham as saying that Abu-Jamal was bleeding—a contradiction of her just-given testimony.

Buried within Durham's testimony was the fact that the prosecution did not produce the original "dictated" statement Durham claimed to have given her supervisor the day after hearing Abu-Jamal's "confession." In more capable hands than Jackson's, the defense could have used the hocus-pocus of that typed document to discredit her claim that she even made a report to her supervisor. Further, Jackson should have interviewed Bartelli in the next day or so to determine if Durham had ever made a report to him about Abu-Jamal's alleged confession. And if he were to have said she had not, Durham's entire testimony could have been impeached.

But Jackson, not Clarence Darrow, was defending Abu-Jamal. As a result, Durham's testimony, the hodgepodge of backtracking and contradictory statements that it was, was likely the most damaging testimony brought against Abu-Jamal. McGill would use Durham's testimony to corroborate what his next witness—Officer Garry Bell—would testify to: not only that Abu-Jamal had shot Faulkner but also that he had hoped Faulkner would die. A corroborated confession such as this, particularly when the victim is a police officer in the line of duty, would make a death penalty conviction a near certainty.

Bell was Faulkner's partner and considered Faulkner his best friend. Durham had identified him as the officer who had prompted Abu-Jamal's confession. Under questioning by McGill, Bell testified that at the hospital he went over to Abu-Jamal to see who had shot his partner. He looked at Abu-Jamal, and Abu-Jamal said "these exact words" to him: "I shot the motherfucker, and I hope the motherfucker dies." McGill asked him what he did next. Bell said he told Abu-Jamal, "He shouldn't be the one that dies, you should."

McGill: Could it have been something like—
Jackson: Objection.
McGill: "If he dies, you die"?
Jackson: Objection. He's putting words in his own witness's mouth.
Judge Sabo: Yes. Could you rephrase that?
McGill: Could it have been another way?
Bell: It's possible. I was angry at the time.

Jackson began the cross-examination by asking Bell if he had given a statement to the assigned detective or to Night Command or anyone within twenty-four hours. Bell answered, "No." Jackson then asked him if he had written up an Incident Report (a report that police officers fill out, according to Bell's subsequent testimony "on any radio call or any contact you have with any individual. . . . It's a form, it's duplicated and you sign your name, badge number and fill in the details as to the exact time, location and anything else for your assignment"). Bell answered, "No, I did not."

> JACKSON: Indeed you're telling us that in fact the first time that you ever told the police that Mr. Jamal made those remarks was on the 25th of February after Mr. Jamal made a complaint about being beaten. Isn't that true?
>
> BELL: I gave a statement on the 25th of February, that's correct.
>
> JACKSON: Officer Bell, again, isn't it a fact that you were interviewed on 2/25/82 as a result of a complaint that was lodged by Mr. Jamal through me with regard to some complaint?
>
> BELL: That's correct.
>
> JACKSON: At no other time prior to Feb. 25, 1982 did you give a statement relevant to anything that Mr. Jamal may have said?
>
> BELL: No. I did not.

Jackson asked Bell if he knew on the night that he was at the hospital who the assigned detective on the Faulkner case was. Bell said he did not. How about on February 25, 1982? No, again. Did Bell ever make any efforts to find out who the assigned detective was? Bell answered that there was no reason for him to find out.

> JACKSON: Well, didn't you think the information with regard to the statement you said Mr. Jamal gave you, didn't you think it was relevant and important?
>
> BELL: Yes, I did.
>
> JACKSON: But you didn't take any steps whatsoever to convey it to anyone?
>
> BELL: At the time it was a very, very emotional time for me.
>
> JACKSON: I can appreciate that, sir. But again, not until Feb. 25 when you were asked—didn't you think again—
>
> BELL: When I was directly asked I responded with my answers.

JACKSON: I understand you responded when you were asked back in February. My question is: At that time didn't you think what you heard, what you said you heard, was important enough for you to seek out an investigator and tell him that the man who's accused of shooting my best friend told me he shot him?

BELL: I did tell him that.

JACKSON: When?

BELL: When he asked me.

JACKSON: In February?

BELL: That's correct.

JACKSON: But the question is: Didn't you think it was important enough to tell him before then?

BELL: Yes, I did think it was important enough. I wasn't thinking clearly. I put it in the back of my mind at the time.

JACKSON: Did you tell anybody else before you spoke to Sergeant Vargas?

BELL: I don't believe I did, no.

JACKSON: You never told that to anybody?

BELL: No, I did not.

JACKSON: Just kept that a secret?

BELL: Kept it in my mind, yes.

Jackson, a few questions later, asked Bell how many police officers were around Abu-Jamal when he was brought into the hospital. Bell said there were several. (Durham had estimated that there were fifteen or twenty officers around Abu-Jamal.) Were they in physical contact with him? Bell said he didn't believe so. (Durham had said one officer was holding his legs, another his arms, in an attempt to control him.)

JACKSON: So that he was just lying on the floor by himself?

BELL: He was handcuffed.

JACKSON: Behind his back?

BELL: That's correct.

JACKSON: And he was lying on his back?

BELL: Lying on his side. [Durham had said Abu-Jamal was lying on his back.]

JACKSON: Lying on his side. Was he doing anything to anybody?

BELL: No, he wasn't. He was lying there—he was moving around, squirming, but he wasn't doing anything to anybody.

JACKSON: Wasn't kicking anybody with his elbows and shoulders, was he?

BELL: Not that I can recall he wasn't.

JACKSON: Was he hollering?

BELL: He was mumbling something. [Durham had said Abu-Jamal was hollering.]

JACKSON: Do you know what?

BELL: I couldn't understand exactly what he said at times and other times when he told me he shot Danny then I heard what he said. He said it very loud.

Jackson then brought out that Bell had not quoted what Abu-Jamal had said to him about shooting Faulkner in the same words that Durham had attributed to Abu-Jamal. Durham had testified that Abu-Jamal had shouted out, "Yeah, I shot the . . ." Bell said he was almost positive Abu-Jamal had not said "Yeah" first.

Asked about security guard Durham, Bell said he knew of her but did not know her personally. He wasn't sure he'd seen her at the hospital that night.

Jackson wrapped up by asking Bell if he ever discussed "with his brother officers, his wife, his girlfriend, uncle, brother, somebody, anybody what he heard this man [Abu-Jamal] say." "No, I didn't," Bell said.

The double-barreled testimony of Durham and Bell concerning Abu-Jamal's alleged confession on the sixth day of the trial—with Abu-Jamal banished from the courtroom toward the end of Durham's testimony and for all of Bell's—was in essence the end of the trial. It should not have been, but it was. Although Jackson succeeded in bringing out important discrepancies and holes in Durham's and Bell's testimony, particularly their tardiness in reporting the confession to the D.A.'s investigators, the best he could do when it came to debunking the "confession" itself was to quibble over whether Abu-Jamal had said "Yeah" at the beginning of it. At the end of the day the jury had every reason to believe that Abu-Jamal had defiantly said, "I shot the motherfucker, and I hope the motherfucker dies."

17

TESTIMONY OF MICHAEL SCANLAN

O n the seventh day of trial, Judge Sabo allowed Abu-Jamal
back into the courtroom.

McGill's first witness was Michael Scanlan—the only
"clean" eyewitness to Faulkner's shooting the prosecution chose to call.
Scanlan told the police he was driving home from a date and had
stopped at a traffic light at the intersection of 13th and Locust. His
position put him about forty feet behind Faulkner's police car. He testified that he saw a black man being spread-eagled in front of a police
car by a police officer. He said the black man swung around and struck
the officer in the face with his fist and then the officer attempted to
subdue the black man. Scanlan said he then saw another man come
running out of the parking lot across the street toward them. He said
he saw the running man's hand come up and then he heard a gunshot.
He said he next heard another gunshot when the man got to the police
officer and the man the officer had been talking to. "And then the officer fell down on the sidewalk and the man walked over and was standing at his feet and shot him twice. I saw two flashes." Scanlan
concluded his testimony to McGill by saying he could not identify
either the driver of the VW or the man who ran over and shot Faulkner.

Under cross-examination by Jackson, Scanlan said he had just
dropped off a friend at the Academy House Apartments. He said he'd
had "a few cocktails" a couple of hours before he arrived at the intersection. At this point Abu-Jamal interjected by asking Scanlan if he

could describe the second man "that you saw run across the parking lot?" Judge Sabo excused the jury. After a couple of heated exchanges between Sabo and Abu-Jamal, the judge again ordered him removed from the courtroom. Before he left, Abu-Jamal reiterated his request to have Jackson removed as his counsel and replaced by John Africa.

When Jackson's cross-examination resumed, Scanlan said the man in the VW and the police officer were standing in front of the police car but behind the VW. He observed the police officer looking at a piece of paper in his hands, saying he thought it was a driver's license. Then he saw the driver of VW hit the officer, who responded by spread-eagling the man on the front of the police car and hitting the man two or three times in succession on the shoulders with a blackjack or a long flashlight. He said the blows caused the man's knees to buckle and he ducked down. After the officer hit the man, Scanlan said he saw a man running from the parking lot with his hands together, implying he was holding a gun at chest level. He said that the first shot did not make Faulkner fall, but after the second shot—fired five or six seconds later—the officer went down on the sidewalk. (Scanlan's observation that the officer did not fall to the sidewalk after the first shot and that it was five or six seconds later that he fell is the precise timing that Robert Harkins described to the police in his statements.)

Jackson referred Scanlan to the testimony he had given on March 29, 1982, before Judge Myer Rose in a related hearing, and referred Scanlan to page 119 of that testimony, when Scanlan was asked, "Is it your testimony that the first time the officer was on the sidewalk was when he fell as a result of being struck by that first bullet"? To that question, Scanlan had answered, "Yes, sir."

Jackson resumed his questioning.

JACKSON: You testified earlier this year that the officer fell after the first bullet. Is that correct?

SCANLAN: That's correct.

JACKSON: So would it be fair to say, with refreshing your recollection with the statement, that the officer did indeed fall after the first bullet, after the first shot?

SCANLAN: He didn't fall immediately down on the sidewalk. It was a few seconds. There was confusion when all three of them were in front of the car. He didn't fall directly down as a result of the first shot.

JACKSON: So your best recollection is that he fell after the first shot?

SCANLAN: Yes, sir.

Jackson did not realize it, but what Scanlan was saying about Faulkner not falling as a result of the first shot was that the first shot was fired by Faulkner himself at the oncoming Abu-Jamal. Abu-Jamal went down to the curb, replaced now by Freeman who, in the next few seconds, wrestled Faulkner to the ground and then shot the officer first in the back and then in the face, just as witness Harkins had told police in his two statements. Notice that Scanlan had said there was confusion "when all three of them were in front of the car." Cook was back inside the VW, while Freeman was outside the VW just as Faulkner was shooting Abu-Jamal. By the time Harkins arrived to observe the scene, Abu-Jamal had already crumpled to the curb. What had blinded Scanlan from seeing what was actually happening was his assumption that the man running from the parking lot was doing the shooting. Although Scanlan described the shooter as having an Afro and wearing a black knit cap, it never dawned on him that anyone other than the man running from the parking lot would be the one to shoot the police officer.

Jackson then read from Scanlan's handwritten December 11 statement to the police, referencing a question-and-answer exchange the police officer interviewing Scanlan had written down. The officer had asked Scanlan, "Did you see this male [the man running from the parking lot] shoot the officer?" Scanlan had responded, "No, all I saw was the flash from the gun. I didn't follow the flash back to the gun, but when I saw the guy running across the lot towards the cop I knew he was going to help the guy that was getting hit from the billy club."

Jackson asked him if it would be fair to say, based on his second statement to the police, on December 11, 1981, that he had not seen who fired the first shot.

"Well, what I meant, I couldn't identify them. I was worried about identifying the person. As of now, I still can't identify them, only through clothing," Scanlan answered.

In his December 11 statement to police, Scanlan had said the shooter "had a long-sleeved sweater on. I think it was red and black, or yellow and black." In his trial testimony, Scanlan said the shooter had on "I think a red and blue striped coat or sweater." (Abu-Jamal was wearing a red-quilted, waist-length ski jacket with a vertical blue strip on the front.)

When Jackson asked Scanlan who had told him the colors were red and blue, McGill's objection was sustained.

Under further questioning from Jackson, Scanlan said the shooter ran across the lot and got as close as three or four feet to Faulkner before he raised his hand and fired the first shot. (Abu-Jamal was shot from within twelve inches of Faulkner, so what Scanlan was now saying could not have happened.) Jackson brought out that Scanlan had told the police the shooter had "an Afro" haircut and was wearing a black knit cap. If Jackson had been aware of Kenneth Freeman's presence at the scene, he would have realized that the shooter Scanlan was describing as having an Afro and wearing a black knit cap was Freeman and could not possibly have been Abu-Jamal, who wore his hair in dreadlocks and had on a green beret. One would be hard-pressed to confuse a green beret with a black knit cap, but it would be impossible to confuse an Afro with dread-locks. Scanlan proved he knew the difference when he told police that the driver of the VW (Billy Cook) wore his hair in dreadlocks. Jackson did not realize that Scanlan saying that the shooter had an Afro meant Abu-Jamal could not have been the shooter.

Jackson asked Scanlan if he had seen Faulkner shoot his gun. Scanlan testified he had Faulkner in sight during the entire incident but he did not see Faulkner shoot his gun.

Scanlan estimated that it took the shooter "two seconds" to get from the parking lot to Faulkner.

On re-direct, McGill showed Scanlan Abu-Jamal's jacket. Scanlan identified it as the jacket worn by the shooter, saying, "I remember the stripes, the big stripes."

18

TESTIMONY OF ALBERT MAGILTON

McGill then called Albert Magilton, an eyewitness who testified he saw Faulkner pull over a VW at the corner of 13th and Locust. He told McGill that he saw Abu-Jamal run across the street toward Faulkner with his hands behind his back. (Scanlan, the previous prosecution witness, had just testified that the man who ran across the street from the parking lot was holding his hands in front of himself.)

Magilton told McGill that the police at the scene had taken him to the paddy wagon to identify the man he had seen running across the street. At the paddy wagon, he said, he identified Abu-Jamal as that man.

McGill asked Magilton, who was on foot at the scene, if he lost sight of the man running across the street. Magilton said he did, about halfway across the street. "I had turned to proceed crossing the street."

McGill asked him what happened next. Magilton said he heard some shots, looked over, and did not see the officer any longer. He said he then proceeded back across the street to see what had happened to the officer. When he got to the pavement, he looked down and saw the officer lying there. He said he did not see "the other gentleman" (Abu-Jamal) until he moved up closer and saw "he was like sitting on the curb" by the front of the Volkswagen.

McGill asked Magilton if he had seen Faulkner in his police car earlier that day. Magilton answered, "Well, I had seen him down the street, just before he pulled away around Juniper and Locust."

Jackson's cross-examination immediately put Magilton in a compromising light. A few minutes before Faulkner pulled over the VW, he had spotted Magilton peering into the back of a parked limousine at the corner of Juniper and Locust. Faulkner had driven up to him, asked him what he was doing and what his name was, and told him he looked familiar.

Jackson asked him what he was doing looking into a car at 4 A.M. "Well, it was a big limousine and it had stuff in the back of it," Magilton answered.

Magilton said he was walking on the south side of Locust but when the VW got pulled over, he stood at the corner of 13th and Locust and watched. This would put him just to the right of Scanlan's car, about fifty feet behind Faulkner's car. He said the VW drove through the intersection and pulled over behind a couple of cars. He noticed there was a Ford in front of the VW.

Although there were people moving about on both 13th Street and Locust, according to Magilton's testimony, Magilton did not see anyone just standing around other than some people over on the southwest corner of Locust Street by an old church or movie house. When asked if he saw anyone standing on the southeast corner of Locust, Magilton said, "No. I noticed a gentleman come from through there (pointing to a diagram of the crime scene), and he started moving across the street, and that man was Mr. Jamal." When Jackson asked Magilton if he saw a taxicab, he answered that there were cabs moving all around but he had not seen any parked.

In testifying that he did not see anyone on the southeast corner, Magilton, like all the other eyewitnesses McGill and Jackson would call to testify, was saying he did not see the prosecution's main eyewitness, prostitute Cynthia White, who claimed she had been standing on the corner directly ahead of Magilton throughout Faulkner's encounter with Cook and the officer's subsequent shooting. In saying he did not see a cab parked at the scene, he was also saying he did not see another key prosecution witness, taxicab driver Robert Chobert, who claimed to be parked two car lengths directly behind Faulkner's car.

Jackson asked Magilton if he heard "one shot, two shots, in rapid succession." He replied that he'd heard "Pow, pow, pow and then pow, pow."

Jackson closed his cross-examination by having Magilton admit that he did not see who shot the officer.

19

How Faulkner Died

At the end of the seventh day of trial, Dr. Paul J. Hoyer, an assistant medical examiner for the City of Philadelphia who specializes in forensic pathology, testified for the prosecution. He said he conducted an autopsy of Faulkner at 9 A.M. on December 9, 1981, finding that Faulkner died from gunshot wounds. He said the bullet to Faulkner's face, which entered the right-hand corner of his left eye, caused death to occur instantaneously. He also said that the bullet that went through the upper side of his back caused Faulkner pain but did not hit any vital organs and did not incapacitate him.

Abu-Jamal was in court as the eighth day of the trial began.

The state's first witness was Dr. Charles S. Tumosa, the criminalist supervisor for the City of Philadelphia. Prosecuting attorneys regularly call such experts in capital cases to create an air of scientific certitude for the jury. In that sense their testimony is usually pro forma window dressing used to reconfirm authoritatively the prosecution's theory of the case. In regard to Tumosa, McGill would disclose at a sidebar conference with Judge Sabo and Jackson during Jackson's subsequent cross-examination of Tumosa that he had called Tumosa as a preemptive tactic because he knew from Jackson's witness list that Jackson might call him when the defense presented its witnesses. As such McGill viewed Tumosa's testimony as something of a wild card that he thought would be better played under the auspices of a prosecution—rather than a defense—witness. It was a calculated gamble that forced McGill into making his biggest blunder of the case. Instead of confirming through scientific findings the prosecution's version of how Faulkner was shot to death, Tumosa's testimony would destroy it, leaving McGill to reel as the doctor's testimony unfolded.

McGill began his direct examination by asking Tumosa if he had examined any of the evidence in the case involving the death of Faulkner. After Tumosa said he had, McGill asked him if he had a report with him that showed the results of his examination. Tumosa said he did. He then asked him to identify the patrol jacket and sweater Faulkner had worn the night he was killed.

Tumosa proceeded to read from the report he had written about the jacket, noting the presence of primer lead on the back of Faulkner's jacket. Tumosa said that lead traces on this jacket could come primarily from two sources, either from a bullet going through the jacket's material or from the powder inside the bullet's cartridge.

McGill asked him if he had made "any kind of findings in relation to any comparison of the primer lead around the hole in Faulkner's jacket."

"We determined that the weapon must have been twelve inches or less when discharged."

Only two prosecution witnesses—Cynthia White and Michael Scanlan—stated that they saw Faulkner being shot. White testified at trial that Abu-Jamal shot Faulkner in the back from two or three feet away, with both shots being fired from the same distance. In her original statement to the police, given on the night of the shooting, she stated that Abu-Jamal "had fired the gun four or five times" before Faulkner fell to the ground. Scanlan testified at trial that the shooter ran across the parking lot and got "as close as three or four feet" to Faulkner before he raised his hand and fired the first shot. Scanlan testified that his best recollection was that Faulkner fell "a few seconds" after the first shot.

Tumosa had just said that the shot that hit Faulkner in the back was fired by a weapon that was twelve inches or less away from him—at point-blank range. What White and Scanlan had testified to, by deduction, could not have physically happened—neither had seen what they had claimed to have seen. McGill's two most important eyewitnesses had been debunked by the prosecution's own expert. With his case unraveling before him, McGill's next set of questions dug the hole deeper.

> McGILL: How can you determine that? Tell me what you do.
>
> TUMOSA: This is just as I described. If you hold a hose out, water from the hose will come and at particular points will hit the ground. The water itself won't go on forever. The same thing is true with the products of combustion. When a firearm is discharged, when a cartridge is discharged from the weapon, at a particular distance, you will not find this particular material anymore. Usually, it is around nine to twelve inches where this falls off so that when we detect it, when we know it is there, we know that the distance must have been less than that distance, twelve inches.
>
> McGILL: We have a ruler here. Would you hold that up? Would that be twelve inches?
>
> TUMOSA: Well, one foot, twelve inches, or less.
>
> McGILL: Or less?
>
> TUMOSA: Or less.
>
> McGILL: Twelve inches is the outside figure?
>
> TUMOSA: Yes, it is the outside estimate.

McGill, after questioning Tumosa extensively about two other bullet holes in the collar of Faulkner's police jacket—neither bullet had made contact with Faulkner's body—asked Tumosa what his findings were in reference to Abu-Jamal's jacket. He responded by reading verbatim from his report: "Item number one is a red and blue quilt waist-length jacket with a zipper up the front stained with human blood. There is a hole at the right chest area above the right pocket. Tests for nitrates were negative. Tests for lead indicated the presence of primer lead. Comparisons of this primer lead pattern with patterns from the test firing of Patrolman Faulkner's firearm identified a muzzle-to-jacket distance of approximately twelve inches."

> McGILL: Again, would you explain what you mean by that very briefly. You already stated it before, but state it briefly, again.

TUMOSA: Again, the primer lead is a device on the cartridge which, when the firing pin strikes it, sets off an explosion and ignites the powder in the cartridge sending the projectile out. The primer lead, this compound, this organic compound, is blown out of the barrel of the firearm for about one foot so that if the firearm is discharged at a distance of usually less than one foot we can detect the presence of lead, a large concentration of lead.

McGILL: So, again, that evidence, the primer lead on that jacket that you analyzed, indicated in those comparison tests from Officer Faulkner's gun that this weapon was fired within twelve inches of the jacket?

Jackson should have objected to McGill's last question—McGill was not only putting words in Tumosa's mouth, but he was also misstating what the criminalist had just said—but he did not. McGill wanted very much for the jury to believe that after being shot in the back, Faulkner had somehow gotten off the shot that struck Abu-Jamal in the chest. None of the eyewitnesses at the scene had seen Faulkner fire his gun; none had seen him even attempt to draw his gun. Furthermore, as McGill and Tumosa both knew, the police claimed not to have run any tests on Faulkner's gun to determine if it had been fired the night he had been shot, nor to have run any tests on his hands to determine if he had fired a gun. All Tumosa was testifying to was that the lead pattern found on Abu-Jamal's jacket was consistent with the lead pattern that a test firing of Faulkner's gun produced. Nonetheless, Tumosa, normally a stickler for such nuance, answered "Yes, sir," to McGill's bogus question about Faulkner's gun.

During his cross-examination of Tumosa, Jackson would show himself to be something of a forensic student but not much of a defense attorney. Tumosa's direct testimony had just contradicted the prosecution's account of how close Abu-Jamal was to Faulkner when he supposedly fired the initial shot. Jackson could have taken Tumosa through the pertinent eyewitness testimony of White and Scanlan and had him say they were both in error. If White and Scanlan had been wrong about that, what could the jury rely on them for? Jackson looked like he was going down that road when he eventually brought his cross-examination around to asking Tumosa about Faulkner's jacket.

> JACKSON: Dr. Tumosa, I am going to now refer you to the jacket that was supposedly Officer Faulkner's jacket. I believe you indicated that without any question the muzzle-to-jacket distance was within twelve inches; is that correct?
>
> TUMOSA: That is correct.
>
> JACKSON: Could it have been two-and-a-half feet away?
>
> TUMOSA: No, sir.
>
> JACKSON: What about six-feet away?
>
> TUMOSA: No, sir.
>
> JACKSON: You are certain of that?
>
> TUMOSA: Yes, sir. The hole in the back is less than one foot, probably closer to nine-to-six inches.
>
> JACKSON: Closer to nine to six inches?
>
> TUMOSA: Yes. Twelve inches is the estimate at the outside.
>
> JACKSON: So that I am clear and the jury is clear, too, that means that whoever was holding that weapon and wherever the weapon was, it was, in your view, six to nine inches away from the officer's back?
>
> TUMOSA: About so far, that is correct.

When Jackson said, "So that I am clear and the jury is clear, too," etc., he must have been hoping that the jury would make the connection between what Tumosa had just said and what White and Scanlan had testified to concerning the distance between the shooter and the officer. Instead of making sure the jury was on the same wavelength, Jackson changed the subject to Abu-Jamal's jacket, allowing the trial's most contradictory evidence to drift from center stage.

After cross-examining Tumosa about Abu-Jamal's jacket, Jackson exposed the sham that was the Philadelphia Police Department's investigation of Faulkner's killing.

> JACKSON: Does your unit collect trace evidence relevant to the neutron activation tests?
>
> TUMOSA: No, sir. That is the function of the Mobile Crime Detection Unit.

JACKSON: That is their function to do that?

TUMOSA: Yes. The detective division may ask for it through the Mobile Crime Unit. We will often advise them as to whether or not that should or should not be done.

JACKSON: In this case, sir, did you advise them as to whether or not that should or should not be done?

TUMOSA: I wasn't asked.

JACKSON: No one asked you?

TUMOSA: That is correct.

JACKSON: Now, although the collection is done by—the Mobile Crime Lab, who actually does their test? Is it done in Philadelphia?

TUMOSA: No. sir. They usually give the kits to us and they forward them to the Federal Bureau of Investigation.

JACKSON: As far as you know, no kit was given to you?

TUMOSA: That is correct, sir.

JACKSON: By the way, for the benefit of the jury, could you tell us what the neutron activation test is?

TUMOSA: Basically, it is a way of looking for the residues of the discharge of a firearm. If an individual fires a handgun or a rifle, whatever, a certain amount of residue from the primer which we mentioned earlier also deposits itself upon the hand of the individual firing the weapon. There is a way, using a nuclear reactor, to make a determination as to whether or not what was present on the hand of the individual is consistent with the discharge of the firearm by that individual.

JACKSON: How is this trace evidence collected?

TUMOSA: Basically, it looks like a cotton swab and a 5 percent nitric acid solution is placed on it, and it is wiped over the hands of the individual.

JACKSON: How long would you expect that trace evidence to be present assuming a weapon had been fired by that individual?

TUMOSA: In a living individual?

JACKSON: Yes.

TUMOSA: In a living individual who is not active, up to about four hours.

JACKSON: What about an individual who is not living?

TUMOSA: Depending upon whether or not any moisture is at the scene, it may last for many hours. . . . .

JACKSON: In excess of twenty hours?

TUMOSA: Possibly a day would be more like it.

Jackson's further questioning of Tumosa revealed that the police also had not conducted a trace metal test on Faulkner's hands, another test that is used to determine if someone had fired a gun, nor had they conducted any other type of forensic testing to determine that finding. As Jackson bore in on Tumosa regarding these police investigative lapses, Judge Sabo summoned him and McGill to several sidebar conferences. At one of them Sabo said, "Mr. Jackson, the fact still remains that they took no such test. It doesn't make any difference. They did not take it in this case. So, what difference does it make? Do you want to argue to the jury that they should have done it? Fine."

JACKSON: Yes, I do want to argue about that and I want to lay the basis for it.
JUDGE SABO: The fact remains that they didn't do it.
JACKSON: And I want to call it sloppy police work and it is sloppy because he is accused of shooting a policeman.

At a subsequent sidebar conference held a few minutes later, Judge Sabo said his position was that the tests were not done and whether doing the tests or not was somebody's fault, "it has nothing to do with this case."

JACKSON: I am not so sure.
JUDGE SABO: It is strictly conjecture as to what the outcome [of the tests] would be.
JACKSON: That may be conjecture—
JUDGE SABO: There is so much other evidence in the case.
JACKSON: I understand that and it is the evidence that is not here which seems to be beneficial to the defendant and that is what I am pursuing.
JUDGE SABO: There isn't any. The only evidence is the three people there, Mr. Cook, his brother, the defendant, and the police officer [Faulkner]. Let's not argue at this time.
JACKSON: All right [ending the sidebar conference].

In effect, Judge Sabo had told Jackson that police investigative malfeasance—a staple of defense tactics in thousands of cases—was off-limits. Sabo prevailed. The jury did not get to hear Jackson lay the basis for his claim of "sloppy police work."

The judge's judicial bias against the defendant throughout the trial would create grounds for subsequent appeals by Abu-Jamal's appeal attorneys. In the just-concluded sidebar conference, Judge Sabo, caught up in the moment and speaking extemporaneously, could not have made his bias more palpable. Prior to even hearing the defense portion of the trial, Sabo rendered his own opinion about the case with unvarnished directness when he told Jackson there wasn't any other evidence in the case.

*   *   *

After Tumosa stepped down, McGill would make another strategic mistake when he recalled Police Officer James Forbes to the stand to confirm that he had seen Faulkner's flashlight in the street near the policeman's body. Forbes and Officer Shoemaker were the first police officers at the scene, arriving within minutes of Faulkner's shooting, after having been notified of it by eyewitness Harkins. Given a second chance to cross-examine Forbes, Jackson brought out that there was a white male at the scene right after Forbes arrived. The white male approached Forbes carrying a brown paper bag, and Forbes told him to move away.

> FORBES: I would say [the white male] was in his late fifties. He appeared to be over six feet tall. He was extremely intoxicated and he was wearing a white or a tan trench coat. I believe he was balding, also.
>
> JACKSON: He had no hat on, then, right?
>
> FORBES: No. . . .
>
> JACKSON: You came within one foot of him and he came within three feet, I believe you said, of Officer Faulkner, is that correct?
>
> FORBES: Yes.
>
> JACKSON: How close did he ever get to Mr. Jamal?
>
> FORBES: Around six to eight feet.

JACKSON: And you never saw him again, did you?

FORBES: No, I did not.

JACKSON: You did not get his name or address or anything of that sort?

FORBES: No. I did not.

JACKSON: As far as you know, did anyone interview him?

FORBES: No, as far as I know.

Once again, Jackson did not take advantage of a major defense opportunity. As strange as Forbes's encounter was in its own right—another witness or potential assailant allowed to leave without any police questioning—the defense attorney did not develop it as another way of establishing the sloppy police work he wanted to put before the jury.

After Forbes, McGill called his final witness, Detective William Thomas, the detective in charge of the Faulkner investigation, to identify Abu-Jamal and Billy Cook from police photographs taken the night of Faulkner's shooting. Here, handed to him by McGill, was Jackson's great opportunity to put the police department's investigation on trial. Jackson did not ask him one question about the investigation, choosing instead to limit his cross-examination to a quibble about the type of hat Billy Cook wore that night and to reserve his right to call Thomas as his own witness during the defense portion of the trial.

When McGill heard that Jackson might want to call Thomas, he responded by saying, "Your honor, the detective will be available at any time, as all the police officers will be for Mr. Jackson's defense." How disingenuous that statement was would be revealed when Jackson attempted to call Officer Gary Wakshul as a defense witness on the final day of the defense presentation.

On a Friday afternoon of the ninth day of the trial, the prosecution rested. The tidy part of the trial was over.

20

JUDGE SABO: "I DON'T CARE ABOUT MR. JAMAL"

After the prosecution rested, Judge Sabo conducted an in-chambers session with McGill and Jackson, in which Jackson told them, "I have a strategic problem with regard to what I say in my opening remark and it may be compounded somewhat by the defendant at a later point." Jackson was referring to the character witnesses he might call on Abu-Jamal's behalf. Abu-Jamal had not yet informed him who they were or what they might say. Jackson also said he was unsure if Abu-Jamal would permit him to call any character witnesses.

Jackson then informed the judge and the prosecutor of another problem he had. "One of the difficulties that I have in determining what [other] witnesses to call is that I have to reflect and think and search my notes as to the statements of witnesses since I no longer have a copy of the statement. Mr. Abu-Jamal has copies of statements." In other words, the defense was in shambles. Abu-Jamal had not just been telling the court that he wanted Jackson ousted—he was hardly communicating with him, and he was withholding information vital to his own defense from Jackson.

McGill commiserated with Jackson about the difficulty of his task until Jackson broached a new subject concerning his opening remarks. Jackson said he might want to refer to a report written by an investigator of the Philadelphia Medical Examiner's Office that noted that Abu-Jamal had been shot by arriving police rather than by Faulkner. McGill was keenly aware of this report and said it was "hearsay upon hearsay" and was inadmissible. Judge Sabo, after hearing more about it, agreed.

On the morning of December 9, 1981, a few hours after Faulkner had been killed, the medical examiner investigator called the homicide unit to do a pro forma report on Faulkner's cause of death. In taking down the response he received from a desk sergeant, he wrote in his report that the assailant himself had been shot by arriving "police reinforcements."

As Jackson pressed the issue, McGill grew more agitated. Jackson argued to Sabo that he wanted to question the medical examiner investigator and the desk sergeant to determine what their duties were and to show that no investigative action resulted from the report that said Abu-Jamal was shot by arriving police. Jackson said their inaction "is evidence of police collusion, bias, the whole bit." Finally, it was agreed that Jackson would question the medical examiner investigator and the sergeant in private prior to giving his opening statement on Monday afternoon. He was then to inform the court of what his interviews had discovered.

Back in the courtroom following this spirited in-chambers conference, Jackson requested to schedule his opening remarks for Monday, and Judge Sabo set the time for 1 P.M. Jackson then informed the judge that Abu-Jamal wanted to address the court without the jury present. The judge consented and dismissed the jury, setting up Abu-Jamal's most extensive courtroom exchange of the trial to date.

ABU-JAMAL: Judge, you have heard me say quite a few times that I do not want this lawyer to represent me and the reason is obvious, because he is going to get me convicted and he is going to get me sentenced and when that sentence comes, I want all of you, everyone in this courtroom, to know that I repeatedly told you that this lawyer could not represent me and that this lawyer is going to cause me to be sent back to prison.

You have talked much about how much I need a legal trained lawyer. You have insisted that I have a legal trained lawyer. You have insisted that John Africa does not know the law. So, when I get sentenced, convicted, and found guilty of murder, I want everyone here, all of you, to understand that I was found guilty of murder using a legal trained lawyer and not John Africa, who you repeatedly have refused to let me use. According to you, John Africa doesn't know the law, but Tony Jackson, a legal trained lawyer, does know the law. What you are saying is that I must have an adequate defense and that John Africa cannot adequately defend me and that Tony Jackson can adequately defend me. So, according to that reason, with Tony Jackson, defending me, I should be acquitted because you are insisting that I can't get acquitted by using John Africa. I am insisting that I can.

When you insist that I must use Tony Jackson, a legal trained lawyer, in order to protect myself from a death sentence or from prison, what you are saying is that he can get me acquitted and since I am at the mercy of you, the court, this judge, and him, Tony Jackson, a legal trained lawyer, I expect to be acquitted or else I want you, Judge Sabo, and Tony Jackson, a legal trained lawyer, I want you to tell me why, why you have imposed an inadequate, so-called defense on me and denied me John Africa, who is the defense of my choice.

JUDGE SABO: I have explained the law on that subject to you before. I do not guarantee what a jury is going to do and I don't think anyone can do that. They are the triers of the facts. They will hear all of the evidence and regardless of who defends you, even if it was F. Lee Bailey, nobody can guarantee you what a jury is going to decide.

ABU-JAMAL: However, you have decided—

JUDGE SABO: They are the triers of the facts and they are the only ones who are going to make that decision.

ABU-JAMAL: You decided who to assist me in my defense.

JUDGE SABO: That is right, but Mr. Jackson nor can anyone else change the facts, whatever facts that the jury actually believe and they are the ones who try the facts. They are the ones that make the decision. There is nothing that anybody can do that is going to in any way influence them. It depends on what comes out in the trial. If what you are saying is true, then John Africa, whoever he defends, is going to be acquitted. He would be the best lawyer in the world.

ABU-JAMAL: I think he is.

JUDGE SABO: You may think he is—

ABU-JAMAL: It is my life that is on trial, not yours.

JUDGE SABO: There is no guarantee that he could do anything more or less than anybody else, but he is not trained in the law. He doesn't know what is necessary. I have watched Mr. Jackson, not on this case, but on other cases. He is a very able lawyer.

ABU-JAMAL: Well, if he is able—

JUDGE SABO: That doesn't mean that he can guarantee you anything. Nobody can.

ABU-JAMAL: What is he able to do?

JUDGE SABO: Exactly what he has been doing.

ABU-JAMAL: Which is?

JUDGE SABO: Exactly what he has been doing.

ABU-JAMAL: Following the orders of the court.

JUDGE SABO: No, he doesn't follow my orders.

ABU-JAMAL: Sure he does.

JUDGE SABO: No, he doesn't. There is nothing else. Gentlemen, we will adjourn today until Monday at 1:00 P.M.

THE CRIER: This court is adjourned until Monday at 1:00 P.M.

On Monday afternoon, when McGill and Jackson met with Judge Sabo in chambers, the issue of Jackson's interviewing the medical examiner investigator and the desk sergeant was still afoot. Jackson informed the judge that Abu-Jamal wanted those interviews done in open court—with or without the jury present. Jackson further informed him that he didn't want to question those two "out of the presence of Mr. Abu-Jamal."

JUDGE SABO: I don't care about Mr. Jamal.

JACKSON: I understand that, your honor. Your honor, I am representing him.

JUDGE SABO: I don't do this in front of the general public for anything. I am not going to do it to please Mr. Jamal.

JACKSON: It's not to please him, your honor.

McGILL: Your honor said you didn't care about Mr. Jamal.

McGill was giving Judge Sabo an opportunity to modify his assertion of disregard for Abu-Jamal, because judicial bias that blatant would be cause for appeal. Jackson, incredibly, helped the judge recover ground.

> JACKSON: But, you meant in reference to this particular issue.
> JUDGE SABO: This issue here, yes. It has nothing to do with Jamal nor the public or the press that is out there. I am not going to do it.

Jackson eventually acceded to Judge Sabo's preference that the interviews be conducted on the record and under oath but in chambers. Abu-Jamal refused to attend either interview. Jackson first interviewed Sgt. Frederick Westerman, the homicide officer. Westerman testified that he had talked with an investigator of the medical examiner's office a few hours after Faulkner had been killed but that he had not said anything to him about how Abu-Jamal had been shot.

Next Jackson questioned Stefan Makuch, the investigator. Makuch, a twenty-two-year veteran of the medical examiner's office, was in a most awkward position. After Makuch testified that he recalled talking with Westerman, Jackson asked him if the information he placed on the investigative log accurately reflected the information he received on the phone. "Not necessarily verbatim," Makuch responded.

After further quibbling, Jackson asked Makuch if he had any reason to believe that the information he recorded on that investigative log was incorrect. "I don't," he answered.

Jackson also got Makuch to admit that neither he nor anyone else he knew of had done any further investigation into who had shot Abu-Jamal.

On cross-examination, McGill began none too subtly to put the investigator on the defensive by saying he was not familiar with the name Makuch. He followed that up by asking him if he were a native of this country. Makuch answered that he was not. "What country?" McGill asked. "I am Ukrainian," Makuch said.

The raw implication McGill was making was that a foreign-born person might have difficulty understanding what he was hearing when speaking to a desk sergeant. McGill, a few questions later, led Makuch to posit that what he had written down in his report about the injury to Abu-Jamal might have been in error.

Back in open court, with the jury not present, Jackson informed Judge Sabo of several requests he was making on behalf of his client. Jackson asked that Abu-Jamal be permitted to give the opening remarks to the jury, conduct the examination of up to three witnesses, and deliver the closing remarks to the jury.

"Mr. Jamal is the best person to give that opening remark, and I would ask that Mr. Jamal be permitted to do that in my stead. I feel that he could do it and not be disruptive as your honor has suggested, and I think it would be in the best interests of justice to allow Mr. Jamal to do that," Jackson said.

He then told Judge Sabo that both Abu-Jamal and he wanted the just-concluded in-chambers testimony to be made a matter of public record, noting that with the jury being sequestered there was no opportunity for them to learn about it from the media.

Judge Sabo asked McGill if he had anything to say. McGill responded, "No, sir."

"Well, the court will deny those requests," Judge Sabo announced. "I told you initially that when I appointed you as counsel, once you became counsel you were going to follow this thing all the way through.

"I think it's only fair that the continuity of your representation of this defendant include not only the opening remarks, since you are going to be the one that has to let the jury know what you intend to prove, and the closing remarks as to your arguments as to what you have proven, or as to what the evidence shows."

Judge Sabo also said he was not going to allow the in-chambers testimony of Westerman and Makuch to be made public at that time.

Jackson asked the judge when the transcripts of the in-chambers testimony would be made public. Sabo, over an objection from McGill, said that testimony would be released as soon as the court reporter transcribed the notes. For all practical purposes, that could have been overnight. (Judge Sabo's pledge to release the transcripts proved hollow. The transcripts would not be released until after the trial concluded.)

Following an off-record discussion between Jackson and Abu-Jamal, Jackson asked the judge to allow his client to speak to him about the medical examiner's report.

As the trial unfolded, the defendant had been conferring periodically with MOVE activist Pam Africa (then known as Jeanette Africa) and through her presumably obtaining the advice of John Africa as to his courtroom tactics. Abu-Jamal was not about to let go unknown the fact that a medical examiner's log had reported he had been shot by arriving police. He wanted the reporters covering the trial and their readers and viewers, as well as the observers in the gallery, to know about this potentially explosive revelation. More important, Abu-Jamal, who knew that Judge Sabo had already ruled that what the medical examiner investigator had reported in his log was inadmissible as evidence at trial, wanted the jury somehow to find out about it. McGill, with Judge Sabo in agreement, was adamant that the medical examiner office's log remain suppressed.

Judge Sabo said that the defendant had passed up his opportunity to be a part of the in-chambers discussion. "As far as I am concerned, that closes the issue. I am not going to discuss it with him."

ABU-JAMAL: I chose not to go back in chambers for a very good reason. Because, in chambers, "in camera" as it is called, this matter of a very serious import was discussed.

McGILL: Your honor, I object to this.

ABU-JAMAL: It was discussed in secrecy.

McGILL: I object, your honor.

ABU-JAMAL: What is the court trying to hide, Judge Sabo?

JUDGE SABO: Mr. Jamal, the court is not trying to hide anything.

ABU-JAMAL: Why don't you discuss this investigative log from the M.E.'s Office, the Medical Examiner's Office?

McGILL: Again, I object. It is so obvious what he is doing.

ABU-JAMAL: It is obvious I am bringing out information that they are trying to hide.

JUDGE SABO: And, I am telling you, Mr. Jamal, unless you sit down and allow this court to run the court—

ABU-JAMAL: I will not allow the court to railroad me. I will not allow this court to hide evidence that it concedes—

JUDGE SABO: Nothing is being hidden, and your attorney knows all about it.

ABU-JAMAL: Well, bring it out in open court, judge.

JUDGE SABO: At the proper time.

ABU-JAMAL: The proper time is now [that] the defense is open.

McGILL: Would your honor make a ruling?

JUDGE SABO: I have made a ruling.

ABU-JAMAL: I have said, judge, what I said. This is not an outburst, judge. I am angry because you are obviously hiding and trying to keep something secret. I want this report addressed in court, not in sidebar, right here.

JUDGE SABO: May I see you here?

ABU-JAMAL: I don't want to meet you there. I want you to meet me here in open court. I don't want you [Jackson] going over there. [Jackson] is again disobeying my orders. He is working for me, not for the court.

(There was an unreported sidebar conference.)

ABU-JAMAL: Judge, if it is your intention to remove me, then that is your intention. It will not be the first time. It will not be the fifth time. It wouldn't be the seventh time. That will be your order. I am telling you I am fighting for my life. If you want to hide evidence that you don't want to have submitted in this trial—

JUDGE SABO: That is not evidence.

ABU-JAMAL: Based on your determination. Were you on 13th and Locust?

JUDGE SABO: No, but you were.

ABU-JAMAL: This sergeant was here as well, which is evidence admitted into evidence.

JUDGE SABO: Your attorney knows that that is not evidence.

ABU-JAMAL: My counsel is John Africa. My counsel would be ordered not to hide anything.

JUDGE SABO: Are you going to sit down?

ABU-JAMAL: No, I am not.

JUDGE SABO: You are going to become disruptive.

ABU-JAMAL: No. I am pressing this point.

JUDGE SABO: Are you going to do it in front of the jury?

ABU-JAMAL: I will do it, right. I have no objection to them hearing the truth.

JUDGE SABO: I am not going to allow you to do that in front of the jury. I think it is better I remove you beforehand.

ABU-JAMAL: Judge, I think you know what is better for you to obtain a conviction.

JUDGE SABO: I want to know from you: Are you going to be quiet?

ABU-JAMAL: I want to know from you: Are you going to speak to this medical examiner's report?

McGILL: Your honor, again I object to this obvious ploy. It is so completely obvious.

ABU-JAMAL: I object to this obvious railroading. I object to this obvious attempt to silence and keep information secret in a trial for my life.

McGILL: Will your honor rule on whether he can continue this disruptive behavior?

ABU-JAMAL: I am not.

McGILL: I am convinced he doesn't think so. Your honor, I would ask this court to make a ruling.

JUDGE SABO: I hate to bring the jury and have him act up in front of the jury again.

ABU-JAMAL: Judge, this is not an act. I am not acting up. I want you to address that information. I have been rational. I have been articulate.

JUDGE SABO: It has already been discussed.

ABU-JAMAL: It has not been discussed with me, judge. Here you have a man [Jackson] that goes back in sidebar with this man [McGill] trying to kill me, this man [Jackson] that I don't want here, and you obviously trying to convict me, and you discuss pertinent information that comes from the police department to the medical examiner's office about who shot me, and you don't want me to discuss it.

McGILL: He is completely inaccurate, judge.

ABU-JAMAL: I am not acting up, judge.

JUDGE SABO: You are disrupting this court.

ABU-JAMAL: I am disrupting nothing.

JUDGE SABO: Sheriff, take him out. Take him out.

ABU-JAMAL: I am fighting for my life according to the strategy of John Africa. I don't want you [Jackson] to participate. You are not working for me. I want you to get your ass up and go out of here.

JUDGE SABO: Quiet in the courtroom. If there are any outbursts in the courtroom, you are going to be evicted.

ABU-JAMAL: On a MOVE!

Sheriff's deputies removed Abu-Jamal from the courtroom. Judge Sabo summoned the jury back to court. He then invited Jackson to make his opening remarks to the jury.

21

THE DEFENSE

As Jackson asked for permission to approach the jury, the defense was in tatters. Abu-Jamal's open contempt for Jackson—his repeated requests to have Jackson replaced—made the defense attorney feel like he was walking on eggshells. From the beginning, his defense had been seat-of-the-pants, and it would remain so to the end. In many ways it is easy to understand why. The court denied Jackson's request for an assistant attorney and severely limited his budget for pretrial discovery and expert witnesses. McGill aggressively withheld address information about prosecution witnesses. Until the trial got under way, Jackson had been in the limbo world of backup counsel, assuming Abu-Jamal would be in charge of his own defense. In addition, once the trial began, Abu-Jamal withheld numerous witness statements from Jackson, forcing the attorney to rely on his own scattershot notes. For these and numerous other reasons, Jackson would flounder as Abu-Jamal's court-appointed defense attorney, but the simple fact was that Jackson was in over his head. Abu-Jamal knew it, McGill knew it and relished it, and Jackson no doubt felt it. In short, the defense was doomed from the moment of the third day of jury selection when Judge Sabo barred Abu-Jamal from participating in the selection of the jury, and it was doomed further still on the second day of the trial when Sabo stripped Abu-Jamal of his right to act as his own counsel, forcing the unprepared Jackson into that role.

Jackson never would develop a theory of defense, of how best to rebut the prosecution's charges and assert Abu-Jamal's innocence.

He probably thought his client was guilty. Instead Jackson simply let McGill put onstage the prosecution's version of Faulkner's killing. As the state's witnesses testified, Jackson's cross-examinations did a credible job of showing inconsistencies and contradictions, but he was never able to deliver the knockout blow that could have turned this case on its head. He had just such an opportunity when Durham and Bell testified, but owing to a lapse in memory, he did not recall the bombshell statement he had read several months earlier in going over the statements the various police officers had filed in conjunction with Abu-Jamal's arrest. If he had, the strongest indication of Abu-Jamal's guilt—his alleged confession—could have been gutted in dramatic, Perry Mason–type fashion.

Among the police officers in the area directly around Abu-Jamal when Bell approached him at the hospital was Officer Gary Wakshul. Interviewed by a detective an hour after Abu-Jamal went into surgery, Wakshul stated that he never left Abu-Jamal's side from the time Abu-Jamal was placed in the paddy wagon until he was taken into surgery. Wakshul's signed statement mentioned no shouted confession. Instead he reported, "During this time the Negro male made no comments."

During pretrial discovery Jackson had read Wakshul's statement. It was the only contemporaneous statement Jackson had read that referenced what Abu-Jamal had or had not said the night of his arrest. Most important, it was given by one of the two police officers who had accompanied Abu-Jamal from the time he was placed in the paddy wagon until he was taken into surgery, by an officer who, by his own admission, had never left Abu-Jamal's side. Apparently unknown to Jackson or his client, Wakshul's statement was corroborated by his partner, Officer Stephen Trombetta, who also had accompanied Abu-Jamal from the paddy wagon to the operating room. In a police report taken from Trombetta after Abu-Jamal went into surgery, he was specifically asked, "While at the hospital did [Abu-Jamal] make any statement to you?" Trombetta had answered, "No." (On the morning of the eleventh and final day of the trial, July 1, 1982, Jackson would make a belated, but unsuccessful, attempt to call Wakshul as a rebuttal witness.)

Despite the fact that Jackson had lost the trust and respect of his difficult client, he could have mounted a considerable defense. To do so, he essentially needed to take apart the prosecution's case plank by plank and to open the possibility that someone other than Abu-Jamal shot Faulkner. But Jackson, from Abu-Jamal's preliminary hearing onward, was never on top of the case. His performance as defense attorney was textbook "ineffective counsel" from the beginning of his representation to the end. In retrospect, the best thing Jackson could have done for Abu-Jamal was to refuse to represent him the second day of the trial when the judge stripped Abu-Jamal of his right to self-representation and placed Jackson in the role of lead counsel for the defense. Such a refusal would have most likely caused Sabo to jail Jackson for contempt of court—possibly for as long as six months—but it would have halted in its tracks the charade of a trial that was about to unfold. The court would have been forced to appoint new counsel for Abu-Jamal or to accede to his request to represent himself. Even then, the court would have been compelled to appoint new backup counsel for him. If new counsel had been appointed, the court would have been forced to allow the new counsel several weeks, if not months, of preparation, and would have had to disband the sequestered jury and form a new jury when the trial resumed.

The case that McGill put on was built essentially on three planks: the fact that a gun registered to Abu-Jamal was found at the scene with five spent, empty chambers; the eyewitness testimony of prostitute Cynthia White and felon Robert Chobert; and Abu-Jamal's alleged "confession" at the hospital. Each plank was powerful in and of itself, but combined they carried a big wallop. The defense, however, could parry all three planks. Jackson's cross-examination of White and Chobert already had impugned their credibility, and he had another witness, prostitute Veronica Jones, who could destroy what remained of White's credibility with the jury. There was no forensic evidence to link the bullet in Faulkner to Abu-Jamal's gun in particular. The forensic expert the prosecution put on the stand had to admit that the bullet in Faulkner could have been fired by any of hundreds of thousands of guns. In fact, other than highly compromised and contradictory eyewitness testimony, there was no evidence at all that Abu-Jamal had shot Faulkner. The third plank, Abu-Jamal's alleged "confession," would have been the simplest for Jackson to debunk. And in using Wakshul's report to debunk the confession, Jackson could have thrown wide open the possibility that the police framed Abu-Jamal. He could have parlayed that into laying a foundation for establishing how the prosecution "corrupted" the witnesses it could manipulate, such as White and Chobert, by getting them to "enhance" their testimony against Abu-Jamal each time the police reinterviewed them.

Just as Jackson was unprepared to make an opening statement at the outset of the trial and was forced to forgo it then, he was woefully unprepared now to take advantage of his first opportunity to address the jury directly on behalf of his client. Unlike McGill's aggressive opening statement, in which he said the state would prove that Abu-Jamal murdered a police officer in cold blood and had the "arrogance" to boast of it, Jackson let the jury know right away that he was not going to try to "prove" anything. He did not even know what the witnesses he would call on Abu-Jamal's behalf would say, because he had never interviewed any of them—a negligence of staggering proportions. Jackson had never even asked Abu-Jamal to tell him his side of the story. Instead of making his opening statement a forceful challenge to the main three planks of the prosecution's case, Jackson made no attempt to skewer any of them. His rambling, directionless opening statement was that of a man completely lost and befuddled.

Good afternoon, ladies and gentlemen of the jury.

This, of course, is my first opportunity to talk to you as an assembled jury. You've sat through and listened to the prosecution present a host of witnesses purporting to tell you—and, of course, the prosecution hopes to prove to you—what happened on that fateful evening of December 9, 1981.

Let me just suggest to you—and, it should be obvious to you—that on December the 9th, 1981, Mr. Jamal was a victim himself. You've heard testimony of what did or may have happened to Officer Faulkner. You have heard very little of what happened to Mr. Jamal.

You know from the records, from the testimony that Mr. Jamal himself was, indeed, shot. Mr. Jamal himself was, indeed, beaten. You heard very early at the outset of this case Judge Sabo indicating to you that the defense has no obligation whatsoever to prove anything.

Indeed, it is the choice of the defense to have the defendant say nothing at all. There is absolutely no requirement that we present anything to you at all, that, indeed, you could and would make a determination based on the prosecution's evidence alone that you have just heard; that is, the prosecution's case. You've heard the prosecution rest.

It is now our opportunity to present to you some information. We are not going to stand up here and say we are going to prove this and the other, but what we would like you to do is now have an opportunity to see all of the facts that happened on that evening, on that early morning hour.

What happened December 9, 1981, at or about 4 A.M.? You must as jurors in listening to the proof, in listening to the testimony of both the prosecution and the defense make a determination of what happened, not just of some of the things that the prosecution wants you to hear, but of all the facts, because each and every one of the facts, each and every one of those persons who testified, their testimony is interrelated.

What do I mean by that? If I were to ask you: Does each and every one of you see my hand? Members of the jury, now from that perspective I am sure you are saying, "Yes, we see your hand."

All that I am asking you to do is to reserve making an opinion like that, because what you see is just one side of my hand, just one side. At this point what we want to do is to turn the hand around so that you can see both sides of that hand, so that you know, in fact, what it is that you've seen, what it is that you've heard before making any decision whatsoever. For that I would ask you to listen and to listen closely, as to the cross-examination that has been conducted both of the prosecution's witnesses as well as the witnesses that are going to testify here.

The witnesses that you will hear are witnesses that have been available to the prosecution. You will see that the prosecution has interviewed these witnesses, that they have given statements to the prosecution. For one reason or another, the prosecution has decided not to present those witnesses to you.

So, what we are going to do is to present those witnesses to you so that you have an opportunity of making a decision. You recall you have the power exclusively to decide what the facts are, what the facts were, on December the 9th, 1981, at about 4 A.M.

I ask you to do that in the name of justice. Thank you.

22

WITNESSES FOR THE DEFENSE

Jackson's first witness for the defense was Dr. Anthony V. Coletta, a third-year surgical resident at Jefferson University Hospital who had treated Abu-Jamal in the emergency room. For the prosecution, Coletta was a potential Pandora's box–type witness because he was privy to medical information about Abu-Jamal's condition that only the surgeon who examined Abu-Jamal and operated on him could possess. As such, what he had to say would have great credibility with the jury. For the defense, Coletta held the potential to make the trial take a sharp detour away from the prosecution's version of the events surrounding Faulkner's shooting. Unbeknownst to Jackson, because Coletta had rebuffed Jackson's efforts to interview him prior to taking the stand, Coletta was about to testify that the bullet that struck Abu-Jamal was fired on a downward trajectory, meaning that Faulkner had not gotten off that shot as the prosecution said that he did—as he was falling to the ground.

Under questioning from Jackson, Coletta testified that Abu-Jamal had a gunshot wound to his right chest, lacerations on his forehead about four centimeters (1.6 inches) long that required suturing, swelling over the left eye, a lacerated lower lip, and soft-tissue swelling on the right side of his neck and chin—all indicators of the brutal beatings Abu-Jamal had been subjected to by the police who arrested him and brought him to the hospital. He said Abu-Jamal was coherent but was in "critical condition," meaning that he would die if not treated. He said Abu-Jamal was weak and on the verge of fainting from blood loss, having lost about one-fifth of his blood volume. Two vials taken from him detected no alcohol in his blood serum.

Coletta said he began treating Abu-Jamal at about 4:15 A.M. on December 9. Coletta testified that the bullet he retrieved from Abu-Jamal had entered his chest just below the right nipple at about the sixth thoracic vertebra and ended up lodged in his back at around the twelfth thoracic vertebra—about four or five inches lower. He said the bullet went through Abu-Jamal's right diaphragm, then through his liver, finally lodging in his lower back. He also said the bullet had a downward projectile and did not appear to strike any bones, and thus had ended up lower on a straight line downward.

Coletta's testimony rendered specious the prosecution's scenario—arrived at solely through the testimony of Cynthia White—that Faulkner had shot Abu-Jamal as the officer was falling to the ground after being shot in the back by Abu-Jamal. In that case the bullet would have entered Abu-Jamal on an upward trajectory. What the downward trajectory of the bullet removed from Abu-Jamal meant was that Faulkner, who like Abu-Jamal was about six feet one, probably shot Abu-Jamal while standing on the curb facing Abu-Jamal as he ran up to him from the street.

Based on the evidence provided by Coletta, Jackson was given an immense opportunity to establish a number of entirely new scenarios of how both Faulkner and Abu-Jamal came to be shot, but Jackson made nothing of the young surgeon's revelations. Instead of developing what the evidence of the bullet's downward trajectory might mean—as well as showing that it conclusively disproved the prosecution's version of Abu-Jamal's shooting—Jackson wasted the rest of his examination of the doctor by attempting to show that Abu-Jamal was too weak to have been flailing his arms and legs about as he lay on the floor outside the emergency room prior to being treated by Coletta.

The downward trajectory of the bullet raised the possibility that Faulkner, engaged in an intense confrontation with Cook in the wee hours of the morning in one of the city's most dangerous sections, had responded to the man running toward him by shooting him in the chest. At worst, this scenario would have allowed Jackson to make the case that Abu-Jamal shot Faulkner in self-defense after he himself had been shot. Coletta's testimony—coupled with that of Tumosa's—made it impossible for Faulkner to have shot Abu-Jamal after Abu-Jamal had shot him, because Faulkner himself wasn't shot until he was on the ground on all fours. If there was a chance for Jackson to have salvaged this case, this was it, but it slid right by him.

Jackson next called to the stand Dessie Hightower, a young black accounting student who had witnessed the immediate aftermath of the Faulkner shooting from a parking lot directly catty-corner to the incident. When Hightower saw the police beating Abu-Jamal, he stepped forward to let them know they "were beating the wrong guy." Hightower, with no criminal record and a respectful, straightforward manner about him, represented the most credible eyewitness testimony the jury would hear, if Jackson had only taken the time to interview him before calling him to testify. (Thirteen years later at Abu-Jamal's postconviction hearings, Hightower would reveal that detectives had subjected him to a polygraph test, making him the lone witness administered a veracity check. Had Jackson known this at trial—a fact not revealed to the defense—he could have examined Hightower on the stand about it and later asked the jury in his closing what it said about the police and prosecution that polygraphs were not administered to any government witnesses. In particular, why was prostitute White, who had so obviously altered her statements to comport with the prosecution's version of the case, not polygraphed?)

Hightower testified that he and his friend Robert Pigford had gone to the Whispers nightclub at the northwest corner of 13th and Locust to pick someone up at the club at about 3:35 A.M. on December 9, 1981, but the club had already closed. Hightower saw a police car pull up behind a Volkswagen. He said he saw the police officer get out and walk toward the passenger side of the Volkswagen door, like he was "motioning to hold the door." He said he didn't pay it any attention, thinking it was a routine check, and then went back to the parking lot. When Hightower recalled that Faulkner had approached the passenger side of the VW and motioned to hold the door, he clearly indicated that there was a passenger in the VW who was attempting to get out of the car—just as Cynthia White had described at Billy Cook's March 29 trial for assaulting Faulkner when she testified that the passenger did get out of the VW as Faulkner approached.

Here, handed to him on a silver platter, was Jackson's opportunity to tie together White's previous testimony with what Hightower was now stating to establish the presence of the passenger who fled the scene. In his belated opening remarks to the jury, Jackson said he would try to establish that various witnesses had reported seeing someone flee the scene soon after Faulkner's shooting. This was his golden chance to shift the case dramatically away from Abu-Jamal to the person Hightower told police he saw run away. But Jackson allowed this key revelation to sail right by without probing Hightower further about it.

While walking back to Pigford's car in the club's rear parking lot, Hightower said he heard a series of three consecutive, rapid pops, then a pause, and two more rapid pops. After hearing the first three sounds, Hightower testified that he told Pigford he thought they were firecrackers. When he heard the next two sounds, he said to Pigford, "That sounds like somebody shooting a gun." Hightower said he then walked back up to the corner of the club and cautiously peered around the wall to see what was happening. Pigford followed him. From that viewpoint Hightower said he was able to see clearly across the street to where the VW and the police car had parked—about six car lengths away.

For a second or two, from his secure vantage point, Hightower saw the back of the head of someone about five feet nine or five feet ten, with either dreadlocks or braids, wearing a red and black sweater and running east "from fairly close" to the slain officer toward 12th Street, past the St. James Hotel (where eyewitness Deborah Kordansky happened to live). Because of the hair, he said he wasn't sure whether the person he saw running was a man or a woman. About ten or fifteen seconds later he saw a police officer drive to the scene. As he and Pigford began to walk toward the scene, more police officers arrived. Hightower and Pigford stationed themselves on the sidewalk directly across the street from the VW and the police car. Hightower said that the first officer on the scene told everyone to "Get away, get away" as he went over to where Faulkner lay on the other side of the cars. Hightower saw Billy Cook, wearing a Navy pea coat, standing somewhat stooped over Faulkner, with a look of shock on his face. "It was just like he was frozen. He was standing over top of him, and he was just standing there."

Hightower said he watched as the police took Faulkner to the police van. He said that Faulkner was slumped over and that one of the officers grabbed him by the belt of his gun holster to hold him up; Hightower said he noticed that there was a gun in Faulkner's holster. Jackson made nothing of this observation even though what Hightower had just testified to contradicted the prosecution's version of the shooting, that Faulkner had gotten off the shot that wounded Abu-Jamal as he was falling backward to the ground. In that event, Faulkner would have had neither the time nor a reason to reholster his gun. During cross-examination, McGill referenced the holstered gun several times, quibbling about Hightower's saying that he remembered the holster being on Faulkner's left side, thus reopening the door for Jackson to revisit Hightower's observation of Faulkner's gun being in its holster. Once again, Jackson made no point of the holstered gun.

Instead, Jackson was intent on establishing that the police mistreated Abu-Jamal. Hightower described the arrest of Abu-Jamal as "an attack." He said that shortly after the first police officer showed up, about eight or nine other officers arrived. He then observed three or four of them striking Abu-Jamal with nightsticks while one or two others were kicking him and pulling him by his dreadlocks. He also saw the police, in carrying Abu-Jamal to the police van, ram his head into a no-parking pole and drop him to the ground.

Hightower also testified that he had given "several" statements to the police, one at the police station forty-five minutes after the shooting and then two or three others in the weeks to come. Jackson did not pursue this information in any manner. As a result, he did not find out that two detectives questioned Hightower for about five hours the first time and about a week later came to his workplace and picked him up for more questioning, some of it conducted with Hightower wired to a polygraph machine.

*   *   *

On the ninth day of the trial, Jackson continued attempting to establish the police's mistreatment of Abu-Jamal after his arrest by calling Dr. Regina Cudemo to testify. Cudemo was the psychiatric resident doctor on call in the Crisis Center at Jefferson University Hospital when Abu-Jamal was brought there for treatment. She testified that she saw Abu-Jamal at about 4:20 A.M. on the floor "on what I call the treadles of the emergency room"—the mats outside the emergency room doors. She said four to six police were around Abu-Jamal.

Cudemo was a reluctant witness, but Jackson did elicit from her that she saw one of the police officers around Abu-Jamal raise his leg and then heard Abu-Jamal "moan." After observing this incident, she said she was directed by another police officer to leave the area.

Jackson's next witness was Detective William Thomas, the detective assigned to investigate Faulkner's murder. This was Jackson's opportunity to put the shoddy police investigation before the jury, but the attorney would barely skim the surface of it.

Thomas testified that he did not order either a trace metal detection test or a neutron activation test on Faulkner, Abu-Jamal, or Cook. (The trace metal detection test is used to determine if someone held a gun. The neutron activation test is performed to determine if a subject recently fired a gun.) Jackson asked Thomas if he was aware that the trace metal detection test was effective up to thirty-six to forty-eight hours even if the subject had his hands washed. Thomas answered, "No, sir, I was not."

Jackson asked Thomas if he had ever located the person Dessie Hightower told police he had seen running from the scene right after the shooting or the man prosecution witness Cynthia White had said was standing with her during the shooting and had given a statement to a Highway Patrol officer. Thomas said he had not; he said that other than Abu-Jamal and Cook, he had never located any other potential suspects who were reported to be at the crime scene.

On cross-examination, McGill led Thomas to speculate that the person Hightower said he saw running from the scene past the hotel may have been prostitute Veronica Jones, Jackson's next witness. On redirect questioning, Thomas told Jackson he had not questioned Jones. (Hightower had testified that the person he saw running from the scene was five feet nine or five feet ten and was wearing dreadlocks or braids. Jones is five feet three and was not wearing her hair in dreadlocks or braids the night of the shooting.)

When Jackson called Veronica Jones to testify, he was expecting her to bolster Dessie Hightower's testimony that he had seen someone running from the scene right after the shooting. But like all other witnesses at trial, Jackson had not interviewed her before she took the stand. Jones had told detectives that she had seen two black men "jogging away" from the scene shortly after she had heard three gunshots and seen a police officer fall to the ground. This assertion was contained in a signed, five-page statement that detectives had elicited from Jones at her mother's house in nearby Camden, New Jersey, six days after the Faulkner shooting.

Jackson was in for a major surprise. Jones testified that she had been standing on the northwest corner of 12th and Locust with a young black man whom she said she did not know and had met for the first time. When Jackson asked her if she had seen anyone running away from the scene, she said, "I didn't see anyone do nothing. No one moved." Jackson was stunned by this answer and shortly thereafter asked for a sidebar conference.

*   *   *

At the bench, Jackson told Judge Sabo that McGill knew full well that Jones was now contradicting her signed statement. The judge said Jackson could question her about her statement. When Jackson did, she said she had signed only a blank sheet of paper and that she had not "said what they put there."

Jackson could not get Jones to support any of the relevant statements she gave the detectives on December 15. At one point she depicted the statement as "a bunch of bull."

Her testimony took an unexpected turn when Jackson asked her if she had given any other interviews to the police.

Apparently not satisfied with the contents of Jones's December 15 statement, detectives wanted a second shot at interviewing her. Uniformed Philadelphia police arrested Jones in early January and brought her to the police station, where detectives reinterviewed her for five hours. Under questioning from Jackson, Jones volunteered this about the detectives interviewing her: "They were getting on me telling me I was in the area and I seen Mumia, you know, do it, you know, intentionally. They were trying to get me to say something that the other girl [Cynthia White] said. I couldn't do that."

Jackson asked Jones if she knew Cynthia White. She said she did. He asked her if she had seen her the night of the shooting. She said she had not, thus joining all of the other prosecution and defense eyewitnesses who testified that they had not seen White at the scene.

Jackson then returned to Jones's second interview with the detectives, asking her what the detectives were talking to her about. "They were more so conversating [*sic*] among each other and I guess they expected me to say something in their behalf, you know, but I couldn't. I just saw what I saw."

Jackson asked Jones if the detectives who interviewed her in January had questioned her about the events of December 9. "It more so came about when we had brought up Cynthia's name and they told us we can work the area if we tell them," she answered.

When this "surprise" testimony popped out, McGill objected and Judge Sabo called for a sidebar conference. Sabo asked Jackson where he was going with this witness. Jackson said he wanted to ask her what the police had asked her, adding, "I didn't know she was going to say that. I never talked to her before."

McGill asked the judge to strike Jones's last statement about being told by police that she could work the street if she told them what

Cynthia White had said—that is, that Abu-Jamal killed Faulkner. Judge Sabo agreed, meaning even though the jury had heard Jones testify that the detectives were trying to buy her off for falsely testifying against Abu-Jamal, the jurors would not be allowed to consider that incredibly unfavorable admission. Judge Sabo then called for a ten-minute recess so that Jackson could interview her privately.

When Jackson returned, Sabo asked him at sidebar if he had talked with Jones. Jackson relayed a summary of what she had said: that she had been picked up in the first week of January by uniformed officers, who took her, as well as some other prostitutes, aside and said, "Look, we will let you work the street and we will do you just like we have done Lucky [Cynthia White]. We want to ask you some questions about where you were, because we know Lucky said you were out there that night and saw what happened." Jackson said she told him that if she gave a statement backing up Cynthia White, they would let her work the street. They asked her where she was that night and who she was with.

Judge Sabo ruled that Jackson had to stick to questioning her about the events of December 9 and disallowed him from developing what Jones had just told him about the police's attempts to entice her to corroborate White's testimony. "We are getting too far a field in this case," Judge Sabo told Jackson. "We have got to stick to the issue. The issue is who shot the cop and who saw anything that night. That is what I am interested in."

*   *   *

The only question Jackson was able to get in before turning the witness over for cross-examination was whether she had seen a plain-clothes officer that evening. She said she had not. For all intents and purposes, Jones's recanting of her statement that she had seen two black men jogging away from the scene was the end of Jackson's defense.

It would not come out until May 22, 1996, when Abu-Jamal's attorneys filed a sworn statement from Jones, that Philadelphia detectives had coerced her into disavowing her claim about seeing two black men hurriedly exiting the scene. In her sworn statement, she asserted that Philadelphia detectives visited her in jail shortly before she was to testify as a defense witness at Abu-Jamal's trial; at the time, the twenty-one-year-old Jones faced major felony charges for armed robbery, assault, and possession of an instrument of crime. She stated that detectives "threatened and coerced" her to change her testimony in exchange for not going to prison. Her reward for doing so would turn out to be a sentence of five years' probation on those charges.

Jackson used the next day to call six character witnesses and to nitpick with two police officers involved in Abu-Jamal's arrest.

23

"THE NEGRO MALE MADE NO COMMENTS"

On the morning of July 1, 1982, the day Judge Sabo had scheduled the case to go to the jury, Jackson called nine more character witnesses before either remembering or being prompted by Abu-Jamal to ask Judge Sabo to allow him to bring in Police Officer Gary Wakshul to testify. Wakshul was one of the two police officers who had accompanied Abu-Jamal to the hospital and had remained with him until the latter went into surgery. In the police report Wakshul stated, "We [he and his partner Trombetta] stayed with the male at Jefferson Hospital until we were released. During this time the Negro male made no comments."

> McGILL: He is not around. I am going to object to bringing this guy in. He is not around. [Wakshul, in fact—as he would later testify at Abu-Jamal's Post-Conviction Relief Act hearing—was at home and could have been in court within thirty minutes to an hour. Wakshul further testified then that either McGill himself or one of his police supervisors had instructed him to remain in Philadelphia until the conclusion of Abu-Jamal's trial in the event he might be called by the defense to testify.]
>
> JACKSON: That is what [McGill] says.
>
> McGILL: I am not bringing him in at the last minute.
>
> JUDGE SABO: You knew about this before. I am not going to hold up this trial.
>
> JACKSON: I didn't.

JUDGE SABO: What do you mean you didn't? Didn't you get statements from the detectives months and months ago?

JACKSON: Absolutely right, judge.

JUDGE SABO: I am not going to delay the court. [Judge Sabo wanted the trial concluded, including any sentencing, prior to the July 4 holiday.]

JACKSON: We can get the man by this afternoon. His testimony would be very limited. This is what he says, that [Abu-Jamal] made no comments. You can understand with regard to at least the statements of Officer Bell and—[Judge Sabo interrupts]

JUDGE SABO: Let me see his statement.

JACKSON: I was forced to try and remember everything that everybody said; I couldn't do it.

McGILL: I object to this. I think if Mr. Jamal, the defendant in this case, decides he is not going to give statements until the very last minute to his attorney, that is on him. I don't see any reason why this trial should be delayed.

JUDGE SABO: I don't know what he means by this: "During this time the Negro male made no comments." That may be as far as he is concerned.

JACKSON: He remained with him the entire time.

JUDGE SABO: Look, there were a lot of police officers in that room. There were other people that were there that may not have heard it.

JACKSON: Judge, he didn't say "I didn't hear anything." He said he made no comments.

JUDGE SABO: Made no comments as far as he was concerned. There were other police officers that were in that room and only two that heard anything was [hospital security guard Priscilla] Durham and I forget who the officer was [Officer Garry Bell]. There was nobody else that made any statement that they heard anything. There was no other officer brought in that they heard a statement and there were a lot of officers there.

JACKSON: I understand that, your honor.

JUDGE SABO: It is a fact he didn't hear it. It doesn't mean it wasn't said.

JACKSON: It isn't a matter of him not hearing it. He is saying, in fact, that he made no comments.

JUDGE SABO: As far as he is concerned. He can't speak for everybody else that is in that room. I am not going to delay the case any longer.

McGILL: Judge, this defendant has nothing else to do except this case. It seems to be the strategy to delay it. We are getting closer to the July 4 holiday and it would seem to me to get this jury disgruntled and upset.

JUDGE SABO: It may hurt the defense, too.

JACKSON: I think it would hurt us more than the prosecution. Again, I think in this instance, with regard to Officer Wakshul, we have a specific denial that he said anything.

JUDGE SABO: He didn't say that. He said he didn't hear it. What else could he testify to? He can't testify to what somebody else may have heard.

JACKSON: There is a difference as to whether he heard anything or he said he didn't say anything.

JUDGE SABO: You could have had this man long ago. I am not going to delay. It is a quarter after 11:00. I am not delaying the case any longer.

JACKSON: I think it is a matter that is crucial enough for us to do it. How long does It take to get a police officer here?

JUDGE SABO: How do I know? He could be on vacation.

After a short recess, McGill returned to inform Judge Sabo that he had been informed that Wakshul was on vacation until July 8, neglecting to inform the judge or Jackson that Wakshul was at home and available to come to court.

* * *

The question of Abu-Jamal taking the stand in his own defense was the next order of business. In open court, but with the jury out of the courtroom, Jackson asked Abu-Jamal if he intended to take the stand in his own defense.

ABU-JAMAL: My answer is that I have been told from the duration of this trial, the beginning of the trial, the inception of the trial, that I had a number of constitutional rights. Chiefly among them the right to represent myself. The right to select a jury of my peers. The right to face witnesses and examine them based on information they have given. Those rights were taken from me. It seems the only right that this judge and the members of the court want to confer is my right to take the stand, which is no right at all. I want all of my rights, not some of them. I don't want it piecemeal. I want my right to represent myself and I want my right to make closing argument. I want my rights in this courtroom because my life is on the line and I don't want no gift.

JUDGE SABO: Mr. Jamal—

ABU-JAMAL: (Interposing) I heard what you said.

JUDGE SABO: I already ruled on that issue. I ruled on all those issues. You have the perfect right to take the stand and give your version of what happened in the early morning hours of December 9 of 1981.

ABU-JAMAL: Like I had the perfect right to represent myself in this case.

JUDGE SABO: If you choose not to let the jury know your version of it you do not have to. That is your own free will.

ABU-JAMAL: It is no question of free will. You have taken every right I have and you want to save one right. You have taken all my rights and you want to say "You can have that right but you can't have the other four that I said you had." I mean it is horseshit.

JUDGE SABO: If you choose not to take the stand and if you asked me for that instruction that I mentioned, Mr. Jackson will advise the jury that you have the constitutional right not to take the stand and that they are not to draw any adverse inference from that fact. Whether or not you elect to take the stand and give your version of what happened in the early morning hours on that date is for you and you alone to decide. Whichever you want to do. It is up to you.

ABU-JAMAL: I have given you my answer.

JUDGE SABO: You say you have given your answer?

ABU-JAMAL: Yes.

JUDGE SABO: You don't wish to testify?

ABU-JAMAL: It means I want all of my rights and not some of them.

JUDGE SABO: Then you are saying you don't want to testify, is that it?

ABU-JAMAL: I said what I said, Judge. You are a smart man.

Judge Sabo asked Jackson if it was his interpretation that his client did not intend to take the stand.

JACKSON: If you don't allow him to exercise all of his rights to the fullest he is not going to select his right to take the stand.

JUDGE SABO: He is not going to take the stand.

McGILL: That is my interpretation.

A few minutes later Jackson told the court, "The defense rests."

ABU-JAMAL: The defense does not rest. There are two statements from Gary Wakshul, police number 3763. I have informed this court-appointed lawyer that you have appointed to defend me of the existence of pertinent information. It was your decision that he not be allowed to come in here and that he not be allowed to testify.

JUDGE SABO: That is not true.

ABU-JAMAL: It is true. Whose decision was it, judge?

JUDGE SABO: The officer is on vacation.

ABU-JAMAL: On here it says no vacation. He was an officer who arrested me at the scene. It has pertinent information that differs substantially from information that I was provided.

JUDGE SABO: That is not true. It does not differ.

ABU-JAMAL: I am telling you it does. Here on the statement it says that I made no comments. That is different, isn't it?

JUDGE SABO: What I am saying to you is you had a right to ask for him before and you didn't do it.

ABU-JAMAL: I had a right to represent myself, but you stopped that, didn't you?

JUDGE SABO: He is on vacation and will not return until July 8 or 9.

ABU-JAMAL: Why would a policeman be on vacation if he is ordered not to be on vacation?

JUDGE SABO: There is no order.

ABU-JAMAL: It says no vacation, judge. I am reading this.

JUDGE SABO: It may be there, but he is on vacation.

ABU-JAMAL: This is an investigative interview record from the police department.

JUDGE SABO: Your attorney and you goofed.

ABU-JAMAL: You goofed.

JUDGE SABO: I didn't goof, you did.

ABU-JAMAL: You stole my right to represent myself.

JUDGE SABO: You did by your own actions.

ABU-JAMAL: By fighting to defend myself I stole my right? That is a lie, judge.

JUDGE SABO: You should have told Mr. Jackson you wanted him [Wakshul] from the beginning of the trial.

ABU-JAMAL: I told him at the motion to suppress and he didn't show up.

JUDGE SABO: Yes.

ABU-JAMAL: What do you mean "Yes"?

JUDGE SABO: All right.

ABU-JAMAL: Are you going to order him to come in?

JUDGE SABO: He is not here. He is on vacation.

ABU-JAMAL: I am sure he can be located, judge. Do you want me to go out and find him?

JUDGE SABO: I don't blame you, but I am afraid it is not possible.

ABU-JAMAL: It is possible if you direct the police department to find him. You are saying this is not pertinent. Here is a man who says—he arrested me at the scene and took me to the hospital and he said I made no comments.

JUDGE SABO: The district attorney has another witness that he wanted to bring in who heard you make the statement and I have ruled he can't bring him in.

ABU-JAMAL: He is not standing here in my defense, he is in your defense. Just like McGill is the attorney for the Commonwealth because he is being paid by the same Commonwealth. He is not fighting. I told him [Jackson] about pertinent information. He had the statements for months and he can't find the man. The man is on vacation. It is not my fault, judge.

JUDGE SABO: It is not my fault.

ABU-JAMAL: It is the fault of the police department. They knew he was there. They knew he was at the scene, because they had statements from December the 9th. Then they allowed him to go on vacation.

JUDGE SABO: Mr. Jamal, are you going to allow the court to proceed?

ABU-JAMAL: I am not going to allow this court to proceed to lynch me without speaking in defense of my life. Damn. I know you want to kill me. It has been made abundantly clear.

JUDGE SABO: I have nothing to do with killing you. The people that sit in that jury over there they are going to decide your fate.

ABU-JAMAL: Those people I didn't have a right to select. I didn't have a right to select.

JUDGE SABO: They will decide what the true facts are and what happened in the early morning hours of December 9.

ABU-JAMAL: You don't want the jury to hear what the cop has to say?

JUDGE SABO: He is not available.

ABU-JAMAL: You can find him. Do you want me to find him?

McGILL: Your honor, maybe the record should be clear in the officer's statement he clearly says—do you want to give it to me?

ABU-JAMAL: I will read it to you. It is damn near the same thing. "During this time the Negro male made no statements." This is December the 9th.

McGILL: I would also point out that Mr. James LaGrand is now present in the waiting room area and has come into—

ABU-JAMAL: (Interposing) There are other statements.

McGILL: Can I finish? Or do you want to ramble?

ABU-JAMAL: The point is he was there on the scene and you weren't.

McGILL: Will you let me speak?

ABU-JAMAL: Knock yourself out.

McGILL: We have Mr. James LaGrand who is ready to come in and testify to what he heard, which was the exact same thing that Priscilla Durham heard and Garry Bell. Your honor ruled I am not permitted to bring him in.

ABU-JAMAL: Bring him in and bring Gary Wakshul. You are trying to hide the truth.

JUDGE SABO: I am not hiding anything. You have the perfect right to take the stand.

ABU-JAMAL: I have a right to call witnesses and you want to say what rights I have.

JUDGE SABO: It is your choice.

ABU-JAMAL: You said I couldn't defend myself. You are the one who said I couldn't select a jury of my own choice. You pinned me with this inefficient bungler over here.

JUDGE SABO: Don't blame him. He is an excellent lawyer.

ABU-JAMAL: Would you put your life in his hands?

JUDGE SABO: Absolutely. Absolutely.

ABU-JAMAL: Then you do that, because I have not chosen him. I have said consistently I didn't want him to defend me. That is a legal trained lawyer?

JUDGE SABO: He has a difficult job. You won't assist him.

ABU-JAMAL: Assist him in hanging me? What is the use if I tell him something and you tell him no?

JUDGE SABO: I only rule on the law.

ABU-JAMAL: That is a lie. You rule on convictions.

JUDGE SABO: I have nothing to do with your conviction.

ABU-JAMAL: That is a lie, judge. You have everything to do with that. You stopped me from my right to represent myself. Here I am sitting here on trial for my life essentially gagged silent until I have to protest. I talk to this man and he says what he wants to say and not what I want to say.

JUDGE SABO: Never in a million years could you do as good a job as Mr. Jackson.

ABU-JAMAL: I don't think you have any knowledge of what is going on.

JUDGE SABO: Anything else before we bring the jury in?

ABU-JAMAL: Bring this cop in here, judge.

Jackson requested, and Judge Sabo agreed, that the defense would present its closing argument before the jury in the afternoon session.

24

JACKSON'S CLOSING STATEMENT

Jackson made his closing statement to the jury that afternoon. It would essentially be a ramble, in which he seemed to mention various aspects of the case as they popped into his head. As he talked, he stood at a distance from the jury. He began by apologizing for the length of the trial and then praised the U.S. judicial system, a ridiculous statement given the total charade this trial had been for his client. His next words were almost inconceivable: Jackson told the jury they had heard "all of the evidence." He apparently had forgotten that a few hours earlier that day Judge Sabo had denied Abu-Jamal's request that the jury hear the testimony of Officer Gary Wakshul that would have undermined, if not destroyed, the defendant's alleged confession.

Although the jury instructions Judge Sabo would deliver later that afternoon involved four possible determinations: (1) guilty of murder in the first degree, (2) guilty of murder in the third degree, (3) guilty of voluntary manslaughter, or (4) not guilty—Jackson adopted the risky strategy of urging the jury to decide on only the first charge. It must have never dawned on Jackson that Abu-Jamal may have shot Faulkner in self-defense after Faulkner had shot Abu-Jamal as he ran right up to him. This scenario, a highly plausible one if developed properly, would have given the jury reason to consider a verdict of voluntary manslaughter. Instead Jackson blundered ahead.

I say to you now, if you believe beyond a reasonable doubt that Mumia Abu-Jamal committed the crimes as the Commonwealth has suggested, then you should find him guilty of murder in the first degree. I am his defense lawyer and I am telling you that. I don't want you to compromise this verdict. I don't want you to say, well, I am not really sure if he is guilty of murder in the first degree. Maybe he is guilty of murder in the third degree, or maybe he is guilty of voluntary manslaughter. I am saying to you if you are not convinced that he is guilty of murder in the first degree then he is not guilty, because that is what the Commonwealth said they would prove—that he was guilty of murder in the first degree. Don't compromise your verdict in any way whatsoever. Face it head on. That guilt must, again, be proven beyond a reasonable doubt.

Jackson tiptoed around the subject of why Abu-Jamal had not taken the stand in his own defense. Instead of explaining the real reason why he did not do so, he urged the jury not to assume that his client was "hiding some guilt of his own." Jackson could have enlightened the jury about a wide number of issues that had been raised by Abu-Jamal while the jury was out of the courtroom. The jury never was allowed to understand the substance or cause of Abu-Jamal's many defiant exchanges with the judge, exchanges that resulted in Abu-Jamal being barred from the courtroom for more than half of his trial. To the jury, these exchanges were simply outbursts, the rantings of an arrogant young man who did not respect the judicial system. Jackson could have explained that the real reason Abu-Jamal had not taken the stand in his own defense was because he had insisted to the judge that he wanted all of his rights, not just some of them. He did not want his rights "piecemeal," as he told Judge Sabo when the judge asked him if he wanted to take the stand. Jackson could have explained that for Abu-Jamal the trial was a sham from the moment that Sabo stripped him of his right to participate in jury selection, and that it had careened out of control the second day of the trial when Sabo stripped him of his right of self-representation.

Jackson passed up this once-in-a-trial opportunity to allow the jury to make sense of what must have been to them a bizarre experience that had taken two weeks of their lives to sit through. This was his final chance to build some rapport with the jury for his client and for himself by confiding in them, but he let it go begging.

In desperation, Jackson said Abu-Jamal was a "peace-loving man" who happened to be on the scene when either his brother or some other person shot Faulkner.

Jackson then attempted to impeach the government's key witness, Cynthia White, by reminding the jury of her many inconsistent statements and her probable deal making, how her statements were enhanced each time she gave the police a new one. He forgot to mention that none of the eyewitnesses, whether for the prosecution or for the defense, had even seen White at the scene.

Jackson turned next to Veronica Jones, citing her inconsistent statements. She had originally told the police she had seen two black men "jogging" from the scene after the shooting, but on the stand she changed that to seeing two black men only standing around. Jackson could have tried to slip in her testimony that had been struck, that the police had tried to bribe her to corroborate White's testimony.

Turning to Chobert, Jackson said that he had described the shooter as being six feet tall and weighing 220 to 225 pounds. Jackson also mentioned that Chobert had claimed to have seen a man with an Afro at the scene near Faulkner, but both Abu-Jamal and his brother, Billy Cook, wore their hair in dreadlocks. Again, Jackson neglected to mention that none of the eyewitnesses had seen Chobert at the scene.

Jackson then spoke about the man with Cynthia White. White had testified that she had seen that man talking to a Highway Patrol officer after the shooting but never saw him again. "You haven't seen him either," Jackson said. "I certainly haven't seen him. Where is he? Who is he? We don't know his name and we don't know his whereabouts. I think you want to know who he is. I think you want to know which police officer he talked to and what he told that police officer."

Jackson asked the jury to consider why no fingerprints were taken from either Abu-Jamal's or Faulkner's gun, and he stated that there were no conclusive ballistic results.

According to witness Dessie Hightower, Jackson said, Faulkner's gun was in his holster. Jackson said that a bullet from Faulkner's gun was in Abu-Jamal, "but who fired it?" "How easy do you think it is to get [a gun] out of the holster, particularly after being shot in the back?" he asked.

Jackson then turned his focus on Abu-Jamal's alleged confession at the hospital, pointing out that the confession did not surface until more than two months later, during the formal investigation into the charges that Abu-Jamal had been beaten by the arresting police. He pressed the point that none of the numerous other police officers around Abu-Jamal ever claimed to have heard Abu-Jamal blurt out the damning confession that security guard Durham and Officer Bell testified to at trial.

"What about the other seven or eight officers or fifteen or so officers? Why didn't they come in and say, 'Yes, we heard him too'?" Jackson asked.

Jackson's final remarks to the jury were pathetic. He would even undermine his own argument about Abu-Jamal not having blurted out a confession.

Our system of criminal justice says that the defense addresses the jury first and then the prosecution will then give its summation to you when I finish here. I will not speak to you again. I would ask you when the prosecution begins to give its summation listen and ask the prosecution, or consider when the prosecution has given its summation what argument will be advanced by Anthony Jackson in response to the argument being presented by Mr. McGill. Is there some other reason, some other way the circumstances could have happened other than the way Mr. McGill would suggest to you? Ask the Commonwealth, silently of course, why didn't you take those tests? Why didn't you take the Neutron Activation Test and why didn't you take the Trace Element Test? Why didn't you find out who that man was that Cynthia White was talking to? Why didn't you? Why didn't you explore the possibility or probability that Billy Cook was the one who shot Officer Faulkner, or someone else shot Officer Faulkner? Is it because Mr. Jamal was a well-renowned journalist in the black community and is it because having him somehow adds to it? I mean I don't know. I mean why him? There is everything to suggest that Mr. Jamal's character is such that shooting a weapon would be inconsistent and shooting a police officer would be inconsistent with what his character witnesses have said. They know him. They have told you they have known him over a number of years.

It was easy since he was shot to make that assumption [that Abu-Jamal had shot Officer Faulkner].

Tell me this, even if you accept for a moment what the security officer Priscilla Durham said and what Officer Garry Bell said, "Yes, I shot him, I hope he dies," what would the love of your brother cause you to do if you thought you were dying? If you thought you were dying and your brother was all right would you say "Yes, I shot him, I am going to die anyway"? Would you say that?

Ladies and gentlemen of the jury, I am going to close now and I hope that I have been of some benefit to you not just in this summation, but throughout the trial in attempting to seek the truth, because you sit as a board of truth to determine what the truth was on December the 9th at 13th and Locust. There have been a number of heated debates between counsel and if you hate me, fine, but don't transfer that hate to Mr. Jamal. I have attempted to do the best as I could to assist you in seeking the truth as to what happened on December the 9th at about 3:51 A.M. that morning. I just suggest to you, ladies and gentlemen, if you have been attentive you will know that Mumia Abu-Jamal did not shoot Officer Faulkner. You are not asked to assume the responsibility of deciding who it was. You only have to decide whether or not Mr. Jamal did it.

I think it is clear and it ought to be very clear to you that the Commonwealth has not proven him guilty beyond a reasonable doubt and he did not commit that crime. I would ask you to find him not guilty.

Thank you very much.

25

McGill's Summation

When McGill approached the jury to deliver his closing argument, he might as well have been frothing at the mouth, the avenger come to collect his due. There was nothing fair about the way the Commonwealth developed its case against Abu-Jamal, and McGill would not play fair now. He told the jurors that if they found Abu-Jamal guilty, "there would be appeal after appeal and perhaps there could be a reversal of the case, or whatever, so that may not be final." (McGill knew better than to use such language in his summation, but he could not help himself despite the risk of having a higher court declare a mistrial as a result.)

A few minutes into his summation, McGill said, "Let us look at the evidence." This was pure bravado. If any oddity marked this case more than other murder trials, it was its lack of hard evidence: no fingerprints on the alleged murder weapon, no trace metal tests to determine if the defendant had shot a gun, not even a simple smell test to determine if Abu-Jamal's gun had been fired recently. Two bits of crime scene evidence McGill never suggested the jury look at—and the defense did not raise—were both exculpatory to Abu-Jamal. A blood sample recovered at the murder site did not match the blood types of Faulkner, Abu-Jamal, or Cook. (A report by the criminalist referenced the presence of type O blood at the crime scene; the blood type of Faulkner, Abu-Jamal, and Cook was type A.) In addition, a copper jacket from a bullet was recovered at the scene despite the fact that both Abu-Jamal's and Faulkner's guns could fire only jacketless bullets. The only "evidence" McGill really had was the enhanced testimonies of White and Chobert and the hospital "confession," which he undoubtedly knew was a tissue of lies, just as he knew that White and Chobert had repeatedly perjured themselves in altering their testimony at trial to fit the prosecution's version of the case.

"Ladies and gentlemen, you have four witnesses that testified from different times," McGill continued. "As you recall all of the testimony that you heard you will see that they had a consistency throughout." How much calculated contempt did McGill have for this jury? White and Chobert's testimonies were riddled with inconsistencies. Jackson had demonstrated in his cross-examination that their testimonies had only begun to comport with each other's after each gave subsequent statements to the police. Of McGill's other two witnesses, Magilton had not seen the shooting and Scanlan testified he thought the shooter had an Afro and that Abu-Jamal was the driver of the VW. The only thing consistent about the testimony of the state's four witnesses was that they had seen a black man running from the parking lot toward the spot where Faulkner had pulled over Cook's VW. White was the only witness to claim that she saw a gun in the runner's hand, a gun that she initially told police he had begun firing four or five times from ten feet away as he ran toward Faulkner.

McGill, with Judge Sabo's repeated assistance in suppressing information favorable to the defendant, had every reason to believe that by now the jury had bought his story line. It was such a simple story: the defendant ran from the parking lot, shot Faulkner in the back, was shot by Faulkner as the officer was falling to the ground, stood over Faulkner and shot him right between the eyes, and then collapsed to the curb and was arrested within a minute or two of the shooting by arriving police. The simple beauty of it, to McGill, was that the defendant was unable to flee the scene.

McGill reminded the jury that the defendant "was observed by the witnesses . . . and never left the scene. Who was arrested on the scene. Who was on the scene and taken to a wagon at that very time and who was identified while in the wagon by the people who did not leave the scene either." (Only Magilton and Chobert identified Abu-Jamal in the paddy wagon. Scanlan said he thought Abu-Jamal was the driver of the VW, and White, most likely because she had not witnessed the shooting, was not brought to the wagon to identify Abu-Jamal.)

"When you talk about identification evidence," McGill continued, "when you talk about that type of evidence, one would wonder whether you would even need an identification, since you never lost sight of the man who shot."

Never need an identification? The next step from there would be not needing a trial.

Time and again during his summation McGill displayed a flagrant disregard for the truth. "None of those people closest to the scene see anybody going anywhere except firing and staying there. I mean how much common sense do we need!"

This was another bald-faced lie and McGill knew it. He knew that Veronica Jones was close to the scene and told police within a week of Faulkner's slaying that she saw two black men jogging away right after Faulkner was shot. He knew that Dessie Hightower told police that he saw a person run away. He knew that tow-truck driver William Singletary as well as the woman in the nearby hotel, Deborah Kordansky, also had reported seeing people flee the scene. Most critical, McGill knew that there was an unaccounted-for passenger in Cook's car who had managed to flee the scene.

"You wouldn't have to see somebody's face, let alone know a person runs, shoots, and then slumps down, or falls down to the curb and is arrested and taken to a wagon," McGill stated. "He hasn't left your sight. What more compelling identification testimony would you need than that? That is where he was and that is what you heard. . . . Recall Cynthia White's testimony, Robert Chobert's testimony, and Albert Magilton's testimony. Those three people clearly saw that man and he never left the scene. All of those witnesses have some strange motive."

As the prosecutor well knew, Magilton did not claim to see the shooting. White and Chobert, as he ironically stated, did have "some strange motive" to frame Abu-Jamal with Faulkner's killing, motive supplied by the police and McGill himself to get the testimony he wanted from them.

A major problem facing McGill in his summation was to account for how Faulkner could have possibly shot Abu-Jamal after Faulkner had been shot in the back and had fallen to the ground on his hands and knees. The physical evidence to which the medical examiner testified revealed that Abu-Jamal was shot from a foot or less away and that the bullet struck him on an unimpeded downward trajectory. Scanlan had testified that the officer was shot only after he fell down. Only White, McGill's most unreliable witness, had given the prosecution any way to explain how Faulkner shot Abu-Jamal, testifying that Faulkner seemed to grab for something after he was shot and was falling to the ground. This, of course, could not explain the downward trajectory of the bullet that hit Abu-Jamal in the chest. The best McGill could offer the jury was a rush of rigmarole about the trajectory of Faulkner's gun.

When you are dealing with the barrel of a weapon—I won't use the weapon at this time. This would be the barrel of the weapon. It would depend, ladies and gentlemen, as to exactly where the weapon is with respect to the position of the body. I am holding my left-hand as the body and what the trajectory would be. As a matter of fact, both of you are standing up next to each other. You are pointing a weapon like my finger at this point and you move that finger somewhat, either up or down, just a little bit, even though you are standing straight up right at him that trajectory would change depending on where the barrel is pointed. If you turn the body down a little bit then you get a different angle if you are like that. If you turn the body down further you get a different angle. And further the same thing.

So, when you are dealing with both sides and two individuals you are dealing with a target body and you are dealing with a weapon . . . the slightest change of either of those two things would change the trajectory, because there is no absolute thing. It is not nailed to the body so it won't change. The slightest change of either, the slightest difference in angle would get a different trajectory.

Ladies and gentlemen, I will ask you not to be confused about this particular piece of evidence.

In other words, what McGill had just said did not make sense, but he hoped the jurors, like defense counsel Jackson, would not put two and two together and realize that Faulkner could not have shot Abu-Jamal after the officer himself was shot. McGill, of course, made no attempt to account for how Faulkner's pant leg had been split at the knee and his knee scraped as he fell on his back.

The real point of McGill's summation was to get a verdict of guilty of murder in the first degree. To McGill, two things about Faulkner's death demonstrated more than anything else Abu-Jamal's intent to kill the officer: the high-powered bullets McGill alleged to be in Abu-Jamal's gun and Abu-Jamal's alleged hospital confession, in which he shouted out that he had killed the officer and hoped he would die. "That has to be the supreme arrogance that can be associated with such a vicious act, because it would take somebody with that frame of mind to shoot down a man on the ground. To shoot him in the back and then straight on in the face. That same kind of arrogance that would carry on through to the hospital and would be stated," McGill said.

McGill created more grounds for appeal by alluding to the fact that Abu-Jamal had not taken the stand in his own defense, inferring that by not doing so he was attempting to hide his guilt or possibly protect his brother, Billy Cook. When Jackson objected to this reference, Judge Sabo should have cautioned McGill or instructed that those comments be stricken. Instead he simply said, "Your objection is noted," which allowed McGill to continue in this vein by stating, "Are they suggesting that there was a third man, a fourth man, or is he doing this all for his brother? I ask you to look through all of this, as well as any other strategy or tactics you have seen during the course of this whole particular trial and recognize it for what it is."

To bolster security guard Priscilla Durham's claim about Abu-Jamal's hospital confession, McGill claimed there was another security guard [James LaGrand] who also overhead his confession. It was out of bounds for McGill to mention LaGrand because he had not been called as a witness. Jackson objected immediately. Judge Sabo should have ordered the reference to LaGrand stricken, but he said nothing to the jury about it.

Jackson, in his summation, had done a good job of discrediting the prosecution's two primary witnesses, cabdriver Robert Chobert and prostitute Cynthia White, showing how their testimony had been "enhanced" each time they gave new statements to the police. Through the testimony of Veronica Jones, the jury had heard how White had been allowed to continue to work as a prostitute as a reward for her cooperation, a reward similarly offered to Jones, who had rebuffed it. The jury did not know that Chobert was currently serving five years of probation for felony arson and had twice violated his parole by being arrested for driving while intoxicated and was in continuous violation of his parole by driving his taxi with a suspended license. If his probation were to be revoked, Chobert faced up to thirty years in prison.

McGill knew all this about Chobert only too well. Like White, Chobert was a highly motivated witness in need of currying favor with the police and the powerful prosecutor. In fact, when he testified at Abu-Jamal's postconviction hearing in 1995, he admitted that before or during the trial he had sought McGill's intercession in getting his chauffeur's license reinstated. So no one knew better than McGill how motivated a witness Chobert actually was. He was so compromised by his parole violations that McGill, ethically speaking, should not have used him at all. In using witnesses such as Chobert and White, in making these two witnesses the centerpiece of his evidentiary case against Abu-Jamal, McGill put himself on the slippery slope of intentionally using perjured testimony, a felony in and of itself. It could not have been more obvious to anyone than McGill the degree to which Chobert had so obviously altered his account of the shooting from the time of his first statement to what he was willing to testify to later.

Chobert had originally described the shooter as being in his mid-thirties, six feet tall, and heavyset, weighing up to 225 pounds, and wearing a gray-colored dress shirt with a green picture on the back. No aspect of his description—other than the height—fit Abu-Jamal. After the shooting, he had said that the shooter walked thirty to thirty-five steps away and that another man had run away after the first shot. By the time McGill called him to testify, Abu-Jamal had walked only about ten feet away and there was no mention of another man running away.

In a shameless rhetorical flourish, this is how McGill vouched for Chobert's credibility: "Ladies and gentlemen, he knows what he saw and I don't care what you say or what anybody says, that is what he saw. Do you think anybody could get him to say anything that wasn't the truth?"

McGill even made an attempt to vouch for Cynthia White's credibility by misrepresenting to the jurors that "she came out with the same story substantially as every one of those other witnesses, substantially the same story. The man running over and doing the shooting."

The man whom White had running over to the officer got off four or five shots from ten yards away, one of the shots causing the officer to fall. It took homicide detectives three more sessions with her—plus immunity from being arrested for prostitution in Philadelphia thenceforward—to get her account to reflect what the physical evidence showed.

McGill's final sally to the jury was another ethical breach, one he had initiated earlier in his summation when he depicted Faulkner's killing "as one uncompromising vicious act. This is one act that the people of Philadelphia, all of them, all of you everywhere is [sic] outraged over. This act demands action." McGill was talking then as though he wanted the jury not just to find Abu-Jamal guilty but to take him out of the courtroom right then and lynch him. Now, in his final statement to the jury, he would again sustain this incendiary tone by putting pressure on the jury to deliver a capital verdict.

McGill told the jury it was not just he who wanted the jury to find Abu-Jamal guilty of first-degree murder but also the people of the state and of Philadelphia, who were reaching out to the jury members and were demanding that they provide justice. "Ladies and gentlemen, I ask you, all of us, the Commonwealth, the people of this city, reach out to you and demand justice. Look right at that intent to kill and that man who did it with that weapon and say, 'The evidence is clear to us. You are guilty of first-degree murder.' Thank you very much."

26

GUILTY!

Judge Sabo's instructions to the jury offered the possibility of four verdicts: (1) guilty of murder in the first degree, (2) guilty of murder in the third degree, (3) guilty of voluntary manslaughter, or (4) not guilty.

"You must ask yourself the question: did the defendant have the willful, deliberate, and premeditated specific intent to kill at the time of the killing," Judge Sabo instructed.

Sabo explained that the law in Pennsylvania fixes no length of time as necessary to form an intent to kill, "which design to kill can be formulated in a fraction of a second." He said, "An intent to kill may be inferred by reason of the killer's use of a deadly weapon on a vital part of the body of the victim."

There was no charge of second-degree murder. It pertains when the death of the victim occurs while the defendant was engaged as the actual perpetrator or as accomplice in the commission or attempt to commit another type of felony such a robbery, rape, or kidnapping, or was in flight from such a crime.

Third-degree murder is unlawful killing with malice but with an intention merely to inflict bodily harm. It carries a maximum sentence of twenty years.

Voluntary manslaughter—which carries a ten-year maximum sentence—is the intentional and unlawful killing of a person without either expressed or implied malice but under the immediate inference of a sudden and intense passion resulting from serious provocation by the individual killed. The killer acted intentionally under sufficient provocation brought on by a state of terror, anger, fear, or rage or resentment without time to cool down so that he was placed beyond the control of his reason and was suddenly impelled to kill.

The voluntary manslaughter option gave the jury the opportunity, based on the fact that Faulkner had been subduing Cook by hitting him repeatedly in the head with a long flashlight, to find that Abu-Jamal, in the heat of the moment, had been so provoked that he killed Faulkner out of rage or resentment, or even out of fear, considering that Faulkner was armed.

Abu-Jamal was also charged with possession of an instrument of crime. To convict on this, Judge Sabo told the jury, they would have to find that "the defendant possessed the item with intent to commit—to employ it criminally."

The jury commenced deliberations at 11:48 A.M. on July 2. At 2:50 P.M. the judge met with the jury in open court to answer its question regarding definitions of the charges for first-degree murder, third-degree murder, and voluntary manslaughter.

At 5:18 P.M. the jury returned its verdict: guilty of murder in the first degree and guilty of possessing an instrument of crime. During the ten minutes it took the jury foreman to read the verdict, Abu-Jamal sat slouched in his chair. As guards were leading him out of the courtroom, he turned to the gallery and said, "On a MOVE. Long live John Africa" and "The system is finished."

27

THE SENTENCING HEARING

In Judge Sabo's determination to get the sequestered jury home in time for the Fourth of July holiday, the sentencing hearing was held the next morning to determine if Abu-Jamal was to be sentenced to death or to life imprisonment. Usually, because all of its previous focus has been on preparing for the guilt phase, the defense is given at least a week to ten days—and sometimes a month or more—to prepare for the sentencing. It would have been a simple matter, even with a sequestered jury, to send the jurors home under orders not to discuss the case with anyone or read or listen to news accounts of the trial, then reconvene them a few days later. That would have been the fair thing to do, but Jackson did not request it and Sabo never broached the subject.

When the hearing opened, Jackson called upon Abu-Jamal to make a statement, one the defendant had not provided to Jackson or McGill. Finally, now that it was too late for Abu-Jamal to prove his own innocence, Sabo would allow the jury to hear from him directly. And in a move termed "highly unusual" by a legal expert consulted for this book, the judge would allow the prosecutor to cross-examine him, even though Abu-Jamal was not a witness for the defense and his statement was not sworn.

If there ever were a time to make a good impression on this jury, this was it. Abu-Jamal would proceed to do just the opposite.

He began by telling the jury that its decision came as no surprise to him. He called Jackson "inadequate" and Judge Sabo "a black-robed conspirator." He informed the jury of Judge Sabo's refusal to allow the defense to call Officer Gary Wakshul to the stand so that his statement the morning of the shooting, that "the Negro male made no comments," could be presented to the jury.

Abu-Jamal also criticized Jackson for telling the jury that they had heard "all the evidence," when they got to hear only what the judge wanted them to hear.

"Many jurors were told I would cross-examine witnesses, make opening and closing arguments, and explore evidence," Abu-Jamal said. "What they also heard was I would act as my own attorney, my own lawyer. What they saw was a man silenced, gagged by judicial decree. So what they heard was nothing."

Abu-Jamal said that "every so-called 'right' was deceitfully stolen from me by Sabo," particularly when the judge denied Abu-Jamal's "demand that the defense assistance of my choice, John Africa, be allowed to sit at the defense table."

I am innocent of these charges that I have been charged of and convicted of and despite the connivance of Sabo, McGill, and Jackson to deny me my so-called rights to represent myself, to assistance of my choice, to personally select a jury who is totally of my peers, to cross-examine witnesses, and to make both opening and closing arguments, I am still innocent of these charges.

According to your so-called law, I do not have to prove my innocence. But, in fact, I did have to by disproving the Commonwealth's case. I am innocent despite what you twelve people think and the truth shall set me free.

This jury is not composed of my peers, for those closest to my life experiences were intentionally and systematically excluded, peremptorily excused. Only those prosecution prone, some who began with a fixed opinion of guilt, some related to city police, mostly white, mostly male remain. May they one day be so fairly judged.

Long live John Africa! For his assistance in this fight for my life! It is John Africa who has strengthened me, aided me, and guided me, and loved me! Could John Africa have done worse than this worthless sellout and shyster who promised much and delivered nothing? Could he have done worse than Tony Jackson? . . .

On December the 9th, 1981, the police attempted to execute me in the street. This trial is a result of their failure to do so, just as police tried to kill my brothers and sisters of the family Africa on August the 8th, 1978, they failed and hence, a so-called trial was conducted to complete the execution. But long live John Africa for our continued survival!

This decision today proves neither my guilt nor my innocence. It proves merely that the system is finished. Babylon is falling! Long live MOVE. Long live John Africa!

With the permission of Judge Sabo to address the defendant, McGill now took his turn. Abu-Jamal had no legal duty to answer any of McGill's questions, but with a good deal of bravado for a man just convicted of first-degree murder, he stepped right into McGill's trap.

At the top of McGill's agenda was to make sure the jury was aware of Abu-Jamal's former association with the Black Panther Party. Before getting to that, McGill asked the defendant why he did not stand when Judge Sabo entered the courtroom. Jackson objected; Judge Sabo overruled. "Because Judge Sabo deserves no honor from me or anyone else in this courtroom because he operates—because of the force, not because of right. [Whereupon the defendant stands up at defense counsel's table.] Because, he is an executioner. Because, he is a hangman; that is why."

McGill spent most of the rest of his time going over a news article that had appeared in the *Philadelphia Inquirer* on January 4, 1970, some twelve and one-half years previously. It included a quotation from the then-fifteen-year-old Abu-Jamal, who was acting as lieutenant of information for the Philadelphia chapter of the Black Panther Party, referencing Mao-Tse-tung's famous quote that "political power grows out of the barrel of a gun."

McGill asked Abu-Jamal if he thought his actions and his philosophy were consistent with the communist dictator's quote about political power. "I believe that America has proven that quote to be true," Abu-Jamal answered.

McGill concluded by asking Abu-Jamal if he remembered being in front of Judge Ribner on April 29, 1982. Abu-Jamal said he did.

McGILL: And do you recall over about two or three actual pages of testimony saying such things as, and this was in court, open court: "I don't
give a damn what you think, go to hell. What the hell are you afraid of?
What the hell are you afraid of, bastard?" Do you recall saying that to
Judge Ribner?

ABU-JAMAL: Sure do. (Nods head affirmatively.)

McGILL: I have nothing further, judge.

Jackson then asked Abu-Jamal if he had anything further. Abu-
Jamal, waving his hand away, said, "No." Jackson then announced
that the defense "would rest."

Judge Sabo took this as his cue to begin his sentencing instructions to the jury. Before the judge could finish his first sentence,
which had so far only mentioned the death penalty, Jackson inter-
rupted him for a sidebar conference. Jackson was entitled to address
the jury one last time, as was McGill.

The task before Jackson was to lead the jury away from impos-
ing the death penalty. He had a number of ways to do this, but as
he admitted at Abu-Jamal's postconviction hearing in 1995, he had
given no preparation to the penalty phase of the trial and not even
talked with his client about it.

Jackson began by quibbling over whether Faulkner, a police officer, was covered under the state statute that allowed the imposition
of the death penalty on defendants convicted of the first-degree murder of a fireman, peace officer, or public servant in the line of duty.
"If they [the legislature] meant police officers, why didn't they say
police officers?"

Jackson then moved to the more fertile area of mitigating and
aggravating circumstances. He said the legislature had unfortunately
not presented guidelines to assist a jury in weighing aggravating versus mitigating circumstances.

Jackson then listed the mitigating circumstances the legislature
had enacted for juries to consider in death penalty deliberations.
First, the defendant's prior police record. Jackson said Abu-Jamal

had no record and that if he had one, McGill would have certainly informed the jury about it. Two, the defendant was under the influence of extreme mental or emotional disturbance. He said the jurors' verdict suggested that they had assumed Abu-Jamal had come to the rescue of his brother in response to Faulkner's beating of his brother. "If that is indeed your assumption, the question then would be was that circumstance sufficient to provoke anger, fear, to such an extent that the offense occurred."

Jackson told them that they must decide that mitigating circumstance by a preponderance of the evidence, which is not the same as deciding something beyond a reasonable doubt.

Federal District Judge Yohn's ruling in 2001 vacating Abu-Jamal's death sentence was based on this very point. In Judge Sabo's oral and written sentencing instructions to the jury, he informed the jurors that "a verdict must be a sentence of death if the jury unanimously finds at least one aggravating circumstance, or if the jury finds one or more aggravating circumstance which outweighs any mitigating circumstance."

Judge Yohn ruled that Judge Sabo's instructions "created a reasonable likelihood that the jury believed that it was obligated to consider only mitigating circumstances that were found to exist by a unanimous panel."

Jackson should have spent more time explaining the importance of the jury's consideration of mitigating circumstances. Mitigating circumstances, whichever ones apply in a particular case, must be weighed against the heft of the aggravating circumstances in the case. If the jurors come to the belief that the mitigating circumstances outweigh the aggravating circumstances, that would cause them to return a sentence of life imprisonment, not death. Jackson did inform the jury that the mitigating circumstances that he was indicating "are not things that you may or may not consider; you must consider these mitigating circumstances when you look at the aggravating circumstances as suggested by the Commonwealth."

The problem was that Jackson was not making the mitigating circumstances that applied to Abu-Jamal clear enough and detailed enough for the jury to feel their weight. He only mentioned in passing Abu-Jamal's clean record or the extraordinary circumstances Abu-Jamal found himself in when he saw a police officer clubbing his brother in the street at four o'clock in the morning. Both of these mitigating circumstances were profound and weighty. In addition, Abu-Jamal had numerous prominent friends, including elected officials and respected journalists, whom Jackson could have brought in as character witnesses to attest to his peaceable nature, his community-oriented past, and his accomplishments in radio journalism. Abu-Jamal also had strong family ties and was a devoted father. If anything struck those who knew Abu-Jamal best, it was their utter dismay that he could have possibly been involved in the killing of a police officer, or the killing of anyone for that matter. But Jackson did not call any character witnesses to speak on Abu-Jamal's behalf during the penalty phase, a strategic error of staggering proportions.

After rambling on for a good while about a host of issues that only served to dig the hole deeper for his client with this death penalty–vetted jury—Abu-Jamal's Black Panther association, some of the quotes McGill had attributed to Abu-Jamal, the unevenness of the death penalty applied to blacks, the United States' status as the only advanced nation in the world to impose the death penalty—Jackson returned to his discussion of mitigating circumstances. He said the jury "was permitted" to impose the death sentence if it found aggravating circumstances and no mitigating one. The only other way it could return a death sentence, he said, was for the jury to find that one or more aggravating circumstances outweighed the mitigating circumstances. Absent those two conditions, the jury must impose a sentence of life imprisonment, Jackson said.

Jackson had been in tears earlier in his summation and was now beginning to sob again. At this juncture, the court stenographer noted in the transcript that "there was an extended pause while counsel drinks water and composes his emotions."

Jackson's disjointed, emotional thirty-nine-minute summation had broken him. He composed himself long enough to conclude by saying, "I ask you at this moment before Mr. McGill addresses you again, is there some compelling reason [to impose a life sentence rather than a penalty of death]? Thank you."

With the courtroom crackling with sympathy for the crestfallen Jackson, McGill asked for, and received, a five-minute break before presenting his summation.

"All right, ladies and gentlemen," McGill intoned, "the purpose of this hearing as you clearly know is to determine the sentence for this defendant. You've heard a number of things. You had the opportunity to actually hear this defendant who chose to testify; he didn't have to, but he did. You had an opportunity of seeing the person, the type of person he is, and how he is. That way you again have an opportunity to reflect back upon the incident—the events at the time."

McGill got right to the point. "Now, ladies and gentlemen, what we're talking about in terms of sentencing is aggravating and mitigating circumstances. That is it." He reminded the jurors that they were no longer dealing with a defendant presumed to be innocent, but "a convicted murderer." Pointing to Abu-Jamal, McGill said, "This man over here is a killer. You're looking at and have heard a killer. That's who we're dealing with."

McGill, like Jackson before him and Judge Sabo to follow, made a muddle of his explanation of aggravating and mitigating circumstances. First he said there were two scenarios, then remembered there were actually three. He described the three alternatives: aggravating and no mitigating, no aggravating and no mitigating, and both aggravating and mitigating.

He said in the case of aggravating circumstances and no mitigating, the law mandates the death penalty, as it would also in the case where both circumstances were present but the aggravating outweighed the mitigating. He neglected to inform the jury that it must impose a life sentence if it found that the mitigating circumstances outweighed the aggravating.

The aggravating circumstance in this case was that the defendant had been convicted of murdering a police officer in the line of duty. Jackson had quibbled that a police officer is not a peace officer as defined by the state statute, so McGill debunked that notion by reading the statute's definition of a peace officer: "The peace officer is any person who by virtue of his office or public employment is vested by law with a duty to maintain public order or to make arrests for offenses."

While Jackson's summation might have elicited an emotional response from the jury, McGill's intent was to incite a visceral one. He wanted the jury to feel his own outrage at Abu-Jamal and to take vengeance for it. Why should the jury put so much weight on the aggravating circumstance of Abu-Jamal's killing a police officer? Because, McGill said, "The fact of the matter is simply this: it's all called law and order. That is why that is so important, that aggravating circumstance. Law and order. And, ladies and gentlemen, this is what this trial is all about more than any other trial I have ever seen."

McGill told the jury to ask themselves this question: "Are we going to live in a society with law and order, and are we going to enforce the laws consistent with the intention of law and order, or are we going to decide our own rules and then act accordingly? That's really what we are talking about."

How plain could McGill have made it for the jury? Either they would sentence Abu-Jamal to death or Philadelphia would turn into a jungle of lawlessness.

To offset any emotional connection Jackson may have made with the jurors in pleading in tears for them to spare Abu-Jamal's life, McGill praised Jackson's "extreme competence" in defending Abu-Jamal over the last six months despite Abu-Jamal's continuous criticisms of him. When Jackson objected to this improper reference, Judge Sabo responded, "It's noted."

Encouraged by Judge Sabo, McGill pushed on, saying that Abu-Jamal viewed Jackson as a "traitor" because Jackson obeyed the rulings of Judge Sabo and the state supreme court that he act as Abu-Jamal's lead counsel.

To push the jury to render the death penalty, McGill wanted the jurors to view Abu-Jamal as the embodiment of a lawlessness steeped in arrogance. Not only had Abu-Jamal murdered a police officer, McGill said, but he had done so "with the arrogance that has been displayed in front of you over this period of time" and bragged about it "defiantly" afterward.

McGill was shooting fish in the barrel. Abu-Jamal was arrogant and defiant, yet he was something even worse as well. "Let's look at this as we're talking about the individual who executed a police officer as you saw. What else did he do besides that? You know, ladies and gentlemen, if you look at that, you can see in that act an extreme amount of cowardice. Because, in order to be sure we're going to kill and shoot [Officer Faulkner] in the back when he's not even looking at us; we'll get him in the back."

As he had in his final argument to the jury during the guilt phase of the trial, McGill told the jurors again that they were not being "asked to kill anybody" by rendering a death verdict. All he was asking of them was to follow the law: "the same law that will provide him [Abu-Jamal] appeal after appeal after appeal."

Jackson, properly, objected. Judge Sabo's response was to tell McGill to "Go ahead."

To bolster his point that the jury did not have to worry about sentencing Abu-Jamal to death, McGill informed them that no one had been executed in Pennsylvania since 1962. McGill knew that saying that was improper summation, but he so wanted a death verdict that he said it anyway—let some future Philadelphia district attorney worry about the appeal consequences.

McGill then thanked the jurors for the "courage" they had shown in convicting Abu-Jamal of first-degree murder and asked them to continue with that courage in their verdict deliberations. He urged them to make their decision without "in any way being intimidated," a reference to Abu-Jamal's MOVE and family supporters in attendance throughout the trial and sentencing procedure.

The jury was excused to begin its deliberations at 12:27 P.M. At 4:20 P.M. the jury returned with its verdict. The court crier asked the jury foreman, juror No. 9 (George Ewalt), to stand and asked him, "Having found the defendant Mumia Abu-Jamal guilty of murder in the first degree . . . what is your verdict as to penalty?

The foreman said, "Death."

28

THE FREE MUMIA MOVEMENT

Abu-Jamal's climb from an obscure left-wing prison writer to the world stage was long, uphill, and unexpected. He's told those who've asked him about his international celebrity that nothing has surprised him more, that he is baffled by it. "I wish I knew," he told *Inquirer* staff writer Julia Cass in 1995 during an hour-long interview she conducted with him at Graterford Prison, where he spoke to her from behind wire mesh in handcuffs. "If I told you I could have predicted the controversy and support that has exploded around my trial, I would be lying to you. I don't know. If I did, I'd write the formula down myself. All I can say is, I write, people read."

Cass wrote that Abu-Jamal "was at his most eloquent—and startling—when he described his life on death row, where he occupies a 6-foot-by-8-foot cell for 22 and in some cases 23 hours a day, with the other hours spent in an exercise cage."

Cass said that Abu-Jamal remained an intensely loyal MOVE follower. "I must confess, when I first met them, I was far from attracted. But the old saying, 'You live and learn.' I found them to be deeply and totally committed to revolution. I share their view of the injustices, racial and otherwise, in America. They are extremely loyal, loving to a fault. They are people. I love them. They are my family. That's it," Cass quoted him as saying. When she asked him what he would do if he were set free, he told her he would work as a journalist and that he spent "dream time" thinking about visiting Africa and Europe. He said he was unsure if he would return to Philadelphia to live.

When Abu-Jamal entered prison in 1982, he was in disciplinary custody—"the hole"—for the first seven years for refusing to cut his dreadlocks. By 1990 he was allowed to watch some television and to receive books and magazines. He was also permitted to complete the requirements for his B.A. degree from Goddard College and earn an M.A. from California State University. In a phone interview in 1994, he told a reporter that he spends most of his time reading, writing, and studying, "trying to stay abreast of changing stuff." He said he reads "a lot of African history and African-American history, as well as a bit of science fiction. One of the few psychological and mental escapes I have is to read."

For his first five years in prison, his active supporters were MOVE members, principally John Africa—until he was killed in 1985 when the police firebombed MOVE headquarters—and Pam Africa, and some local black leaders such as state representative David Richardson, who died in 1995. Pam Africa and other MOVE members distributed copies of Abu-Jamal's polemical prison essays to small leftist publications and black-owned newspapers. MOVE members also protested Abu-Jamal's conviction and sentence when public opportunities to demonstrate arose. MOVE's support for Abu-Jamal would prove to be unwavering.

The Partisan Defense Committee—a radical international socialist labor organization—took up Abu-Jamal's cause in the late 1980s. It held rallies to build awareness of his case in New York City, Philadelphia, Atlanta, and California, unfurling banners that read: "Free Mumia Abu-Jamal! Abolish the Racist Death Penalty!"

After the Pennsylvania Supreme Court unanimously rejected Abu-Jamal's first appeal of his conviction and refused to commute his death sentence in 1989, the Quixote Center, a social-activist Catholic group based in Hyattsville, Maryland, took up his cause. In issuing the Pennsylvania Supreme Court decision, Justice Stephen Zappala wrote that the court found "not a trace of support for the assertion that the prosecution challenged black jurors to keep them off the jury." Jane Henderson, founder of the Quixote Center's Equal Justice USA project, said the center saw Abu-Jamal's case as a "microcosm of the biases that permeate the death penalty and overall justice system." (That appeal had been filed on Abu-Jamal's behalf by Marilyn Gelb, an attorney appointed by the court to handle it.)

On February 2, 1990, the Pennsylvania Supreme Court denied Abu-Jamal's petition to reargue his appeal, potentially leaving only the U.S. Supreme Court and the governor of Pennsylvania between Abu-Jamal and his date with the electric chair. Abu-Jamal still retained the right to a Post-Conviction Relief Act hearing in the Philadelphia Court of Common Pleas and to file a writ of habeas corpus in U.S. district court. To utilize these options effectively would require considerable financial resources.

Led by Pam Africa, MOVE members set up International Concerned Family & Friends of Mumia Abu-Jamal to raise money to obtain new legal counsel.

In an *Inquirer* article on July 14, 1990, it was reported that Abu-Jamal's supporters "have written tens of thousands of letters and collected thousands of signatures on petitions urging Governor Robert Casey to commute Abu-Jamal's death sentence."

By the early 1990s Abu-Jamal's essays about racism and politics in the criminal justice system, the death penalty, and prison conditions finally reached the more mainstream media. The *Yale Law Review* published his article about the death penalty, and *The Nation* ran an article Abu-Jamal wrote about conditions on death row. By then he had written over three hundred essays. In 1993 when radio producer Noelle Hanrahan read one of them in a black San Francisco newspaper, she arranged to begin taping Abu-Jamal reading twenty-five of his commentaries for the Prison Radio project, to be broadcast on California radio stations and on public radio's stepchild, Pacifica Radio Network.

Abu-Jamal's rich, resonant, baritone voice, silenced for years, was reborn.

An olive branch comment by Governor Casey—that he was willing to meet with advocates of both sides of the mushrooming Abu-Jamal debate if there was something new to hear—would bring more than 200 Abu-Jamal supporters to the governor's office in the statehouse on April 12, 1994. The Fraternal Order of Police (FOP) countered the Abu-Jamal rally by sending 150 members, including Maureen Faulkner, who had flown in from California, to the Capitol to petition the governor to sign Abu-Jamal's death warrant. In a confrontation in the hallway outside the governor's statehouse office, the opposing sides, according to the *Inquirer*, stood "toe to toe," but the Capitol police kept them from coming to blows. The governor was out of town.

Within hours of the statehouse standoff, a bill requiring the governor to sign death warrants within sixty days of receiving records of the cases was approved by a state senate committee. It had previously been passed by the General Assembly.

On May 14, 1994, National Public Radio's evening news program *All Things Considered* hired Abu-Jamal to do monthly three-minute commentaries for six months on the subject of crime and punishment. The network agreed to pay its standard fee of $150 per commentary, stipulating that he not discuss his own case. The program producer, Ellen Weiss, said she first heard of Abu-Jamal through his commentaries on Prison Radio. "We read his material and evaluated its content. He is a good writer and brings a unique perspective to the air."

Weiss was a bit naive. Two days later, in an unusual Sunday announcement, NPR's managing editor, Bruce Drake, said the network had decided not to air any of Abu-Jamal's commentaries, disingenuously adding that the cancellation was "purely an editorial decision." Drake said Abu-Jamal would be paid a $75 "kill fee" for the cancelled commentary that was set to air that week. What Drake didn't choose to reveal was that Maureen Faulkner and the National Fraternal Order of Police had pressured NPR to cancel the commentaries and had solicited Republican presidential hopeful Senator Bob Dole to denounce the scheduled broadcasts and threaten NPR's funding. In a speech from the Senate floor, Dole said, "This episode raises sobering questions, not only for NPR but for the taxpayer-funded Corporation for Public Broadcasting, which has oversight authority over NPR and provides much of its funding."

In March 1995, Abu-Jamal's first book, *Live from Death Row*, was published by Addison-Wesley. For it he was paid a $30,000 advance. It contained the commentaries NPR had banned as well as other essays, including those that had appeared in the *Yale Law Review* and *The Nation*. Abu-Jamal did not reference his own case, only mentioning in the preface that his conviction and sentence were "unjust." Celebrated black author John Edgar Wideman wrote the introduction to the book; attorney Leonard Weinglass wrote a sixteen-page afterword. Blurbs endorsing it were written by Alice Walker, E. L. Doctorow, the *Village Voice*, and *LA Weekly*. On the day *Live from Death Row* was released, Maureen Faulkner, who had moved to Southern California after Abu-Jamal was sent to death row, hired a plane to circle the book publisher's Massachusetts headquarters with a banner stating, "Addison-Wesley supports convicted cop killer."

The publisher later reported that the book had hit the bestseller lists in San Francisco and Toronto, had sold more than seventy thousand copies, was in its sixth reprinting, and had been translated into seven languages. Avon Books purchased the paperback rights and reissued the book in June 1996.

In 1992, MOVE enticed attorney Rachel Wolkenstein of the radical Partisan Defense Committee to take up Abu-Jamal's case. When she in turn recruited Leonard I. Weinglass, a civil rights lawyer skilled in handling high-profile "political" cases, including the Chicago Seven trial in 1969–70 and the Pentagon Papers case in 1971, to head up Abu-Jamal's defense in late 1992, the Free Mumia movement finally had teeth. Actors Mike Farrell and Ossie Davis were brought on by Weinglass to cochair the New York–based Committee to Save Mumia Abu-Jamal. Other celebrities soon appeared on the committee's letterhead, including Ed Asner, Whoopi Goldberg, E. L. Doctorow, Ruby Dee, and David Mamet. With them, and the fundraisers the committee staged, came some of the financial resources needed to mount Abu-

Jamal's remaining appeals. By 1995 the Committee to Save Mumia Abu-Jamal reported raising about $100,000 of the projected $1 million it said it needed to pursue Abu-Jamal's appeals.

After newly elected Pennsylvania governor Tom Ridge signed Abu-Jamal's death warrant in June 1995, setting his execution date for August 17, the Free Mumia movement intensified significantly. Shortly after Ridge's announcement, two bombs went off in American-owned banks in Greece. A group called to say the blasts were to protest Abu-Jamal's death sentence. In Paris, demonstrations were held every Wednesday for the next three months outside the U.S. Embassy. "Mumia Abu-Jamal . . . is not just an innocent man in the eyes of many people around the world. Now, he is a hero," a writer for the *Inquirer* wrote.

Abu-Jamal supporters responded to the death warrant by running a full-page ad in the *New York Times* calling for a new trial. Maya Angelou, Alec Baldwin, Derrick Bell, Noam Chomsky, E. L. Doctorow, Spike Lee, Norman Mailer, Paul Newman, Joyce Carol Oates, Salman Rushdie, William Styron, and other notables signed it.

On July 7, 1996, HBO premiered the one-hour documentary *Mumia Abu-Jamal: A Case for Reasonable Doubt?* It left little doubt that Abu-Jamal's trial raised grave questions of fairness: less than $1,500 was provided for defense expenses such as experts and investigators; Judge Sabo was known as a "hanging judge"; the prosecutor used eleven peremptory challenges to exclude blacks from the jury; the jury ended up with only two blacks; the defendant could not have been shot the way the prosecution said he was; forensic work was practically nonexistent; the "confession" was concocted; the prosecution's main witness, Cynthia White, lied about what she saw. Court TV re-aired the documentary four days later and followed it up with a one-hour panel discussion entitled *Fair or Foul? The Case of Mumia Abu-Jamal.*

Jacques Chirac, the president of France, and Klaus Kinkel, the foreign minister of Germany, issued public statements urging U.S. officials to spare Abu-Jamal's life. In Rome a petition to halt Abu-Jamal's execution was signed by one hundred thousand people. In the United States, city councils in Ann Arbor and Detroit, Michigan; Madison, Wisconsin; and Cambridge, Massachusetts, passed resolutions calling for a new trial.

After Amnesty International's Secretary General Pierre Sane visited Abu-Jamal at the super-max state prison in Greene County on November 24, 1997, he called Pennsylvania's death penalty "one of the most racist and unfair in the United States." He said it was "worse than Georgia, worse than Mississippi, worse than Alabama." Sane, just as the Pennsylvania Bar Association had done three weeks earlier, urged Governor Ridge to "initiate a full investigation into the racist and unfair application of the death penalty in the state, and to call for a moratorium on executions." The Philadelphia Bar Association passed a resolution the next day calling for a moratorium on executions. Governor Ridge declined to order either an investigation or a moratorium.

Abu-Jamal's second collection of essays, *Death Blossoms: Reflections from a Prisoner of Conscience*, was published by Plough Publishing House in late 1997. Plough is owned by the Bruderhof, a Christian communal society with a number of members living in Waynesboro, Pennsylvania, near the SCI Greene penitentiary, where Abu-Jamal has been incarcerated since 1995. After authorities at Greene clamped down on Abu-Jamal's access to visitors in an attempt to cut off the distribution of his essays and radio commentaries, Bruderhof leader Steve Wiser signed on as Abu-Jamal's spiritual advisor, a role that allowed him unlimited visits and the right to provide Abu-Jamal reading material and to distribute his essays to others.

In April 1998, the *Inquirer* reported, Free Mumia rallies were held the same day in San Francisco and Philadelphia that attracted a combined twenty-five thousand people. That summer Rage Against the Machine and the Beastie Boys did a benefit concert to raise funds for Abu-Jamal's legal defense before a sold-out audience of sixteen thousand at the Continental Airlines Arena in New Jersey.

Amnesty International subsequently reviewed Abu-Jamal's entire case record and found not only chilling violations of U.S. law but also a trial that "clearly failed to meet minimum international standards safeguarding the fairness of legal proceedings." It published its findings in 2000 in a special edition of its Open Media Pamphlet Series entitled *The Case of Mumia Abu-Jamal: A Life in the Balance.* While taking no position on Abu-Jamal's guilt or innocence, Amnesty International deemed him a "political prisoner" and recommended a new trial.

Six thousand people attended a teach-in on Abu-Jamal's case at New York City's Madison Square Garden on May 7, 2000, while similar teach-ins were held in cities around the world. Two weeks later an article in the Sunday *New York Times* "Week in Review" section called Abu-Jamal the "new face of the death penalty in the United States."

On May 13, 2000, to commemorate the fifteenth anniversary of the firebombing of MOVE headquarters, two to three thousand demonstrators brought the busiest intersection in Paris to a standstill by marching and shouting, "Free Mumia—the voice of the voiceless." Similar protests have been held in England, Germany, Switzerland, Norway, and the Czech Republic.

On June 27, 2000, twenty-two members of the British Parliament filed an amicus curiae ("friend of the court") brief in federal district court in Philadelphia, calling on Judge Yohn, the judge assigned to consider Abu-Jamal's habeas corpus petition, to vacate his death sentence. The members of parliament wrote, "The decision to refuse Mr. Abu-Jamal the assistance of John Africa effectively prevented him from meaningfully exercising his right to self-representation at his trial." Similar briefs had been filed earlier in the year by the Pennsylvania branches of the NAACP and the ACLU. Both those groups cited the prosecution's improper use of Abu-Jamal's former Black Panther Party affiliation during the penalty phase of the trial. Judge Yohn refused to consider any amicus briefs.

On October 4, 2003, Abu-Jamal was made an honorary citizen of Paris in a ceremony presided over by the mayor of Paris, Bertrand Delanoe. The last such recipient was Pablo Picasso in 1971. Earlier

Abu-Jamal had been anointed an honorary citizen of Palermo, Italy, and the central district of Copenhagen, Denmark.

Two things account for the unprecedented national and international interest in this case. First and foremost is the man himself. Despite twenty-five years of the bleakest existence possible in isolation on death row, Mumia Abu-Jamal remains what he has always been: an articulate, compassionate righter of wrongs. When he eventually walks free, it will be in large part because he wrote his way out, one essay at a time. The second thing that makes his case so compelling to such a wide audience is that his trial represents such a monumental abuse of government power to frame one man that it really says no citizen is truly free until this wrong has been undone.

29

THE POST-CONVICTION RELIEF ACT HEARINGS

Pennsylvania's Post-Conviction Relief Act (PCRA) is the second stage of appeals in all the state's death penalty cases. Under the act, three issues may be appealed: did the defendant receive ineffective counsel; did the judge improperly suppress evidence; is there new evidence so significant that had jurors heard it, they "likely" would have acquitted the defendant.

Embedded in the act is a Catch-22 that doomed Abu-Jamal from the start: the original trial judge, if still active, presides at the appeal. Although by this time Judge Sabo was seventy-four and on senior status, trying only asbestos cases, he continued to handle appeals of the murder cases he had tried. Higher courts had already overturned a record six of the record thirty-one death sentence verdicts Sabo had presided over.

Abu-Jamal's new defense team, headed by Leonard Weinglass, began preparing his PCRA petition for a new trial in 1994. Although Abu-Jamal had been sentenced to death in 1982, no death warrant had ever been signed by the governor of Pennsylvania, because of the appeals—both state and federal—still available to Abu-Jamal. Republican Tom Ridge made signing Abu-Jamal's death warrant one of his campaign pledges when he successfully sought election as governor of Pennsylvania in 1994.

With Ridge in office, Weinglass wrote a letter to the new governor in April 1995, informing him—without specifying a date—of his intention to file a petition under Pennsylvania's PCRA. This statute authorizes inmates to contest their convictions even after all other state-allowed appeals have been denied. Abu-Jamal's last appeal had been turned down by the Pennsylvania Supreme Court in 1989. According to Daniel Williams, a lawyer on Weinglass's legal team, in his book *Executing Justice* (published in 2001 by St. Martin's Press), Weinglass hoped that this "notification would foreclose the governor from issuing a death warrant before the PCRA petition was litigated."

Unknown to Weinglass, David Horowitz, the assistant general counsel at the SCI-Green prison, where Abu-Jamal was incarcerated at the time, was grossly violating Abu-Jamal's civil rights by opening, photocopying, and forwarding to the Office of General Counsel in Harrisburg all of the mail sent to Abu-Jamal, including the privileged mail he was receiving from his defense attorneys. Among other things, the Office of General Counsel advises the governor on questions concerning the signing of death warrants. Abu-Jamal suspected that his mail was being tampered with and filed a civil rights lawsuit against prison officials. By the time a federal court took up Abu-Jamal's suit in September 1995, the PCRA hearing was over. A federal magistrate, in a finding adopted by a federal judge for the U.S. District Court for the Western District of Pennsylvania, ruled that the impermissible interception of legal mail "interfered entirely with counsel's ability to represent [Mumia Abu-Jamal] during his collateral [PCRA] appeal." The court, incredibly, ordered no remedy to cure the damage caused Abu-Jamal for the violations of his Sixth and Fourteenth Amendment rights.

The most immediate damage to Abu-Jamal was that Governor Ridge, armed illegally with Abu-Jamal's privileged client/attorney correspondence, preemptively signed Abu-Jamal's death warrant five days before Weinglass intended to file Abu-Jamal's PCRA petition. It would have been an absurd gesture for Ridge to have signed the death warrant after the PCRA proceedings had begun, because the entire point of the postconviction hearing was to look at Abu-Jamal's trial anew. As it was, it was still absurd because in addition to the postconviction hearing about to take place, Abu-Jamal, like all death row inmates, was entitled by the Constitution to one habeas corpus challenge of his conviction and sentence in federal district court—and that was several years off in the future.

The death warrant ordered the execution of Abu-Jamal on August 17, 1995, just eleven weeks away. So instead of the PCRA procedures having no time pressure associated with them, Ridge had now concocted the pretext of an execution date to allow Judge Sabo to act as though the hearing must be conducted on a fast-track basis and concluded before the execution date. This trumped-up deadline would enable Sabo to ramrod the proceedings. As Daniel Williams wrote in *Executing Justice*, the impending execution date "provided a justification for him [Judge Sabo] to create a climate of haste, which heightens the likelihood of mistakes and omissions. Mistakes and omissions would then be exploited by the prosecution in any future proceedings in federal court, where the real fight would take place." Just as Abu-Jamal's trial had been rigged, the postconviction hearing would be rigged.

On June 5, Weinglass filed the long-awaited Petition for Post-Conviction Relief. The appeal contained forty-seven exhibits and thirteen affidavits from key witnesses; it ran three hundred pages, advancing nineteen claims why a new trial should be granted.

"Mr. Abu-Jamal will prove that his conviction was the product of widespread police and prosecutorial misconduct, countenanced and advanced by a hostile and biased trial court which stripped him of his ability to raise a defense and then violated his fundamental rights to a fair and impartial trial," the appeal asserted.

The petition asked the court to:

1. Vacate the conviction and sentence of death;
2. Order a new trial;
3. Stay Mr. Abu-Jamal's execution;
4. Permit further investigation into the circumstances of Mr. Abu-Jamal's conviction, and if necessary, to permit the filing of an amended petition;

5. Grant the discovery motion filed herewith;

6. Grant a protective order to prevent the Commonwealth from harassing, including, intimidating, or coercing potential witnesses, experts or investigators in this matter, or otherwise communicating with such witnesses about this case, without prior notice to and the presence of Mr. Abu-Jamal's counsel.

7. Direct the Commonwealth to file the complete record of the prior proceedings, including any portions not presently transcribed;

8. In the alternative, direct that a hearing be held in order that all factual issues raised herein can be fully and fairly litigated.

Weinglass further filed a motion requesting that Judge Sabo recuse himself from Abu-Jamal's postconviction hearing. The motion cited sworn statements from various Philadelphia lawyers attesting to the judge's blatant favoritism toward the prosecution. In this motion, Weinglass argued that Sabo had made numerous biased trial decisions, including not allowing Abu-Jamal to represent himself, barring him for over half of the trial, withholding from the jury the parole status of key prosecution witness Chobert, and not allowing the defense to call Police Officer Wakshul to testify.

*   *   *

The day of the PCRA hearing, July 12, 1995, Abu-Jamal supporters began lining up at 6:30 A.M. to gain access to the courtroom. By the time the hearing started, the *Inquirer* estimated that five hundred marchers had descended on City Hall to demand a new trial for Abu-Jamal and a new judge for his appeal. Present were MOVE members, FOP members, three lawyers from Japan, and two from Germany. Abu-Jamal made his first public appearance in thirteen years, receiving a standing ovation from his supporters when he entered the courtroom.

Judge Sabo refused to withdraw from the case. In typical fashion, he also denied all of the defense's discovery requests from the state and quashed more than twenty-five witness subpoenas requested by the defense, including a subpoena for Governor Ridge and one for his attorney pertaining to tampering with Abu-Jamal's attorney/client mail.

Weinglass asked Judge Sabo to stay Abu-Jamal's August 17 execution date so that there would be time for the court to hear the three-hundred-page appeal that Weinglass had filed on Abu-Jamal's behalf on June 5. The judge told Weinglass that he would have to bring some witnesses to be cross-examined about their contentions in Weinglass's appeal "to show a stay is justified."

Another lawyer for Abu-Jamal, Steven Hawkins of the NAACP Legal Defense Fund, then rose to say that the U.S. Supreme Court standards on appeals do not call for witnesses at hearings for a stay of execution. Hawkins, an expert on death penalty cases, said witnesses appear at a later evidentiary hearing when the substance of the appeal is heard. Sabo was unfazed.

Two days later, with Abu-Jamal again present in the courtroom, Judge Sabo ruled that Abu-Jamal would get a hearing on his wrongful-conviction appeal but refused to grant him a stay of execution. He said that if testimony was not completed by August 17, "then I will make a decision on a stay." He again declined to recuse himself from the case.

An expert on death penalty law from Duquesne University Law School, Bruce Ledewitz, said that it was "unprecedented" for a judge not to rule on the stay while calling for an evidentiary hearing on the merits of the appeal. "No judge in Pennsylvania has asked the defense to go forward on the merits of the case before deciding on a stay of execution. I don't know why Judge Sabo would not grant a stay when the state supreme court under similar circumstances has granted them," he said.

Weinglass told Sabo that defense claims of nineteen trial errors that could justify the court's reversing Abu-Jamal's conviction "couldn't possibly be heard in the five weeks before the scheduled execution." He told the judge, "You are an experienced jurist. There is no way this can be done."

Hawkins told the judge, "Even in a civil case, a fender bender outside this courtroom, more time would be granted to read documents and prepare arguments and witnesses."

Weinglass told the judge he was prepared to proceed but at an "orderly pace" to allow time for prosecutors and defense attorneys to exchange documents. He estimated the process would take about sixty days, saying that period of time had been established as normal by other Common Pleas Court judges.

Judge Sabo responded that a judge who does not handle murder cases applied those guidelines. Weinglass said that capital cases should be given more time, not less, adding that he needed the time to consider the district attorney's recent response to his request for the names and addresses of the eighty witnesses the police interviewed in connection with Faulkner's death. Weinglass pointed out that this information was not available to the defense in 1982 and that his investigator had been unable to locate many of those witnesses.

Sabo told Weinglass he was denying his request, to which Weinglass responded, "But I haven't made any argument yet."

"I don't need any argument," Judge Sabo retorted. "I researched it myself and I couldn't find some excuse or reason."

The following day, a Saturday, U.S. senator Arlen Specter, in a speech to the Republican National Committee, criticized Judge Sabo for moving too quickly on Abu-Jamal's current appeal. A former Philadelphia district attorney, Specter said he did not know the merits of Abu-Jamal's appeal but that "once the judge says he is entitled to a hearing, it has to be a realistic hearing and a meaningful hearing and a hearing that has adequate time for preparation." He said he supported a bill in Congress to shorten the time of appeals in death penalty cases but cautioned, "We have to be careful we do not rush to judgment."

In a Sunday *Inquirer* editorial the next day Judge Sabo's bias against the defense was taken on: "The behavior of the judge in the case was disturbing the first time around—and in hearings last week he did not give the impression to those in the courtroom of fair-mindedness. Instead, he gave the impression, damaging in the extreme, of undue haste and hostility toward the defense's case."

That Sunday about fifty Abu-Jamal supporters protested for two hours at Judge Sabo's home in the old-line Chestnut Hill section of

Philadelphia. Police arrested eleven of them. The next day sheriff's deputies began providing Judge Sabo with twenty-four-hour protection, driving him back and forth to his court chambers.

Abu-Jamal supporters were also bombarding the courthouse with letters and faxes. "Right now the mood is very nasty," the chief deputy administrator at the courthouse told an *Inquirer* reporter. "The faxes are coming in from all over the world. . . . There's a huge national and even international interest in this case from all kinds of people." Over the weekend, Abu-Jamal's supporters held rallies in twelve U.S. cities and several European cities.

On Monday, July 17, 1995, the day Judge Sabo had scheduled Abu-Jamal's appeal hearing to begin, Weinglass filed a four-point petition with the Pennsylvania Supreme Court. In it he requested that Sabo be removed from the case; that the prosecutor turn over police logs and documents not produced at trial; a stay of execution; and a delay in the hearing. The next day state supreme court justice Frank Montemuro ordered the hearing delayed, but only for one week. His ruling ignored the other three points in Weinglass's petition.

On July 26 the appeal hearing began in what the *Inquirer* reported as "raucous" fashion, Judge Sabo and the front of the courtroom separated from the rest of the packed courtroom by bulletproof glass, in a courtroom used for organized-crime trials known as "the Mob room." The judge's first act was to order MOVE member Pam Africa to remove herself from the defense table. Weinglass told the judge she was assisting the defense team. "She is not a lawyer," Sabo said. "I am asking her to take a seat back there in the audience."

Weinglass noted that Pam Africa had sat at the defense table "without disruption of any kind for the last court session."

"I am not talking about disruption," Judge Sabo rejoined. "I am saying that is not the proper place for her to sit. She had too much to say in the last trial [Abu-Jamal's 1982 trial] and that's why we had a lot of trouble." (Pam Africa had conferred with Abu-Jamal throughout his murder trial, most probably to relay information and advice from John Africa.)

"Your honor, the court's last comment about the first trial is reflective of an attitude—" Weinglass began to say before the judge cut him off.

"It's not reflective of anything. I am just telling you plain ordinary facts that occurred, counselor," Judge Sabo said.

Weinglass, holding in his hand photocopies of several newspaper articles critical of the judge's handling of the proceedings to date, pressed again for Judge Sabo to recuse himself from the hearings.

"Community sentiment does not control, counselor. This court does not buckle under community pressure. Let's go! The recusal motion request is denied. For the tenth time, the twentieth, the thirtieth time, it is denied. Let's proceed with the case, counselor," Judge Sabo stated.

There would be no getting rid of Judge Sabo.

The defense proceeded to launch its claim of ineffective counsel by presenting an affidavit from Anthony Jackson, the court-appointed attorney who defended Abu-Jamal at his trial. In the affidavit Jackson stated he had not prepared for the sentencing part of the trial. The defense then presented six character witnesses who testified on Abu-Jamal's behalf, contending that the testimony of such witnesses should have been presented at the sentencing phase of Abu-Jamal's 1982 trial and was a prime example of the ineffective counsel rendered Abu-Jamal. Defense attorney Daniel Williams argued that if the jurors had heard about Abu-Jamal's accomplishments, concerns, and character, they likely would not have "looked at him as a person so lacking in human worth that we ought to exterminate him from the planet."

State representative David Richardson was the first character witness called. "We were very actively involved in the community through a number of organizations, groups, to try to help promote and motivate the community around cultural and positive aspects of the African American community here in the city of Philadelphia," Richardson testified. "It was Mumia's compassion for people and compassion for those issues that impacted directly on vital issues, such as housing, such as health care, such as feeding the homeless, that drew me closer to Mumia." Richardson described Mumia as a "strong advocate" for peace, and as a "peacemaker" who abhorred violence.

E. Steven Collins, a local radio reporter, testified that he could not "remember one time where there was ever a discussion, any hostility, verbal or otherwise, towards any law enforcement, or even a philosophical view that would suggest that."

Another character witnesses was Abu-Jamal's junior high school math teacher, Ken Hamilton, who said he called on Abu-Jamal to mediate disputes between warring gang factions. Hamilton said that Abu-Jamal was a surrogate father for his brother Billy Cook and had discussed with teachers how to get Billy back in school after he had dropped out.

Another was Abu-Jamal's half-sister, Lydia Wallace, a nurse and a social worker. When an assistant district attorney asked her how she could reconcile the peaceful image she presented of her brother with the fact that police found him sitting four feet away from a murdered police officer, his .38 revolver just inches away with five spent shells, she answered: "He told me he didn't do it and I believe him. It's not characteristic of him. He's not like that."

Charles "Joey" Grant, one of three prosecutors representing the Philadelphia D.A.'s Office at the hearing, was so impressed by what he heard the character witnesses say about Abu-Jamal that he told the court, "From all the descriptions of everybody that has come here—and they all are good people from what I can see—I don't think the shooting of Officer Faulkner is characteristic of this defendant."

Over the next three weeks that the hearings would run at Judge Sabo's pell-mell pace, Abu-Jamal's attorneys raised all three grounds of appeal that the Post-Conviction Relief Act allows, claiming that Jackson provided ineffective counsel, that the judge improperly suppressed evidence from the jury, and that new, important evidence not available at trial had been uncovered.

INEFFECTIVE COUNSEL

Weinglass's defense team put Jackson on the witness stand for two days. By this time Jackson had been disbarred by the state court for over three years for "mishandling" nearly $60,000 in clients' funds held in his custody. Jackson admitted, sometimes in tears, to making numerous mistakes but overall defended his representation, saying he did the best he could under the incredibly unusual circumstance that his own client did not want him to represent him. In addition, Jackson argued that it was impossible for any defense attorney to put on an adequate defense when limited by the court to a budget of $1,400 for investigators and experts.

Jackson admitted that he did not interview some witnesses until the day they came to court. He also accepted blame for his failure to put on character witnesses during the sentencing phase of the trial. He said he did not properly challenge some of Judge Sabo's rulings that harmed the defense, particularly Sabo's not allowing the jury to learn that key prosecution witness Robert Chobert was on probation for throwing a Molotov cocktail into a school yard in the middle of a school day. (Jackson did challenge the judge's ruling in this matter, but not on the correct legal basis.)

SUPPRESSED EVIDENCE

Jackson's biggest blunder at trial was waiting until the last day of the trial, the day scheduled for closing arguments, to inform the court that he wanted to call to the stand Police Officer Gary Wakshul, who had accompanied Abu-Jamal from the crime scene and was with him at the hospital. When Wakshul testified at the post-conviction appeal hearing in 1995, he was no longer a member of the Philadelphia Police Department. He had been fired in 1986 for "conduct unbecoming a police officer." His suspension notice stated that while on duty at the Sixth Precinct he had struck a handcuffed prisoner in the face with his blackjack, fracturing his jaw; choked him; and dragged him by his handcuffs. Wakshul now held a patronage position. A few days before the postconviction hearing was set to begin, two Philadelphia undercover vice squad officers assaulted him in open court, with the judge present, in the Common Pleas courtroom where he was employed as court crier. The beating was so severe that Wakshul was undergoing a regimen of physical therapy when he took the stand at the PCRA hearing. (After Abu-Jamal's postconviction relief hearings concluded in 1997, Officers Kenneth Fleming and Jean Langen were suspended without pay for assaulting Wakshul in 1995.)

If the beating was a warning about his upcoming testimony, it worked as planned. Under questioning by the defense, Wakshul said he would have testified at trial that he, too, had heard what Bell and the security guard had said they'd heard, but when he wrote his report, he was "so upset he forgot to report it." This was the same tack Officer Garry Bell used at trial in trying to explain why he had not mentioned the confession he claimed Abu-Jamal had defiantly uttered to him at the hospital. One thing Wakshul did divulge was that he did not recall seeing Bell at the hospital when Abu-Jamal confessed. He also revealed that it was prosecutor McGill who had introduced the subject of Abu-Jamal's confession at an early-1982 meeting he'd held with the police officers involved in Abu-Jamal's prosecution.

Weinglass subpoenaed Deborah Kordansky to testify at the hearing. She was one of four witnesses who informed police that they had seen a man running east after Faulkner's shooting. She had refused Jackson's request to testify at Abu-Jamal's trial, telling him that she had once been raped by a black man and did not want to get involved in a trial of a black man. Kordansky lived in a hotel that overlooked the crime scene. After the police arrived at the scene, she came down from her room to inform them that shortly after she heard gunshots, she went to her window and saw a "male running on the south side of Locust Street." Her statement supported the defense's theory that the real killer ran away. Now on the witness stand for the first time, Kordansky, claiming a foggy memory of events, hedged her original statement to contend she saw the man running away only after the police arrived, thus gutting its relevance.

EXPERT TESTIMONY

Two expert witnesses hired by the new defense, one in pathology, the other in ballistics, testified that Abu-Jamal needed the assistance of expert witnesses at his trial but the defense did not have the money to hire them. Dr. John Hayes, an assistant medical examiner in New York City, testified that Abu-Jamal's defense needed a forensic pathologist to disprove the prosecution's theory of how Abu-Jamal came to be shot—that is, that he could not have been shot by Officer Faulkner in the manner advanced by the prosecution. George Fassnacht, the ballistics expert Jackson retained pretrial to assist him, testified that he quit the defense team prior to trial because the defense was unable to pay his fees.

Fassnacht then testified that the police, for reasons never explained to the jury, had claimed not to have conducted several routine tests that would have determined if Abu-Jamal had fired his gun or even if his gun was warm or smelled of gunpowder. (A simple lead residue test of Abu-Jamal's hands and face would have shown if he had fired a gun. Touching and smelling the gun would indicate if it had been fired recently.) Fassnacht depicted these tests as so routine that it would be difficult to imagine the tests not being conducted. Crime scene investigators did conduct lead residue tests on Faulkner's tie and on a nearby wall, a fact that makes their claim of not having done the tests on Abu-Jamal or his gun exceedingly suspicious. In *Executing Justice*, Williams wrote:

> Because these sorts of tests were easy to perform and customary for crime scene investigators, it simply made no sense that law enforcement accidentally bypassed them when positive results could have definitely proved Mumia's direct involvement in the killing. The suspicious nature of the claim [that no such tests were conducted] was heightened by the fact that this was a crime scene investigation involving the killing of a police officer—a crime that undoubtedly provokes enhanced efforts to produce inculpatory evidence [evidence that incriminates the defendant]. Although we never ferreted out direct proof that test results were withheld from the defense, we felt that the inference was compelling that that was precisely what happened.

The defense also subpoenaed Robert Harkins, the eyewitness McGill chose not to have testify because the two statements he gave to the police demolished the version of the shooting that the state's other witnesses rendered at trial. Harkins told police he had seen a man larger than Faulkner wrestle the officer to the ground, shoot him in the back, and fire two shots at his face. Williams said the defense's main purpose in calling Harkins was to find out if the police had shown him a photo array of possible suspects in an attempt to get him to identify Abu-Jamal as the shooter. If such a photo array had been shown to Harkins, under *Brady* rules, the prosecution was constitutionally bound to disclose to the defense all evidence of failed identification. If such results had been hidden from the defense, "we would have grounds for a reversal of Mumia's conviction," Williams wrote in his book.

Harkins, a heavyset fifty-six-year-old with a prior conviction for sexual abuse that included corrupting a minor, had—with hostility, according to Williams—spurned all attempts by Weinglass's defense team to interview him prior to the PCRA hearing. When Williams called him to the stand, the defense did not know if he had been shown a photo array or not. Williams also wanted to use Harkins to expose how his account of Faulkner's shooting differed so substantively from those of Cynthia White, Robert Chobert, and, to a lesser extent, Michael Scanlan. None of those witnesses had reported a struggle between Faulkner and his killer. After numerous objections from assistant D.A. Grant to Williams's delving into the two statements Harkins had given police in 1981—all sustained by Judge Sabo—Williams did get Harkins to mention the struggle between Faulkner and his assailant, but at a very steep price.

WILLIAMS: And you told them [the homicide detectives interviewing him] that the person, the police officer fell down and that's when the shooting happened?

HARKINS: Well he leaned over and two, two to three flashes from the gun. But then he walked and sat down on the curb.

WILLIAMS: The guy that done the shooting walked and sat down on the curb?

HARKINS: On the pavement.

Williams, now reeling, held an impromptu conference with Wein-glass. Harkins had never mentioned anything about the shooter sitting down in either of his statements. His saying so now directly implicated Abu-Jamal as the shooter. Harkins had told the police that he drove away immediately after seeing the officer shot, because he was afraid for his own life.

When Williams resumed questioning Harkins, he wanted to show that what Harkins had just said about the shooter sitting down on the curb did not comport with what he had originally told the police in 1981. But Grant objected, Judge Sabo sustained, and Williams was stuck with what Harkins had just said. Desperate to clear the record of Harkins's last two answers, Williams moved to strike them. "If I can't inquire into it, I move to strike it," Williams told the judge.

JUDGE SABO: You asked the question.

WILLIAMS: No, that was not responsive to my question.

JUDGE SABO: Well, you should have objected then and asked to strike it.

WILLIAMS: I now move to strike it.

JUDGE SABO: Too late, it's there.

WILLIAMS: Your honor, I have never read any evidence code that puts a time-frame on when I can move to strike.

JUDGE SABO: Well, sorry about that, counselor. I can't help what you read.

New Evidence

The defense presented two new witnesses at the hearing who testified that they saw someone other than Abu-Jamal kill Faulkner. William Singletary testified that he told police shortly after the shooting that he saw a passenger with dreadlocks in the Volkswagen Billy Cook was driving get out of the car, shoot Faulkner, and run away before Abu-Jamal arrived on the scene.

Singletary, a tow-truck operator at the time of the shooting, and a cousin of former Chicago Bears linebacker Mike Singletary, testified that he told police within hours of Faulkner's shooting that he saw someone other than Abu-Jamal shoot Faulkner. He said that a black detective tore up his first two statements at the police station and made him sign a fabricated one under threat of physical harm. That statement had Singletary averring that he had not witnessed the shooting but had seen some of the events taking place soon afterward.

Under cross-examination by prosecutor Arlene Fisk, Singletary said Faulkner was "sitting on the ground and he was saying could I get some help. . . . And he said get Maureen [Faulkner's wife] and he mumbled something else and I couldn't make out what it was. I thought it was something about some children or something, I don't know." Singletary's claim that Faulkner spoke to him greatly undermined his credibility on two counts: Faulkner died instantly from the gunshot to his forehead, and he and his wife, Maureen, had no children.

The other witness was William Harmon, a prison inmate who volunteered to testify on behalf of the defense midway through the hearing. He was put on the stand by Judge Sabo after Weinglass informed the court that he had changed his mind about calling him. After the Singletary debacle, Weinglass did not wish to further damage the defense's credibility with another bizarre tale, but Judge Sabo, saying the purpose of the hearing was to get to the whole truth, insisted Harmon's testimony be taken. If Sabo's intent was to compromise the defense, he succeeded. Harmon's account of Faulkner's shooting was more far-fetched than Singletary's and differed so significantly from it that it was a discredit to the defense.

The pure implausibility of Harmon's account, coupled with Singletary's evidentiary misstatements, prompted a columnist in the *Philadelphia Daily News* to dub Abu-Jamal's defense attorneys "The Scheme Team," writing that they had "learned a few tricks from O.J. Simpson's Dream Team."

The postconviction hearing ended on that sour note. Judge Sabo's dispatching the proceedings at the pace of a forced march did cause, as attorney Williams predicted, the defense to make numerous strategic and tactical blunders. With Sabo presiding at the postconviction relief hearing, the defense knew going in that it would not get any sort of justice. The defense's main thrust should have been to expand the record of judicial and prosecutorial misconduct at Abu-Jamal's trial and sentencing for use in appeal at the federal level. Its best avenue for creating such a record would have been to put former prosecutor Joe McGill on the stand. The postconviction relief hearing provided the defense with its first and last chance to take sworn testimony from McGill on a host of questions about his prosecution of the case.

What, if any, race-neutral notations did McGill make in using ten or eleven of his peremptory challenges to exclude blacks from the jury? Why did he not call Inspector Giordano to testify at trial after using Giordano's claim at Abu-Jamal's preliminary hearing that Abu-Jamal confessed in the police wagon that he killed Officer Faulkner? What deals did McGill make with key witnesses White and Chobert? Could he explain how their trial testimony varied so sharply from their original statements to the police given within less than an hour of Faulkner's death? Why is it that not one eyewitness even saw White or Chobert at the scene? Was McGill aware of the intimidation tactics detectives used on defense witness Veronica Jones? Was he not the one who asked Officer Bell and security guard Durham if they had heard Abu-Jamal confess to killing Faulkner? Why did he not allow Officer Wakshul to testify when he knew Wakshul was at home awaiting a call from him to appear in court? Did he not think that Bell's and Durham's recounting of Abu-Jamal's yelled confession to be suspect considering that the two officers who had accompanied Abu-Jamal from the time he was arrested until he entered surgery had officially reported he had made no comments? How did McGill—in the midst of the trial—come up within one hour with the typed statement from Jefferson Hospital wherein witness Durham recorded Abu-Jamal's alleged hospital confession? Why did he use the same type of language in his summation to the jury during the guilt phase that had previously resulted in a judge's order of a new trial for that defendant? Why the same improper language during the sentencing phase? What was McGill's basis for bringing out during the sentencing that Abu-Jamal had belonged to the Black Panther Party, when he was only fifteen and sixteen years old at the time?

All these immensely fruitful and constitutionally important areas of inquiry went begging when Weinglass opted not to put McGill on the stand, even though the defense had subpoenaed him and he was present at the hearing. In fashioning his petition, Weinglass had made McGill's conduct at trial the basis of five of the nineteen claims filed with the postconviction court.

Another witness the defense should have called was Stephen Trombetta, the other officer who, along with Wakshul, had accompanied Abu-Jamal from the paddy wagon to the ER. He had given numerous statements that Abu-Jamal had not made any statements, including in the paddy wagon or at the hospital.

The two witnesses most obvious for their absence were Abu-Jamal himself and his brother Billy Cook. Abu-Jamal did not testify on the advice of Weinglass. Cook, according to his attorney, Daniel Alva, was willing to testify, but Alva speculated that Cook feared being arrested on two outstanding bench warrants on theft charges. Alva told an *Inquirer* reporter that he had asked Judge Sabo "to protect Cook from arrest," but the judge told him he "could not make such a ruling."

*   *   *

Because Abu-Jamal's appeals were far from exhausted, Judge Sabo ultimately had no choice but to stay the August 17 execution. But he waited to do so until August 7, just a week before the PCRA hearing ended. For Sabo, the trumped-up execution date had accomplished its purpose.

Four days after the hearing concluded, Sabo issued a 154-page decision, denying all claims and making 290 findings of fact, none favorable to the defense. "Given the fact that he quashed half of our subpoenas and rejected a large number of our exhibits, and indicated from the first day we could raise our issues on appeal, the court telegraphed in every way conceivable what this decision would be," Weinglass told reporters in response to Sabo's decision.

In September 1996, at the request of the defense, the Pennsylvania Supreme Court ordered the hearing reopened for Sabo to hear the testimony of Veronica Jones, the prostitute who had recanted at Abu-Jamal's trial that she had told detectives she had seen two black men run from the scene immediately after Faulkner's shooting. Under

the threat of perjury, which Judge Sabo made clear to her at the outset, Jones testified that she had been coerced into fabricating her trial
testimony to avoid going to prison for five to ten years on unrelated
felony charges. She testified that about a month after Faulkner's shooting she had been arrested on the street and taken to the Sixth District
Police Station. Weinglass's questions and Jones's answers follow.

Q. I want to just ask you one other question about the month going back
to January of 1982. Were you questioned at all by police in the Sixth
District?

A. Yes, I was picked up on the street. And, umm, I thought I was going, I
was going in for the night, you know. That's what we called going in for
the night. And when I got there I was put in this room. I was never
processed. They usually just sit us to the side for a few minutes, then
take us out and fingerprint. I never got none of that. But they started,
two guys came and just started questioning me. These weren't the
same two detectives that questioned me before. And, umm . . . they
were just questioning me.

Q. Did they say anything to you about what you should testify to?

A. Asked me if my mind had been made up what I was going to do. And
these were two policemen that were usually in that area. These were
suits that I met. I'm sorry. They wear suits.

Q. By the way, who is, you mentioned a person named Lucky. Who is
Lucky?

A. Cynthia White. She was, she was supposed to have been a friend of
mine on the street but we, we just friends out there like that. But her
name was Cynthia White, we just called her Lucky.

Q. Did her name come up with that conversation?

A. Yes. They said you don't see Lucky around here, do you. In other
words, they didn't pick her up. See, a number of us got picked up but
I didn't get processed, okay. And when we got picked up Cynthia was
not in the bunch.

Q. To your knowledge, was she arrested at that time?

A. Not to my knowledge.

Q. Was there discussion among the other women about that?

A. I really couldn't say because I was in a different room. I was in a room by myself.

Q. I see. And when the police mentioned Lucky to you did they say anything about your testimony as compared to what Lucky would do?

A. Just told me I would be able to work, I wouldn't have to worry about my charges, I could work. Basically, that was it.

Q. And did they say what you would have to do in order for you to be able to work?

A. Just name Mr. Jamal as the shooter.

Q. They made that clear to you?

A. Hmm-hmm.

Q. That was in January?

A. This was around, I would say around the ninth or the fifteenth, somewhere in between there. Because it was really cold. Somewhere in there.

Q. So just so to summarize—

A. Okay.

Q. —you were visited at your home about a week after the incident on December 15 by two detectives?

A. Yes, yes.

Q. And you were questioned?

A. Yes.

Q. Then in January of 1982 you were taken to the Sixth Precinct?

A. Yes.

Q. And questioned again?

A. Yes.

Q. And then just prior to your testimony you were visited by two detectives when you were in lockup?

A. Yes.

Q. And questioned a third time?

A. Yes, but they weren't the same people.

Q. Each time they were different detectives?

A. Yes, yes.

Q. My last question to you, Miss Jones: It's clear that on the night of the occurrence shortly after you heard the shooting you saw two men run away from the scene?

A. Yes, sir.

Q. You're clear on that?

A. Very clear.

WEINGLASS: Thank you. Nothing further.

Weinglass filed an appeal for a new trial based on Jones's testimony. Judge Sabo wrote a fourteen-page opinion filed with the Pennsylvania Supreme Court denying it.

At the final continuation of Abu-Jamal's postconviction relief hearing in mid-1997, the defense called prostitute Pamela Jenkins. She testified that three days after Faulkner's shooting, Thomas E. Ryan, a police officer she said she was "sleeping with" at the time, tried to get her to corroborate Cynthia White's story by saying that she too had seen Abu-Jamal shoot Faulkner in cold blood. She testified that she was not at the scene when Faulkner was killed and that Ryan knew that but took her to the Central Division police station to be interviewed by a homicide detective. Jenkins testified that Ryan and the detective pressured her to offer false testimony against Abu-Jamal, but she had refused to do so. She testified that both she and Cynthia White were police informants and that like White in Abu-Jamal's case, she had on numerous occasions provided perjured testimony at various felony trials at the behest of Officers Ryan and John D. Baird.

During a far-reaching federal probe of police corruption within the Philadelphia Police Department conducted in 1995, Jenkins, with great credibility, was a witness for the government. She testified that Ryan and Baird had been paying her $100 per week to offer perjured testimony in a host of felony cases that led to wrongful convictions, including the catalyst case involving a black college student charged in a drug case. Ryan pled guilty and agreed to testify for the government, receiving a ten-month sentence. Baird was sentenced to several years in prison. As a result, the Philadelphia D.A.'s Office was forced to dismiss drug convictions against the student and more than a score of others falsely convicted on charges where the officers had used Jenkins's fabricated testimony to win convictions.

Judge Sabo had no such reaction to Jenkins's testimony, finding her "not credible."

In spring 1999, Abu-Jamal's attorneys again petitioned the Pennsylvania Supreme Court to accept a review of Abu-Jamal's case based on the many new revelations uncovered during the PCRA hearings. A few months later, in September, the high court refused, for the third time, to intervene in the case.

This left only a habeas corpus petition to the U.S. District Court in Philadelphia between Abu-Jamal and his execution date. In 1996, Congress passed the Antiterrorism and Effective Death Penalty Act, a measure that significantly restricted federal court review of state prisoners' petitions for writs of habeas corpus. A habeas petition is a declaration that a state prisoner's conviction or sentencing was unconstitutional. Under the language of the 1996 antiterrorism law, relief can be granted only if the state court decision under review was "contrary to, or involved an unreasonable application of, clearly established federal law, as determined by the Supreme Court of the United States." Weinglass filed Abu-Jamal's habeas petition on October 15, 1999. Federal District Judge William Yohn was assigned to review it.

30

ARNOLD BEVERLY

A s a federal judge considered Abu-Jamal's habeas corpus petition, another potential avenue of defense threatened to fracture his legal team. Defense attorneys disagreed on how to handle new information from a man named Arnold Beverly about the possibility of a shooter other than Abu-Jamal.

In mid-1989, Rachel Wolkenstein had been working pro bono for Abu-Jamal on matters relating to his prison conditions when she heard that a prisoner at Pennsylvania State Correctional Institution in Hunlock Creek had information about Faulkner's murder. According to a declaration Wolkenstein filed in the Philadelphia Court of Common Pleas in 2001, she first interviewed Arnold R. Beverly at Hunlock Creek in 1989. She stated that Beverly told her he was present when Faulkner was shot and that Abu-Jamal had not shot him. Beverly told her that Faulkner was killed at the behest of Philadelphia police officers because he was interfering with payoffs to the police for prostitution and drugs in the Center City precinct where Faulkner was assigned. Beverly denied that he had shot Faulkner and refused to identify who had. He told her he would not testify about Faulkner's shooting, even if under subpoena.

Wolkenstein stated that Beverly identified a black police officer by the name of Boston (whom she later confirmed to be Philadelphia police officer Lawrence Boston) as being involved in the arrangements to kill Faulkner and "that some police officers were on the scene to ensure the 'hit' went off as planned." She stated that Beverly further informed her that the prosecution's main eyewitness against Abu-Jamal, prostitute Cynthia White, "turned tricks" for the police.

In March 1999, Wolkenstein stated in her affidavit, she met with Beverly two additional times at an undisclosed address to interview him. At the first meeting, she stated, Beverly reconfirmed his prior account that Abu-Jamal had not shot Faulkner, telling her that he also had been shot and wounded and that he had bled at the scene. "He also told me that he wore a green Army jacket that night." In the second interview, "Beverly confessed that he himself shot P.O. Faulkner. He told me that someone else fired the first shot that hit P.O. Faulkner [in the back], and then Beverly ran across the street and shot the officer in the face. He stated that Abu-Jamal arrived later and did not shoot anyone. According to Beverly, Mr. Abu-Jamal was shot by a police officer other than Faulkner."

On June 8, 1999, Beverly signed a sworn confession that he and another man, whom he refused to identify, had murdered Faulkner and that "Abu-Jamal had nothing to do with the shooting." In his affidavit, Beverly reiterated that organized crime figures and police officers were involved in the plan to shoot Faulkner and that police officers were present at the shooting.

Lead counsel Leonard Weinglass, according to Wolkenstein's declaration, dismissed the confession "out of hand and offered the excuse that presenting this confession would risk 'losing credibility' with a federal court judge." (By now, Abu-Jamal's federal habeas petition was before Judge Yohn.) Beverly's extensive criminal record would provide any defense attorney with misgivings regarding his credibility. For a wide assortment of felonies, including burglary, theft, receiving stolen property, criminal conspiracy, and weapons possession, Beverly had been sent to prison six times, twice for up to ten years.

The problem with Beverly's account, as Weinglass viewed it, was that it was filled with improbabilities. Although it contained some nuggets of telling detail about Faulkner's shooting—much in the same way that Singletary's testimony at the PCRA hearing had—credible eyewitnesses Michael Mark Scanlan and Robert Harkins saw no such unfolding of events. They each saw Abu-Jamal running toward Faulkner while the officer was still standing.

In an attempt to get Wolkenstein to back off, Weinglass had Beverly take a polygraph exam administered by Earl Rawlings. Wolkenstein stated in her affidavit that the exam was inconclusive on some questions covered but that Rawlings was not qualified to conduct a polygraph test and "performed an incompetent examination." She stated that Rawlings did conclude, however, that "Beverly was being truthful when he said that he was present at the scene of the shooting and that Mr. Abu-Jamal was not the shooter."

Wolkenstein subsequently had Beverly retested by polygrapher Dr. Charles Honts, a nationally recognized expert in administering polygraphs. Honts reported in a sworn statement that "Beverly confessed to him during the polygraph examination and that the polygraph test results supported the truthfulness of Arnold Beverly's confession that he—and not Mumia Abu-Jamal—shot police officer Faulkner."

Despite the bombshell exculpatory evidence that Beverly's confession presented Abu-Jamal's defense team—now supported by Honts's polygraph of Beverly—Weinglass refused to use the confession as evidence of Abu-Jamal's innocence by either presenting it in a supplemental postconviction petition in state court or using it in state court filings to renew motions for discovery, ballistic testing, and DNA testing of the physical evidence.

According to Daniel Williams's controversial book *Executing Justice*, Weinglass refused to advance the Beverly confession because he agreed with Williams that Beverly's "story was insane." In July 1999, in response to Weinglass's refusal, Wolkenstein resigned from the defense team, as did attorney Jonathan Piper, a litigator at the Chicago office of Sonnenschein Nath & Rosenthal. Piper had worked pro bono for Abu-Jamal throughout the 1990s, drafting legal papers and providing legal and factual research assistance, including interviews with FBI sources active in investigating rampant police corruption in Philadelphia at the time of Faulkner's death.

Williams's book itself provoked another shake-up of the defense team. Abu-Jamal claimed that it was a breach of the attorney/client relationship and filed an unsuccessful suit to stop its release. The prosecution, as Wolkenstein predicted, would use passages from Williams's book in court filings to oppose the admission of the Beverly confession as well as to discredit preemptively other defense initiatives such as Singletary's new testimony. Subsequent to the publication of Williams's book in May 2001, Abu-Jamal discharged both Williams and Weinglass.

31

MUMIA'S OWN ACCOUNT

O ne of the most perplexing aspects of the Abu-Jamal case—
for many of his supporters and all of his detractors—is that
Abu-Jamal, in all his books, articles, and radio essays, and
his infrequent interviews with reporters, never gave his version of
what happened the night Faulkner was killed. Not doing so was
partly the advice of his counsel at the time, but mostly it seemed to
stem from his conviction that because he was denied the right to represent himself at his murder trial, he would tell his version of the
events only at a retrial in front of a jury of his peers.

Within days of discharging Weinglass and Williams, Abu-Jamal
would finally break his silence. His new legal team, consisting of
Marlene Kamish of Chicago, Eliot Lee Grossman of Los Angeles,
J. Michael Farrell of Philadelphia, and Nick Brown of the United
Kingdom, issued three sworn affidavits: one from Abu-Jamal, one
from his brother Billy Cook, and the June 8, 1999, affidavit from
erstwhile hit man Beverly that Weinglass had refused to release.
Abu-Jamal's affidavit, which was dated May 4, 2001, contained
thirty-four assertions detailing sequentially his version of the events
surrounding Faulkner's killing. He stated that he did not kill
Faulkner and was himself shot in the chest by a police officer as he
approached the scene. The shot caused him to collapse and to black
out until other police arrived and began beating him. The full text
of Abu-Jamal's affidavit follows.

I, MUMIA ABU-JAMAL, declare:

1. I am the Petitioner in this action. If called as a witness I could and would testify to the following from my own personal knowledge:

2. I did not shoot Police Officer Daniel Faulkner. I had nothing to do with the killing of Officer Faulkner. I am innocent.

3. At my trial I was denied the right to defend myself. I had no confidence in my court-appointed attorney, who never even asked me what happened the night I was shot and the police officer was killed; and I was excluded from at least half the trial.

4. Since I was denied all my rights at my trial I did not testify. I would not be used to make it look like I had a fair trial.

5. I did not testify in the post-conviction proceedings in 1995 on the advice of my attorney, Leonard Weinglass, who specifically told me not to testify.

6. Now for the first time I have been given an opportunity to tell what happened to me in the early morning hours of December 9, 1981. This is what happened:

7. As a cabbie I often chose 13th and Locust Street because it was a popular club area with a lot of foot traffic.

8. I worked out of United Cab on the night of 12/9/81.

9. I believe I had recently returned from dropping off a fare in West Philly.

10. I was filling out my log when I heard some shouting.

11. I glanced in my rear view mirror and saw a flashing dome light of a police cruiser. This wasn't unusual.

12. I continued to fill out my log/trip sheet when I heard what sounded like gunshots.

13. I looked again into my rear view mirror and saw people running up and down Locust.

14. As I scanned I recognized my brother standing in the street staggering and dizzy.

15. I immediately exited the cab and ran to his scream.

16. As I came across the street I saw a uniformed cop turn toward me gun in hand, saw a flash and went down to my knees.

17. I closed my eyes and sat still trying to breathe.

18. The next thing that I remember I felt myself being kicked, hit and being brought out of a stupor.

19. When I opened my eyes, I saw cops all around me.

20. They were hollering and cursing, grabbing and pulling on me. I felt faint finding it hard to talk.

21. As I looked through this cop crowd all around me, I saw my brother, blood running down his neck and a cop lying on his back on the pavement.

22. I was pulled to my feet and then rammed into a telephone pole, beaten where I fell, and thrown into a paddy wagon.

23. I think I slept until I heard the door open and a white cop in a white shirt came in cursing and hit me in the forehead.

24. I don't remember what he said much except a lot of "niggers," "black mother-fuckers" and what not.

25. I believe he left and I slept. I don't remember the wagon moving for a while and then it did [move] for sometime.

26. I awoke to hear the driver speaking over the radio about his prisoner.

27. I was informed by the anonymous crackle on the radio that I was en route to the police administration building a few blocks away.

28. Then, it sounded like [someone] I.D.'d [identified] as "M-I" came on the radio band telling the driver to go to Jefferson [University] Hospital.

29. Upon arrival I was thrown from the wagon to the ground and beaten.

30. I was beaten again at the doors of Jefferson [Hospital].

31. Because of the blood in my lungs it was difficult to speak, and impossible to holler.

32. I never confessed to anything because I had nothing to confess to.

33. I never said I shot the policeman. I did not shoot the policeman.

34. I never said I hoped he died. I would never say something like that.

I declare under penalty of perjury under the laws of the United States that the above is true and correct and was executed by me on 3 May, 2001, at Waynesburg, Pennsylvania.

MUMIA ABU-JAMAL

Like Abu-Jamal, Cook had never previously stated what he had witnessed at the scene. Cook, whom Faulkner was in the process of arresting when the officer was shot to death, exonerated his brother, but he also asserted that a passenger in his car—his longtime street-vendor partner, Kenneth "Poppi" Freeman—had admitted to him that he shot Faulkner as part of a conspiracy to kill the officer.

(Freeman had died in 1985 under suspicious circumstances hours after Philadelphia police firebombed the MOVE house on Osage Avenue. His body was found bound, gagged, and naked in a vacant lot. There would be no police investigation into this obvious murder: the coroner listed his cause of death as a heart attack. He was thirty-one. When asked at Abu-Jamal's Post-Conviction Relief Act hearing if he knew the circumstances of the death, Freeman's friend Arnold Howard answered, "My understanding is he was handcuffed and shot up [with drugs] and dumped on Grink's lot on Roosevelt Boulevard, buck naked.")

The full text of Cook's affidavit dated April 29, 2001:

I, BILLY COOK, declare:

1. If called to testify as a witness in this matter I would competently testify to the following from my own personal knowledge:
2. On the night of December 9, 1981 I was with my partner Kenneth Freeman, my friend from childhood.
3. Mumia had stopped by at my stand [a vending stand in Center City] that night. He would do that periodically. Mumia had been robbed about a week before.
4. I left my gun locked up at my stand that night, but Poppi always carried his gun. It was a .38.
5. I probably was wearing a black knit cap, I had dreds and always tucked them in.
6. We had closed up late at night.
7. Kenny (Poppi) and I had hit a few bars. We were just unwinding. We used to do that all the time after we closed up the vending stand for the night.
8. We were headed along Locust.
9. Poppi had got some beer and gotten back in the car.

10. At Locust at about Juniper I saw flashing lights of a police car. He followed me for about a half a block and I pulled over behind another car in the first empty spot on the south side of Locust.

11. I had wooden bumpers on my car and they were supposed to be metal. I had been stopped for that but he never said anything about that or gave any reason to have stopped me. I never hit him.

12. I had never seen him before. I knew the cops that worked in the district where my stand was. Locust and 13th is an adjacent district but I didn't ever see him before.

13. I got out my car. Poppi stayed in the car in the passenger seat. I let him (the cop) know I was not happy.

14. After that we went back and forth in a verbal confrontation. He pulls out a stick or some kind of object and slaps me in the head three times. By that time he had me on the side of the car, I started bleeding profusely. So I go back to my car to get my paperwork.

15. I never raised my hand to the policeman. I may have gone to block him when he was hitting me. That's all. I am not that stupid. I never hit a cop. He hit me with a flashlight and I was bleeding but then he let me go back in my car.

16. After that I got in the car. I was in the front seat looking in the back seat.

17. There were people on the street. There always were in that area. The bars were supposed to close by two o'clock but the clubs stayed open later. Some until 5 o'clock. They served drinks anyway.

18. I can't say I recall where other people were and I can't describe where anyone was, but there were people milling about. I never saw a taxi that they later claimed was there. I don't really know how many people were on the street. But there were always people out there it didn't matter what time. It could be five in the morning and there would be people.

19. When I heard the first shot I was in the driver's seat facing toward the back of the car looking for something in the back seat to give to the cop like an owner's card. I am not the organized type and I didn't keep papers in the glove compartment. The back seat had a lot of papers and things from the stand, teddy bears, stuffed animals. We

sold all that kind of stuff. Like special stuff for the holidays like on Valentine's Day we'd have Valentines and we sold novelty items and artificial flowers.

20. When I had gotten in my car Faulkner was in front of the car by the hood where he had stopped me and frisked me. When I was in the car looking in the back, I heard gun shots and saw sparks but I didn't see him shot. I saw flashes of a gun out of the side of my eye. He was standing in front of the car but I didn't see him shot. I was facing the back of the car.

21. Out of my peripheral vision I knew, I could feel other people around but I can't say where they were. His car was behind mine and the policeman was standing on the street between my car and what-ever car was parked in front of me.

22. When I first saw my brother, he was running. He was feet away from me. We hadn't made any plans to meet that night or anything like that and I didn't even realize that he came around that area there to pick up fares. He had nothing in his hands. I heard a shot and I saw him stumble. I didn't see who shot him. He was stumbling forward.

23. It is strange people told me later everything happened in a few sec-onds but I could never see it that way. It seemed like everything was happening at once, but it took a long time. I have tried over the years but I can't see it as a few seconds. It seems to me as if it was 45 seconds not three.

24. When I was looking in the back seat Poppi was still there and then I looked and Poppi's door was open. He had been in the passenger seat and I don't know which way he had gone. He left the area right after this happened.

25. Later Poppi talked about a plan to kill Faulkner. He told me that he was armed on that night and participated in the shooting. He was connected and knew all kinds of people. I used to ask him about it but he talked but never said much. He wasn't a talker. I didn't see Poppi for a while after that.

26. Poppi had been in Germany in the army. That night he was wearing his green army jacket. You know just a regulation army jacket. The

jacket he always wore. He had been discharged. I don't know for what.

27. I got out. I wanted to run; maybe I could have gotten away. I even started to run. I did. But I couldn't run because of my brother. Not after I saw my brother down on the ground.

28. I spoke to him. I told him, "I'm here for you." I don't remember his answering, but I remember his groan.

29. I saw a gun on the street. It was in the gutter. I kicked it under my car. Before the cops came.

30. If they asked me something, I don't remember. I didn't answer them anything. I sure don't remember them reading me my rights. I knew [Police Officer] Shoemaker. He used to stop by my stand and sit there and smoke weed. His wife used come to my stand with him.

31. I think they took me away before they took Mumia or the cop. I remember them pushing me. But I can't remember whether I was in a paddy wagon or a squad car or whether I was sitting up or not. My mind was just not to talk.

32. When they had me in the police station they threatened to kill me and throw me in the river.

33. I have been afraid for my life since that night. I have been afraid to tell anything about what happened. Wouldn't you be?

34. They took me in a room. There were two officers black and white. I was saying things to give them something to chew on.

35. I finally came to my senses. I didn't like the whole idea of making a statement. They wanted me to sign a statement but I just wouldn't do it. I told them I wanted to see my lawyer. I didn't like it. So I just wouldn't sign.

36. I think I was in jail a day or two then they let me out on bail.

37. I had been living in Center City, but I couldn't stay there after it happened. I got help and moved out of my apartment in the middle of the night. And moved back in with my mother.

38. I remember [Abu-Jamal's court-appointed attorney Anthony] Jackson coming to my house several times. My mother and sister were there. I don't remember him ever interviewing me. I just remember him trying to calm us.

39. I don't remember meeting with him anywhere else except at my mother's house. He never asked me to testify. [Billy Cook's attorney Daniel] Alva advised me not to testify. My lawyer implied to me that if I came to court I would also be charged with murder. I had to pay him $1,000.

40. Alva was Freeman's lawyer too.

41. If they [Jackson] had said they wanted me to testify I would have done it but they never did.

42. At PCRA, I was expecting to testify. Leonard [Weinglass] and Rachel [Wolkenstein] were giving me cross signals. Rachel wanted me to testify but Leonard didn't. So I didn't testify. In 1999, I was asked to testify again and I said I would.

43. I will testify now.

44. Mumia was not holding a gun. Mumia never intervened in anything between me and the cop.

45. I had nothing to do with the shooting or killing of the police officer. My brother, Mumia Abu-Jamal, had nothing do with shooting or killing the policeman.

I declare under penalty of perjury, under the laws of the State of Pennsylvania and the laws of the United States of America, that the above is true and correct and was executed by me on 4-29-01 at Philadelphia, Pennsylvania.

BILLY COOK

32

WAS FAULKNER AN FBI INFORMANT?

Was Faulkner the FBI informant that Beverly, in his affidavit, said he was and that Cook, in his affidavit, suggested that Freeman had said he was? Although it seems improbable that Faulkner was killed by Freeman for being an informant, and Beverly and Freeman's assertions by themselves may not be persuasive, numerous other signs point to the likelihood that Faulkner was indeed an informant.

- Faulkner was, after all, a good, young police officer stationed in the most corrupt police precinct in a police department rife with corruption.
- A sophisticated Topcon camera, the type used then by the FBI in surveillance, was retrieved by police from Faulkner's patrol car after his shooting and turned over to the lead detective on the case.
- In Rachel Wolkenstein's 2001 affidavit, she stated that in 1998 she interviewed Donald Hersing, whom she identified as the FBI's confidential source during its 1981–82 investigation of Center City police corruption, and he "confirmed that corrupt police were very concerned about possible police informants in the winter of 1981–82." (Hersing operated two Center City nightclubs that were being extorted by high-ranking Philadelphia police officials.)

- In Wolkenstein's affidavit, she references information uncovered by her colleague Jonathan Piper when he spoke with the lead federal prosecutor in the corruption case against John DeBenedetto, the head of the Central Division (Sixth Precinct), where Faulkner worked. Wolkenstein stated that the federal prosecutor told Piper "that Philadelphia police officers were sources in the investigation, including one source who had a brother who was also a police officer." One of Daniel Faulkner's older brothers, Thomas, spent five years on the Philadelphia police force.

- Wolkenstein also stated in her affidavit that George Sherwood, the FBI agent who oversaw the bureau's crime squad in Philadelphia and was involved in the investigation of Sixth Precinct corruption in 1981–82, had subpoenaed Faulkner's army records as part of that investigation. She said former FBI agents advised her that "the most plausible explanation for this was that Faulkner was an informant, confidential source or an investigation target." Wolkenstein stated that Sherwood "advised our investigator that unless the FBI had an investigative interest in a matter the FBI would not have assisted another agency (including the district attorney or the U.S. attorney) with the retrieval of Officer Faulkner's military records."

- According to Wolkenstein, "FBI records on Daniel Faulkner disclosed an FBI-PH airtel [telex] to the director [William H. Webster] dated 12-30-81 that no written summary of the case was being prepared because of the ongoing criminal investigation [into Center City police corruption] and pending legal litigation." Wolkenstein stated that former FBI agents she interviewed about the order for no written summary of Faulkner's death found it "highly unusual."

- She said another curious item that appeared in Faulkner's FBI file after his death was the sentence "Philadelphia [FBI office] strongly recommends letter to wife [Maureen Faulkner] from director."

In the highly unlikely event that Faulkner was killed because he was a police informant, however, he would not have been the first or the last Philadelphia police officer during the early 1980s to die under circumstances suggesting a directed "hit." Officer James Mason was shot to death by a sniper in May 1981. Four years later, Officer Thomas Trench was executed in his police car when a gunman shot him in the face at point-blank range through the open driver's window, indicating that Trench knew and trusted his assailant.

33

JUSTICE DELAYED

On December 6, 2001, Judge William Yohn issued his habeas corpus ruling. He vacated Abu-Jamal's death sentence, finding that the trial judge's sentencing instructions to the jury were unconstitutional. During the sentencing phase of Abu-Jamal's trial, Common Pleas Court Judge Albert Sabo informed the jury that "a verdict must be a sentence of death if the jury unanimously finds at least one aggravating circumstance and no mitigating circumstances, or if the jury finds one or more aggravating circumstances which outweigh any mitigating circumstances."

According to Judge Yohn, "There are numerous aspects of this charge that created a reasonable likelihood that the jury believed that it was obligated to consider only mitigating circumstances that were found to exist by a unanimous panel." Also, he added that Abu-Jamal's jury "was subjected to this sound bite twice."

In their habeas corpus petition, Abu-Jamal's attorneys argued that the written verdict form, reinforced by the judge's oral instructions, "unconstitutionally suggested to the jury that it could not consider any particular mitigating circumstance—something in Abu-Jamal's background that called out for some leniency—unless the jury unanimously agreed to its existence."

The U.S. Supreme Court, in a decision handed down in 1988, had established that jury instructions that do not make the difference between mitigating and aggravating circumstances clear are unconstitutional. While jurors are required to reach unanimous agreement in determining aggravating circumstances, they are free to weigh the importance of mitigating circumstances on their own. In applying that ruling, Judge Yohn wrote that there was a "substantial probability" that Abu-Jamal's jurors would not consider a mitigating circumstance—such as his clean arrest record, his peaceful character, his various journalism awards, or the fact that his brother was being severely beaten by a police officer at the time—if not all twelve jurors agreed that such a circumstance existed.

Within minutes of the 2001 decision's long-awaited release, Philadelphia D.A. Lynne Abraham called it "legally flawed" and said she would appeal the ruling vacating the death penalty to the U.S. Court of Appeals for the Third Circuit. (As shown in the introduction, the Third Circuit agreed in December 2005 to hear that claim as well as three others raised by Abu-Jamal's defense team.)

Although Judge Yohn's ruling ordered Pennsylvania state prosecutors to hold a new sentencing hearing for Abu-Jamal within 180 days, there was little likelihood that such a hearing would be held for several years, if at all. A new sentencing hearing was the last thing—other than a new trial—that the state's current prosecutors would want to face. At such a hearing, a new jury would be impaneled to hear the facts of the case, witnesses and evidence from the original trial could be put before them, and Abu-Jamal's defense attorneys might be allowed to introduce new evidence and witnesses to support his long-held claim of innocence. The hearing could take weeks, and it would be guaranteed to return to full public view, at the Court of Common Pleas in Philadelphia's landmark City Hall, thousands of Abu-Jamal's ardent legions of national and international supporters. It would be the sentence hearing to end all sentence hearings in U.S. history.

And that's exactly why it was never about to happen. The Philadelphia D.A.'s Office was banking on the U.S. Court of Appeals for the Third Circuit not reinstating the death penalty or ordering a new trial based on the constitutional claims put forth by Abu-Jamal's attorneys. Once all appeals before the Third Circuit had been denied, D.A. Abraham most likely planned to allow the 180 days to lapse without holding a sentencing hearing, a strategy that would allow the automatic imposition of a life imprisonment sentence for Abu-Jamal.

"There's not going to be any [sentencing] hearing, or any other legal proceedings, except a properly filed appeal," D.A. Abraham stated following Judge Yohn's decision. "Unless all appeals that we are permitted to pursue are totally exhausted, only then will we get to the other issues."

The Third Circuit's subsequent decision to hear three constitutional claims by Abu-Jamal's attorneys and the one by Abraham's office effectively gutted the district attorney's strategy. Abu-Jamal will most likely get his long-overdue day in court, the one he was entitled to years ago, when his habeas petition was decided by Judge Yohn.

During the two years that Judge Yohn had Abu-Jamal's petition under consideration, he declined to conduct any evidentiary hearings, basing his decision solely on the case's written record and the briefs Abu-Jamal's lawyers and the state's attorneys filed in connection with Abu-Jamal's habeas corpus petition. He also refused to accept four amicus curiae briefs filed on Abu-Jamal's behalf by such groups as the NAACP and the ACLU. Accepting these friend-of-the-court briefs could have broadened Judge Yohn's understanding of the numerous constitutional issues Abu-Jamal's case involved. Holding a hearing could have saved him from the errors he committed in fashioning his ruling.

*　　*　　*

Abu-Jamal's petition included a claim that the prosecution had violated his Sixth and Fourteenth Amendments rights by denying him, through the deliberate purging of blacks from the jury, his right to be tried by a jury of his peers. The U.S. Supreme Court ruled in 1986 in *Batson v. Kentucky* that purging a jury on the basis of race was unconstitutional, and it entitled James Batson to a new trial before a new jury. On those same grounds, Abu-Jamal was entitled to a new trial.

As Lindorff documented in his 2003 book *Killing Time*, Abu-Jamal's attorneys included four documents to support their *Batson* claim in Abu-Jamal's habeas petition.

- A study published by the *Cornell Law Review* in 1998 entitled "Race Discrimination and the Death Penalty in the Post-*Furman* Era: An Empirical and Legal Analysis with Recent Findings from Philadelphia," by David Baldus and George Woodworth. It documented how race and racism influenced juries in deciding on the death sentence during the period 1983–93.
- Research prepared by law professor Baldus in connection with another Philadelphia case (*Hardcastle v. Horn*) that was tried at about the same time as Abu-Jamal's case. This research pertained to jury selection in Philadelphia from 1977 through 1986, including in Abu-Jamal's case. It documented how the Philadelphia D.A.'s Office systematically used peremptory challenges to exclude blacks from the jury on the basis of race.
- Information from the same Baldus research and time period that singles out Joseph McGill, the lead prosecutor in Abu-Jamal's case, documenting his systematic use of peremptory challenges to exclude blacks from the jury in the six death-penalty cases he prosecuted, including Abu-Jamal's.
- Additional data pertaining to the continued role of the Philadelphia D.A.'s Office in excluding blacks from juries during the period 1987–1991 to demonstrate that racial purging of Philadelphia juries was no anomaly peculiar to the 1977–1986 period.

As Lindorff established, Judge Yohn erroneously barred three of the four support documents by misapplying the three criteria established by law and U.S. Supreme Court precedent governing the admission of evidence in a federal habeas petition: Was the evidence from a relevant time period? Was the evidence new? If the evidence was not new, had it been raised in a timely manner and then rejected by a lower court?

Based on those criteria, Judge Yohn had grounds for barring only the *Cornell Law Review* study, which Abu-Jamal's appeal attorneys had submitted to the Pennsylvania Supreme Court too late for consideration in his state appeal.

Lindorff correctly concludes that Yohn erred gravely in barring the other three documents submitted as evidence in support of Abu-Jamal's *Batson* claim, excluding all three on the mistaken assumption that they were not from a relevant time period. The second and third sets of support material were from the relevant 1977–1986 period and included Abu-Jamal's own trial, as well as that of Donald Hardcastle. Moreover, these sets of data—one showing the Philadelphia D.A.'s Office systematic exclusion of blacks from juries in the 1977–1986 period and the other focusing on Prosecutor Joseph McGill's record of excluding blacks from the six murder trials he prosecuted during the 1977–1986 period—constituted new evidence because the Baldus studies did not become known to Abu-Jamal's lawyers until late 1998, when attorneys representing Hardcastle submitted that information to the Pennsylvania Supreme Court for that case. The third set of data was merely supplementary, submitted to show that the Philadelphia D.A.'s Office practice of excluding blacks was endemic even long after Abu-Jamal's trial.

Judge Yohn's errors, therefore, were, as Lindorff states, egregious ones, errors that directly resulted in his not granting Abu-Jamal the new trial to which his *Batson* claim entitled him. Yohn excluded the very data about racial jury-rigging that won Hardcastle a new trial from the same federal district court on which Judge Yohn sits—data, incredibly, that included Abu-Jamal's trial as well as Hardcastle's and several others. On June 27, 2001, the Federal District Court, Eastern District, struck down a Pennsylvania Supreme Court ruling that had upheld the exclusion of twelve of fifteen potential black jurors in the case of *Hardcastle v. Horn*. The court ordered a new trial for Hardcastle—who had been convicted in December 1982, just months after Abu-Jamal's conviction, on two counts of first-degree murder and one count each of arson endangering persons, arson endangering property, and burglary—holding that the prosecution had used its peremptory challenges in a manner that was not "race neutral."

Abu-Jamal's *Batson* claim, as Lindorff shows, is uncannily similar to Hardcastle's. During jury selection for Abu-Jamal's trial,

McGill used at least ten, and probably eleven, of the fifteen peremptory challenges he deployed to strike otherwise qualified black jurors. To establish a *Batson* claim, the defense must only show prima facie evidence of race-based jury selection, not prove it. *Prima facie* means "on the face of it"—or put another way, something that is presumed to be true unless disproved. Such a preponderance of peremptory strikes by McGill against potential black jurors is indicative of racial discrimination and as such may be advanced by the defense to establish prima facie evidence of a *Batson* violation.

In *Batson* the U.S. Supreme Court ruled that a defendant may make a prima facie showing of intentional discrimination in the selection of his or her jury by relying on the prosecutor's exercise of peremptory challenges at the defendant's own trial. To counteract a *Batson* claim, the state needs to establish that the prosecutor's use of peremptory strikes was "race neutral." In neither the Hardcastle nor the Abu-Jamal case did the prosecutors claim to keep notes explaining the reasoning behind their peremptory strikes. In a brief the Philadelphia D.A.'s Office submitted at Abu-Jamal's Post-Conviction Relief Act hearings in 1995, Lindorff writes that the D.A.'s office inadvertently boosted Abu-Jamal's prima facie evidence of race-based jury selection by offering the explanation that McGill struck up to five black jurors on the basis that they had "listened to" or "heard" Abu-Jamal on the radio. The jury-selection transcripts establish that McGill asked only potential black jurors that type of question.

In overturning Hardcastle's conviction, the federal district court ruled that "*Batson* further provides that if the facts establish a *prima facie* case and the prosecutor fails to come forward with a neutral explanation, the conviction must be reversed."

34

ORAL ARGUMENTS

Although the Third Circuit Court of Appeals ordered Abu-Jamal's habeas petition put on a fast track when it agreed to take up the case back in December 2005, the oral arguments would not take place until May 17, 2007, more than sixteen months later. The Philadelphia D.A.'s Office requested its first extension on January 11, 2006, and its second on February 14, putting off the filing of its first-step brief until March 20. On March 16 defense attorney Robert R. Bryan filed his first-step brief and then a month later asked for and received an extension on filing his second-step brief, which he submitted to the court on July 21.

In late July 2006 two separate amicus curiae briefs were filed on behalf of Abu-Jamal. The first was filed by a consortium consisting of the Charles Hamilton Houston Institute for Race & Justice of Harvard Law School, the International Association of Democratic Lawyers, the National Conference of Black Lawyers, the National Jury Project, the National Lawyers Guild, and the Southern Center for Human Rights. The NAACP Legal Defense Fund filed the second amicus brief. These briefs were submitted to supplement and support the briefs Bryan prepared as well as demonstrate broad social concern for the claims the court was addressing.

The court allowed the D.A.'s office two months to respond to the amici briefs.

Hugh Burns, representing the Philadelphia D.A.'s Office, tried an end run on the Third Circuit Court of Appeals when he sent a letter to the court on February 28, 2007, requesting that the entire Third Court recuse itself from the case. Burns wrote disingenuously that the presence of Judge Marjorie O. Rendell, the wife of Pennsylvania governor Ed Rendell, who was the Philadelphia district attorney during Abu-Jamal's trial, might create an inference of bias that the defense could use to file future appeals. An impartial observer might reasonably conclude that the Philadelphia D.A.'s Office thought its chances better in some other circuit court.

The Third Circuit was having none of that, ordering on April 4 that it would not recuse itself, while announcing that Third Circuit Court Judges Marjorie Rendell, Michael Fisher, Richard L. Nygaad, and Theodore A. McKee had recused themselves. The judges were not required to and did not offer explanations for their recusals.

As is its custom, the Third Circuit waited until ten days before the date it set for oral arguments—May 17, 2007—to announce the three-judge panel that would consider the three claims raised by the defense and the one claim brought by the prosecution. These are the same three judges who agreed in December 2005 to certify the four claims. Interestingly, in an indication of the high-profile nature of this case, the Third Circuit's chief judge, Anthony J. Scirica, is one of the judges. The others are Judge Thomas L. Ambro and Judge Robert E. Cowen. Judges Scirica and Cowen were appointed by President Reagan and Judge Ambro by President Clinton.

The much-anticipated oral arguments were held the morning of May 17 in the Ceremonial Room of the Federal Courthouse in Philadelphia, across the street from the Liberty Bell. Supporters for Abu-Jamal—who was not allowed to attend the proceedings—began arriving hours early to try to secure one of the one hundred seats allowed for spectators. In addition to Pam and Ramona Africa of MOVE, Abu-Jamal supporters included activist Dick Gregory, former U.S. representative Cynthia McKinney of Georgia, and civil rights attorney Lynne Stewart. Maureen Faulkner and a few members of the Philadelphia FOP represented the prosecution contingent. Also present was former prosecutor Joseph McGill. The *Inquirer* estimated that some five hundred Abu-Jamal supporters assembled outside the courthouse in a festive, rallylike mood, flashing "Free Mumia" posters and chanting the same slogan loud enough for it to be heard in the courtroom from time to time during the two-and-one-quarter-hour hearing.

By contrast, the atmosphere inside the vaulted courtroom was muted, a polite respectfulness the order of the day.

By the time judges are ready to conduct oral arguments, they have received and reviewed hundreds of pages of briefs from opposing counsel. They know what the briefs state. What they want opposing counsel to do is to narrow the issues the judges must decide and to answer questions for which they seek clarification. Opposing counsel do not actually give presentations per se; they engage in a spirited debate with the three judges.

For opposing counsel, oral arguments give them the opportunity to stress the main issues of their case that might persuade the court in their favor. This is their one and only chance to speak directly to the court on behalf of their client and assert the legal reasons why their client should prevail.

Before Chief Judge Scirica invited Hugh Burns to begin his presentation, he informed both sides that their presentations would be limited to an hour each, which would include any rebuttal time they chose to set aside. As soon as Burns addressed Judge Yohn's ruling overturning Abu-Jamal's death sentence, what followed was a series of pointed questions from all three judges. At the end of Burns's discussion on the first issue, Judge Ambro told him bluntly that in terms of the merits he was "marching up San Juan Hill."

When Burns moved to issue two, prosecutor McGill's misconduct during the guilt phase of the trial when McGill had told the jury that their verdict might not be final because there would be "appeal after appeal after appeal," Judge Cowen asked him if he could deny that the "statements made by the assistant prosecutor were inappropriate for summation." When Burns did deny it, Cowen said, "The purpose of the summation is to argue to the jury the facts which were developed in evidence before the case in light of the charge that will be delivered by the judge. What has the appellate process got to do with evidence that was adduced at trial in light of the instructions to be delivered by the judge?"

Judge Cowen asked Burns if it was not a violation of a defendant's "Sixth Amendment right to a fair trial when a prosecutor tells the jury inferentially—maybe not directly—not to worry about their verdict because whatever you do here is going to be reviewed, corrected by the appellate process." Burns replied that the argument the prosecutor had been making "was just the opposite," saying that McGill had been emphasizing the "gravity" of their verdict.

Issue three involved the *Batson* claim. It pertained to the prosecutor's alleged discriminatory use of peremptory challenges to keep potential black jurors from being impaneled at Abu-Jamal's trial. Burns's primary argument was that the defense had not filed the objection in a timely manner. Judge Ambro cited two cases that he suggested made moot that claim. Judge Cowen commented, "At the very least, the issue is before us on plain error as alleged on appeal."

Judge Ambro then referenced a March 18 preliminary hearing before Judge Ribner where Anthony Jackson, Abu-Jamal's court-appointed defense attorney at trial, "brought up the prosecutor's bent to strike black jurors," and then asked Burns, "Isn't that the equivalent of bringing up the issue contemporaneously?" Burns did not see it that way. He pointed out that Jackson had never made an objection to McGill's strikes during jury selection, which to Burns was proof that McGill was not striking potential black jurors in a discriminatory way. Judge Ambro said that all the defense needed to do to establish a *Batson* claim was to "show an inference [of discrimination] as to one juror who happened to be black." Burns said he agreed with that, but "in this case such an inference does not arise."

McGill did use ten of the fifteen peremptory strikes he deployed to strike black jurors and only five strikes against whites. (This strike number was established at the postconviction relief hearing in 1995.) This imbalance in itself suggests a *Batson* violation on its face, but Chief Judge Scirica was a stickler on this point because no record of the racial composition of the jury pool was preserved. "Many Circuit Courts have said you can't evaluate the strike rate unless you understand what the racial composition of the entire venire was and make a comparison."

A tightly leashed bulldog is one image that comes to mind when assessing Hugh Burns's performance before the Third Circuit. By the time he left the podium to give way to the defense presentation, he had shown himself to be a tenacious and extremely well-versed advocate for the prosecution. Under a barrage of tough questioning, he conceded nothing and had at his fingertips case after case that at least partially supported the stances he took. His knowledge of the case and the case law surrounding the claims before him was encyclopedic. His tone of voice—courteous, not quite indignant—often seemed to be that of a man who could not believe that these three judges had even bothered to think the Commonwealth could have possibly violated any of Abu-Jamal's constitutional rights.

Abu-Jamal's defense team, led by lead counsel Robert Bryan, also comprised local attorney Judith L. Ritter as cocounsel and Christina Swarns of the NAACP Legal Defense Fund, one of the numerous groups that had filed amicus curiae briefs on Abu-Jamal's behalf.

Ritter, a professor of law and the director of the Pennsylvania Criminal Defense Clinic at Widener University School of Law's Delaware campus, went first, in support of Judge Yohn's ruling overturning Abu-Jamal's death sentence. Her assertions that the verdict form and jury instructions used at Abu-Jamal's trial violated his constitutional rights went virtually unchallenged by the judges.

Bryan presented the *Batson* claim. Two enormous omissions by Abu-Jamal's previous defense counsel—Jackson and Weinglass—would heavily weigh him down. During jury selection, Jackson failed to make any comment about how McGill was striking blacks from the jury even though McGill used 66 percent of his peremptory challenges to strike them. At Abu-Jamal's postconviction relief hearing in 1995, attorney Weinglass, although he had subpoenaed McGill to appear, failed to put McGill on the stand and ask him to state the reasoning behind each of his strikes.

The first question from Judge Ambro asked how Judge Yohn was wrong in denying Abu-Jamal's *Batson* claim in his 2001 ruling.

When Bryan said that the 66 percent strike rate was enough to establish the claim, Judge Cowen said that the strike rate absent knowledge of the racial composition of the potential jurors questioned was not sufficient to make the claim. He asked Bryan if there was any way he could go back and determine the racial composition of the jury pool. "I don't know how we could get it. We're a day late and a dollar short on this issue, unfortunately," Bryan conceded.

Bryan then took a broader tack, referencing the March 18, 1982, preliminary hearing before Judge Ribner where Jackson voiced his concern about McGill's penchant for striking black jurors in previous trials. Bryan described the Philadelphia D.A.'s Office at that time as "a culture of discrimination," where a D.A.-sanctioned training tape—prepared in 1986 but based on years-long practice within the office—instructed new assistant prosecutors that "the best jury was an all-white jury." He also referenced the Baldus study, discussed in the previous chapter, which demonstrated a systemic use of peremptory challenges by Philadelphia prosecutors—specifically McGill—to strike blacks from juries when a black defendant was on trial.

Judge Ambro stated that five factors pertain to a *Batson* claim: (1) the exclusion by the prosecutor of a certain racial group, (2) the nature of the crime, (3) the race of the defendant and race of the victim, (4) the pattern of strikes against potential black jurors in this case because the defendant is black, and (5) the prosecutor's questions and statements during questioning of the potential jurors. He then asked Bryan if he thought McGill had revealed bias during his questioning. Bryan's first response was that McGill was too good a lawyer for that, but within the next few minutes he found his way back to that question with an impassioned vengeance.

In 1987, a year after he went into private practice, McGill swore out an affidavit for submission by the D.A.'s office to the state supreme court in conjunction with Abu-Jamal's pending appeal there. The appeal included a *Batson* claim. McGill's purpose was to provide "race neutral" reasons for the peremptory challenges he used to strike blacks. Providing these reasons would give the state supreme court grounds to deny Abu-Jamal's *Batson* claim, which is exactly what the state high court did in 1989.

Bryan began going through the reasons supplied by McGill one at a time, starting with McGill's claim that he struck blacks who had never served on a jury before—yet Abu-Jamal's jury had whites on it who had never served on a jury. McGill struck blacks for being unemployed—yet unemployed whites were impaneled. By the time Bryan got to McGill's third reason, his voice spiked several decibels and his sense of violation with it. McGill said he struck blacks who had heard Abu-Jamal on the radio, but he did not ask any white potential jurors if they had heard the defendant on the radio even though Abu-Jamal had most recently worked for the white audience–dominated local public radio station. McGill said he struck potential black juror Wayne Williams because he had a hearing problem, although Williams had told McGill that as long as his hearing aid was working, he could hear well. McGill agreed to seat a white juror who also said she had a hearing problem. Another category that McGill applied to exclude blacks was "single (unmarried, divorced)"—yet he sat white jurors who filled that bill.

Bryan said McGill struck potential black juror Darlene Sampson because she had heard Abu-Jamal on the radio, but the record showed she had told the prosecutor she had never heard him.

Because a *Batson* claim requires only "an inference" of prosecutorial discrimination in purging blacks from the jury, any and all the points Bryan had just made about McGill's reasoning for striking blacks from Abu-Jamal's jury would appear to meet that standard.

Christina Swarns followed Bryan and immediately took up the *Batson* claim. "The question before this court is not whether Mr. Abu-Jamal has actually proved intentional discrimination in the exercise of peremptory challenges. The question before us today is whether or not he has proved an inference of discrimination." None of the judges took exception to that assertion.

Swarns said the Commonwealth's argument that a *Batson* claim must be lodged contemporaneously to be valid was not an argument it had made previously in any lower court. Speaking directly to Judge Ambro, she said his point in earlier citing the U.S. Supreme Court case known as *Ford v. Georgia* was correct because that case "does dispose and certainly indicate that a contemporaneous objection is not required." Ambro affirmed her point, adding that other cases such as *Riley v. Taylor* also made moot the timeliness issue.

On rebuttal, Burns appeared to make no headway in knocking down the defense's argument for establishing a *Batson* claim. At one point, Judge Cowen called one of his assertions "self-serving."

The third claim certified for appeal—that Judge Albert Sabo was biased against the defendant during the postconviction relief hearings in 1995–97—was not addressed in oral argument because the three-judge panel will decide that claim based on their assessment of the transcripts from those proceedings and the briefs filed by opposing counsel.

Without a doubt, the oral arguments before the Third Circuit Court of Appeals turned out to be Abu-Jamal's fairest and most evenhanded experience with the U.S. justice system. From all outward appearances, all three judges seemed to project grave reservations about the Commonwealth's arguments while seeing legal and constitutional merit in the arguments and answers put forth by Bryan, Ritter, and Swarns.

The judges are under no time demand to issue their decision, but the fact that these judges certified three of Abu-Jamal's claims for appeal bodes extremely well for the defense. If they had not seen merit in the claims, they would have turned them down and heard only the Commonwealth's challenge to Judge Yohn's ruling overturning Abu-Jamal's death sentence. But just as it is impossible to predict how a jury will decide a case, so is it concerning U.S. appeals court rulings.

35

JUSTICE AT LAST

Abu-Jamal's fate now is in the hands of the three-judge panel. If the panel finds no merit in any of his three claims and reverses Judge Yohn's vacating his death sentence, Abu-Jamal's death sentence would be reinstated and a date for his execution by lethal injection set by Governor Ed Rendell. Only the U.S. Supreme Court would stand between Abu-Jamal and his execution date. That court has twice previously refused to intervene in his case. That's the downside.

The oral arguments the three-judge panel conducted on May 17, 2007, foreshadowed the upside.

The first concrete benefit to Abu-Jamal will occur if the Third Circuit rules to uphold Judge Yohn's decision to vacate his death sentence. This ruling, after more than twenty-five years of solitary confinement on death row, would finally place him in the general prison population and greatly decrease the restrictions of his incarceration.

If two of the three judges rule that McGill's summation to the jury during the guilt phase of the trial violated Abu-Jamal's constitutional right to a fair trial, the Third Circuit would set aside Abu-Jamal's conviction and order a new trial. Based on the judges' comments during the May 17 oral arguments, there is a high likelihood a new trial will be ordered. If it is, the judges would not even have to concern themselves with the *Batson* claim or Judge Sabo's alleged bias at Abu-Jamal's postconviction relief hearings. Setting aside Abu-Jamal's conviction and ordering a new trial would make moot the importance of those claims. It might also allow Abu-Jamal to be released from prison on bail, pending his new trial.

If the Third Circuit orders a new trial, the Philadelphia D.A.'s Office will most likely attempt to postpone it by a matter of months by requesting the Third Circuit to render an *en banc* decision, a decision by the entire panel of the thirteen Third Circuit judges, although four of those judges have already recused themselves from the case. By a simple majority vote, the remaining nine active judges would decide on whether to revisit the claims ruled upon by the three-judge panel. *En banc* proceedings are extremely rare to begin with—less than 5 percent of *en banc* requests are granted by all eleven of the U.S. Circuit Courts of Appeal in any given year. It is highly unlikely that the Third Circuit judges would agree to an *en banc* hearing in a case where the constitutional claim advanced by the defendant— the improper summation to the jury—is so clear-cut. The Third Circuit's order for a new trial would undoubtedly stand.

The only option this would leave the Philadelphia D.A.'s Office would be to appeal the ruling to the U.S. Supreme Court. It is remotely possible that the high court would take up the case because of its notoriety. In that event, a final decision would not be expected until the Supreme Court's 2009 term.

If the Third Circuit does not rule in Abu-Jamal's favor on the improper jury summation issue, this would put the *Batson* claim and Judge Sabo's alleged bias back in play. On the *Batson* claim, the Third Circuit would most probably remand the case to Judge Yohn to conduct the evidentiary hearing he should have held prior to rendering his flawed decision in 2001, when he denied that claim. If that hearing convinces Judge Yohn that McGill was discriminatory in striking otherwise qualified blacks from Abu-Jamal's jury, a new trial would be ordered.

If a majority of the three-judge panel finds that Judge Sabo was biased during the postconviction hearings, it could order those hearings reopened and conducted from start to finish before a new judge in the Court of Common Pleas in Philadelphia. Those hearings could lead to a new trial.

One way or another, a new trial is an almost certain outcome for Abu-Jamal.

If Judge Yohn orders a new trial based on the *Batson* claim, the Philadelphia D.A.'s Office could appeal that ruling to the U.S. Supreme Court, but because the law has been settled in this matter since 1986, when the high court issued its *Batson* ruling, it is doubtful the court would take it up.

Were the Court of Common Pleas to order a new trial—after conducting a new postconviction hearing—the Commonwealth could appeal that decision to the Pennsylvania Supreme Court and, if it lost there, to the U.S. Supreme Court, which would most likely refuse to consider the case.

It is difficult to imagine that the Philadelphia D.A.'s Office would even consider retrying Abu-Jamal. Its entire case the first time through was predicated on the perjured testimony of prostitute Cynthia White, the compromised testimony of felon Robert Chobert, and the far-fetched testimonies of hospital security guard Priscilla Durham and Police Officer Garry Bell regarding Abu-Jamal's alleged hospital confession.

But this is no normal district attorney's office. This one carries a vendetta for Abu-Jamal that should not be underestimated. The day Judge Yohn overturned Abu-Jamal's death sentence, D.A. Lynne Abraham put her antipathy for Abu-Jamal this way, "Today, Mumia Abu-Jamal is what he has always been: a convicted, remorseless, cold-blooded killer."

Before becoming Philadelphia district attorney in 1991, Lynne Abraham was an assistant Philadelphia D.A from 1967 until Mayor Rizzo appointed her executive director of the city's Redevelopment Authority in 1972. She became a municipal court judge in 1976 and a judge of the Philadelphia Court of Common Pleas in 1980, presiding over homicides and major felony cases. As a municipal judge she cooperated with Mayor Rizzo's harassment of MOVE in 1977 by issuing eleven warrants for MOVE members on riot and "possession of an instrument of crime," charges that led to the horrific police siege of MOVE headquarters in Powelton Village in August 1978. Immediately following that siege, as recounted in chapter 5, police bull-dozed the MOVE headquarters to the ground. On May 11, 1985, Abraham, then a Common Pleas Court judge, signed arrest warrants against MOVE members that led two days later to the firebombing of MOVE headquarters and sixty other row houses, in which eleven MOVE members were killed.

Abraham's animus for Abu-Jamal has deep roots. It was Common Pleas Court Judge Abraham who went to Jefferson University Hospital to arraign Abu-Jamal at his bedside for the murder of Officer Faulkner. It was her D.A. office that so vigorously opposed the introduction of new evidence at Abu-Jamal's postconviction relief hearing and blatantly used intimidation tactics against defense witnesses Veronica Jones and Pamela Jenkins at that hearing.

D.A. Abraham is known as "the Queen of Death" because of her zeal for seeking the death penalty, and her prosecutors have sent more than one hundred blacks from Philadelphia to death row during her sixteen years in office, a dubious record unmatched by any other district attorney in the United States. An article in the *New York Times Magazine* in 1995 depicted her as the nation's "deadliest D.A."

Abraham can be expected to fight bitterly to keep Abu-Jamal in prison for life and through a blizzard of legal motions and appeals—if needed—postpone Abu-Jamal's retrial for months, if not years. Eventually, though, she will have to retry him or set him free.

It is far from apparent what type of a prosecution her office could muster to convince a jury beyond a reasonable doubt that Abu-Jamal murdered Faulkner in cold blood. In the case of star prosecution witness Cynthia White, Abraham's office claimed at Abu-Jamal's post-conviction relief hearings in 1995 that White died in 1992 in Camden, New Jersey, allegedly of a drug overdose. The D.A.'s office made that claim only after the Pennsylvania Supreme Court ordered Judge Sabo to extend Abu-Jamal's postconviction relief hearing to hear the testimony of Pamela Jenkins, a former prostitute who would testify for the defense that White was a police informant and that both she and White had been pressured by the police to testify that they saw Abu-Jamal murder Faulkner. White, if alive, would now be of more use to the defense than to the prosecution. Abu-Jamal's defense believes that White has been in witness protection, living in a condominium in nearby New Jersey.

The government's other main eyewitness at trial, cabdriver Robert Chobert, admitted at Abu-Jamal's postconviction hearing that he had asked Prosecutor McGill for assistance in getting his chauffeur's license reinstated either before or during Abu-Jamal's trial. The fact that Chobert was a felon on probation at the time he testified, a status Judge Sabo ruled was inadmissible to Abu-Jamal's jury, could not be suppressed at a new trial. In addition, a defense investigator who interviewed the cabdriver in 1995 declared in an affidavit that Chobert told him he had not been parked where he had said he was and had not seen the shooting of Officer Faulkner.

Priscilla Durham, the hospital security guard who testified that she heard Abu-Jamal blurt out a confession that he killed Faulkner and hoped the officer would die, was discredited in an affidavit sworn on April 18, 2003, by her stepbrother, Kenneth Pate, and filed by Abu-Jamal's defense counsel as a remand motion with the Pennsylvania Supreme Court on May 7, 2003. The full text of his affidavit follows.

I, KENNETH PATE, DECLARE:
1. I am related to Priscilla Durham, now known as Priscilla Ahmed, through marriage: My father, Perry Abner, married Priscilla's mother, Dolores Durham, about 20–25 years ago.
2. Sometime around the end of 1983 or the beginning of 1984 I had a telephone conversation with Priscilla Durham in which the subject of Mumia Abu-Jamal came up.
3. I asked Priscilla how she was and she asked me how I was. I was kind of teasing her about her job as a security guard at the hospital, saying "why would a woman need to carry a big old gun like that?"
4. Priscilla began to complain about the way she was treated on the job, about her back hurting, and them "treating her like that" after all she did for them they laid her off [*sic*].
5. Then Priscilla started talking about Mumia Abu-Jamal. She said that when the police brought him in that night she was working at the

hospital. Mumia was all bloody and the police were interfering with his treatment, saying "let him die."

6. Priscilla said that the police told her that she was part of the "brotherhood" of police since she was a security guard and that she had to stick with them and say that she heard Mumia say that he killed the police officer, when they brought Mumia in on a stretcher.

7. I asked Priscilla: "Did you hear him say that?" Priscilla said: "All I heard him say was: 'Get off me, get off me, they're trying to kill me.'"

8. Priscilla also said there was a lot of chaos and confusion going on when the police brought Mumia in and when they were talking to her.

9. I am presently imprisoned at SCI Greene where I have been for about 3 years. At the time of my telephone conversation with Priscilla Durham, described above, I was imprisoned at SCI Graterford.

10. Back in 1982–1984 Priscilla and I had many telephone conversations when I was at SCI Graterford. I would call her house to talk to her or her daughter Sharon. Since then Priscilla and I have written each other many times.

11. Sometime in 1984, after I was transferred to SCI Huntington, I read a newspaper article about the Mumia Abu-Jamal case. It said Priscilla Durham had testified at Mumia's trial that when she was working as a security guard at the hospital she heard Mumia say that he had killed the police officer. When I read this I realized it was a different story from what she had told me.

12. Mumia was also imprisoned at SCI Huntington at that time. I wrote a note to him about Priscilla and gave it to another inmate who was a "tier worker" to pass it on to him.

13. Sometime between December of last year (2002) and February of this year (2003) I was out in the prison yard at the same time Mumia was. I remember that the weather was still cold. We were a couple of cages away from each other. I mentioned to him about the telephone conversation I had with Priscilla back in 1983 or 1984 and that she said she did not hear Mumia say anything about killing the police officer. I told him that I thought she was still scared about telling the truth about what happened but maybe she would.

14. My nickname or street name is "Kenny Stax." That is how I am known by Mumia and other inmates.

15. I am willing to take a lie detector test to prove I am telling the truth
     about my conversation with Priscilla Durham.

This declaration is made subject to the penalties provided for in 18 Pa.
Cons. Stats. Sec. 4904 for unsworn false statements to authorities.

I declare under penalty of perjury under the laws of the United States
of America that this declaration is true and correct and was signed by me
on April 18, 2003, at Waynesburg, Pa.

KENNETH PATE

With Durham admitting that she lied, or at least her stepbrother
testifying that she admitted to perjuring herself at Abu-Jamal's trial,
Officer Garry Bell's trial testimony about the same "confession" goes
out the door with it. In would come the signed statement of Officer
Gary Wakshul in a report taken from him by a detective shortly after
Abu-Jamal went into surgery, in which he said, "The Negro male
made no comments." Wakshul's partner that night, Officer Stephen
Trombetta, likewise reported that he heard Abu-Jamal make no
statements, and he has never backed away from that claim.

The prosecution simply has no case left against Abu-Jamal. There
was never any ballistic evidence or fingerprints to tie Abu-Jamal to
the shooting. Prosecutor McGill really only had Cynthia White,
Robert Chobert, Priscilla Durham, Officer Garry Bell, and Judge
Sabo to orchestrate the frame-up.

Abu-Jamal's defense, capable and well financed, now holds the high
cards. It has Veronica Jones and Pamela Jenkins to detail the frame-
up, it has Billy Cook to testify that his street-vendor partner Kenneth
Freeman either killed Faulkner or assisted in Faulkner's killing, and
for sheer courtroom chaos it has the Arnold Beverly confession.

Once the Third Circuit or Judge Yohn orders a new trial for Abu-
Jamal, the Philadelphia D.A.'s Office, if it had any sense, would state
that it remains convinced Abu-Jamal is guilty of Faulkner's murder
and then spin some reasons why it refuses to retry him. Such a strategy would allow the truth about the death of one of Philadelphia's
best police officers to remain the secret the D.A.'s office has kept all
along. Instead it most likely will file appeal after appeal to postpone
the new trial, to delay the inevitable hour when Mumia Abu-Jamal
will walk free.

INDEX